FRAGMENTS
OF THE SKY

Letters resurface. Truth unravels.
A reclusive artist's legacy is pieced together.

Written & researched by
Julie Lenora Parsons

Copyright © Julie Parsons, 2025
First published 2025

Published by The Book Reality Experience,
an imprint of Leschenault Press,
Leschenault, Western Australia

The right of Julie Parsons to be identified as author of this work has been asserted by them in accordance with sections 77 and 78 of the copyright, designs and patents act 1988.

All rights reserved. No part of this publication may be reproduced or transmitted in any form or by any means, electronic or mechanical, including photography, recording, or any information storage or retrieval system, without permission in writing from the publisher. The book is sold subject to the condition that it shall not, by way of trade or otherwise, be lent, resold or otherwise circulated without the publisher's prior consent in any form of binding or cover other than that in which it is published and without a similar condition, including this condition, being imposed on the subsequent purchaser.

Original illustrations and photographs by Raymond Moult-Spiers, Julie Parsons, Leonard Brokensha.

Except as indicated otherwise, all works of art contained in Part 1 were created by the author.

ISBN: 978-1-923454-09-5 - Paperback

Editor: Kerry Davies AE
Book Designer: Rad Young
Cover Design: Rad Young
Cover Images: Raymond Molt-Spiers 1959
Julie Parsons 1989
Background Image: Moult-Spiers' WWII Burma Railway Diary (detail)

The author asserts that no Artificial Intelligence methods, techniques or tools have been used within the researching or production of this novel. Without in any way limiting the author's [and publisher's] exclusive rights under copyright, any use of this publication to "train" generative artificial intelligence (AI) technologies to generate text is expressly prohibited. The author reserves all rights to license uses of this work for generative AI training and development of machine learning language models.

A catalogue record for this book is available from the National Library of Australia

ALSO BY THE AUTHOR

Books

Rabbits and Other Immigrants: The Alan Parsons Story, self-published, 2018. Second edition, Leschenault Press 2024.

Dorothy Erickson, Metamorphosis, Mookaite and Metropolis: The life and work of an artist jeweller, Co-authored with Phillipa O'Brien and Kathryn Wells; Published by The Western Australian Museum 2025.

Articles

"What Goes Around Comes Around: Juggling Joel Salom", *OZ Arts*, spring edition, 2015. http://www.ozarts.net.au/oz-arts-magazine

"Part 1: Surrealist Artist Raymond Moult-Spiers", *OZ Arts*, spring edition, 2020. http://www.ozarts.net.au/oz-arts-magazine

"Big Sculptures and Other Obsessions: Andrew Hickson", *OZ Arts*, spring edition, 2020. http://www.ozarts.net.au/oz-arts-magazine

"Part 2: The Postmaster Who Would Be Painter", *OZ Arts*, summer edition, 2021. http://www.ozarts.net.au/oz-arts-magazine

Part 3: "The Artist on Stradbroke Island", *OZ Arts*, summer edition, 2021. http://www.ozarts.net.au/oz-arts-magazine

DEDICATION

Dedicated to all creative souls but especially to;
Andrew, Rad, Yasen, Anna, Xena, Luis, and all Ray's mob.

FOR ROO

Sometime between 1 May and 17 May 2024, Roo passed away at the age of 71. As with Raymond, the circumstances of his death remain unclear. Roo had grown thin and, like Raymond, died in his own home but was not discovered for several weeks.

In loving memory of Roo, a delightfully unique character.

I acknowledge the Traditional Custodians of the unceded lands throughout Australia and their connections to land, sea and community. I pay my respect to their Elders past and present, and extend that respect to all First Nations peoples today.

SPOT THE
CARDS. GERMAN ART
EXPERT SAYS I WILL BE
RECOGNISED AS ONE OF THE
GREATS. GREAT WHAT?

AT LAST
THREE MEN OF VERONA.   OLAY.

CONTENTS

9   Preface
10 Prologue

Part 1: The Letter Writer
15 The First Letter
23 The Wedding Guest
29 The Next Letter
35 New Life
41 G-spotting and the Rattlesnake
45 Straddling Straddie
51 The Cat, the Rabbit and the Python
59 The Crocodile Boots
75 The Family Fertility Tree
81 1992 Buckle Your Shoe
89 When Love Calls By
95 The Minister of Bamboo
103 Return to Sender

Part 2: The House Guest
119 Out of the Blue
129 Tailor Made
135 Mr Moult or Mr Spiers

Part 3: The Soldier
149 The New Boy from the Bush Sails Away
157 The Run for Singapore
165 Changi
175 The March of the Slaves
185 The Burma Railway
193 Once in a Blue Moon
203 Kranji

Part 4: The Artist
215 The Artist and His Army of Paintings
223 Paintbox or Letterbox
235 Fantasyland
247 Horsing Around in Horsley
255 A Brush with His Studio
267 Horsley and Away
275 The Artist and the Island
291 The Prodigal Father

299 Epilogue: The Spirit
309 Appendix
310 About the Author
311 Acknowledgements
312 References & Further Reading

Fragments

My eyes water as my gaze deepens entering his definitive brush strokes until I begin to lose myself in his magnificent liberating blues and see they are like stamped addressed envelopes directed across the generations.

My imagination takes hold and I picture a loaded brush plunged into cerulean blue, swirling zinc white through it, until the smell of fresh paint fills my nostrils, and the colour of sky begins to appear.

Just how do I paint sky? It is not a solid surface onto which I peg birds, flying machines and clouds, it is infinite....so how do I paint the sky?

Just how do I understand my Great Uncle Raymond Moult-Spiers? He was never a solid surface onto which I could attach things. He was and is the unfathomable intensity of pure BLUE.

I feel the trepidation the creative urge brings when facing a blank canvas, and I understand he is the foundation of a story, so with a brush and palette of words before me, I overlay, tint, and apply washes, until each eddies against the other in a vibration, suggesting infinity ... suggesting Raymond.

PREFACE

The World War Two diaries of Australian artist Raymond Moult-Spiers were found among his belongings, kept in storage by Lili, his secret daughter. Like her brother, Leonard, and me, she had dutifully kept his gifted effects for twenty-five years without knowing why.

In 1989, when Lili had discovered him to be her birth father, she was thirty-one, and was able to experience the sharing of father–daughter love with him for only seven precious years before his mysterious death.

She could not, however, share this wondrous revelation with everyone, as the man who had raised her and her brother still believed them to be his own. Leonard sadly remained oblivious to his true parentage until Raymond's passing.

The enigma that was Raymond Moult-Spiers occupied a post box in my life for fifteen years. He arrived by mail and exited the same way. By then he was a seasoned artist and I was just starting out.

This book explores my life as his letters fluttered in and out. Twenty years after his death these same letters were delivered back to me, and with good reason eclipsed Australia's 2015 commemoration of the end of World War Two, thus igniting my unresolved curiosity about this man and his death.

Some of the names of the living have been changed, in keeping with Raymond's delight in dubbing close family with names starting with L.

PROLOGUE
Early Autumn 1980

Little did I know the consequences of reaching for it – but my eyes were fixed on the note in the centre of the dining table.

I had been surveying the objects on the table from a distance while listening to Aunty June convey information about the items to her cousin Mavis, my mother. The folded shabby piece of paper occupied the small pile of discard, resulting from the passing of Ethel, June's mother.

My stretch towards it was made as though an onerous weight was laid across me. My arm and chest slid slowly across the shiny veneered table, edging towards the folded paper. My fingers approached the note like the elevated shovel on a digger and retracted it into my heart-felt destiny.

I could hear Aunty June telling the story about the appearance of the mysterious piece of paper left half dangling out of my Great-Aunty Ethel's fuse box.

Apparently the author of the note had called into Ethel's home just a few months before her demise. The author had not indicated he was coming so it was all on the off-chance that someone might be there, but no one was. Ethel was in hospital awaiting her expiry. By plucking the folded paper from the remnants of odd tangible objects, I made the shift from spectator to investigator. The repercussion of this shift was to lead me into a long and curious relationship.

Holding the note, I gazed at the handwriting as it swept across the page, slanting heavily to the right. Everything about the pointy formations seemed to suggest a keen, sharp and imaginative mind. Astonished capital letters were arranged like pickets along an old leaning fence, their versatile importance throwing reckless ideas in all directions. The rhythm of his word placement marched a battalion of letters into a kindly sort of inner battle. It read:

I THOUGHT I WAS ALL ALONE IN THIS COUNTRY, but my BROTHER in england told me we had RELATIVES in WESTERN AUSTRALIA. He gave me your ADDRESS, SO I came here to WA to look you up.
I have called by a couple of times, BUT NO ONE HOME. I am living over EAST. my wife DIED two years ago, and I AM ON MY OWN.
DISAPPOINTED to have missed you. PLEASE get in touch.
RAYMOND MOULT-SPIERS
c/- North STRADBROKE Island, QUEENSLAND

I scarcely read the words; instead, I had seen the sharp lines of an artist's woodcut. I had read the feelings that came from each slice into the paper. I had read the squeezed loops in the letters all rushing into a future yet to be lived. I saw the hope that aloneness drags into the next day. My heart felt each word in ways no one else had.

Before I knew it, I was asking for more about the note. My Aunty June told me that it seemed to her the writer went by their grandmother's maiden name of Moult but had added a second to it.

With Aunty June and my mother, a generation of just two born in Western Australia, both sitting before me, both undecided about this man's legitimacy, and the others, all immigrants, all eight already gone to the grave, I could have given up there and then. But something shouted to me and I responded, saying aloud:

"I will write to this man, and we will see if he is ours."

Everyone nodded, and so I did.

"Blue that will always be there as it is now
after all man's destruction is finished."

– Georgia O'Keeffe, artist, 1887-1986

part one

THE LETTER WRITER

June 18th, 1980

Re. Moult

MAD.MAD.MAD.

Dear Julie,
Thank you for your marvellous letter. I was beginning to wonder why I was such an odd. Ball. Now I know. Sorry I haven't answered before, But I have been to the country seat at Warwick QLD for 4 weeks. which is full of antiques. And some magnificent collages of mine. If you don't come here. I shall be forced to come over there and visit you mob of gypsies. My brother JOHN ran away from his foster parents to live with the gypsies when he was younger in England. He will be thrilled to bits when I tell him the great work you are doing. He like me. Is always tearing off to the continent. Nepal. now it's the Isle of Wight ...

Raymond Moult-Spiers, 1980

1
The first letter

When Uncle Raymond's first letter arrived, I was living in rural Western Australia. Snippi was my nickname back then. It was given to me as a show of affection by my soon-to-be husband when I was vigorously cutting his hair. We were living together in a workers cottage on a dairy farm. I was employed as an art lecturer in the nearby regional centre and he was looking for work. We had a menagerie in the large yard around the little home, surrounded by acres of cows. I was fond of the lamb we were raising – such a personality. One night I arrived home to find the lamb in the fridge. The shock tore at me. Emotion against reason. The shock of my shock tore at him. The sacrifice remained stone-cold silent. I took the side of the lamb, cried and refused to go to the fridge.

I should have known he would exercise his butchering skills sooner or later, but it hadn't occurred to me that the lamb was in his sights. After all, the lamb had been employed to keep the grass down. But by morning I understood and admired his expertise.

In the spring the year before the lamb was cooked and I couldn't eat it, a strange twist had eventuated in my life. The duck farmer with whom I was cohabiting at the time had left one morning to run his leather stall at a country show. He had forgotten his vital tools and had called me to request that I bring the said items at once. I had obliged and there in the show ring, for all to see, was my former beloved (my soon-to-be husband). His cream moleskins, R.M. Williams Cuban-heel boots and pale-blue shirt all moving with a familiarity I could not resist.

A horseman and gentle horsebreaker, he was handing out red and blue ribbons to the riders of show ponies. He had seen me watching him and wove his way through the crowds to my side. With an urgency unsurpassed by any other, I was his, again. Words got in the way of the undercurrent that had already taken me.

The duck farmer willingly gave me back to my former beloved and with wings unclipped took flight to better pluckings.

In the autumn of 1980, having reclaimed his Snippi, my beloved proposed to me in the main street of a timber town, where we had just purchased a small acreage of forest. All my savings, now trees, had made good half their value, and was reason for his urge to be in a union. His contribution was yet to come. With the lamb now in the pot, my upcoming wedding and the emergence of Uncle Raymond happened simultaneously.

Uncle Raymond's first letter, along with all our mail, went to my parents' house in town. Fresh milk was collected from the dairy near our cottage. Lush pasture sprung from the organised cascading irrigation channels from the dam in the surrounding hills. Kikuyu grass, suitable for high-traffic areas, grew under the feet of cows. Two men charged with keeping the kikuyu out of the channels, diligently sprayed the edges of the waterways with poison. A gift from the government, the horrific results of such diligence yet to be realised by the gentle rural community.

A deserted mission for Aboriginal people was nestled in the sumptuous nape of the first rise into the hills. The people had long since been dispersed to housing in the surrounding rural communities. According to the government of the day there was work to be done with these families in community centres. I was there, my skills in the arts called upon. The Aboriginal people who came were also called upon. Interest was measured to be at its greatest during morning-tea time. Forced to learn skills that led nowhere, they cut designs into lino blocks, designs from books their people did not write. Using images stolen from places from whence their people did not come, they printed from inks their people never had, on fabrics their people did not know, and made cushion covers their people never needed. Then they painted "on-glaze" white china tiles to inlay into a wall they would never have thought of.

I always took a leather-burning tool and scraps of leather. Men cut out nature's shapes and burned patterns on shaped small frogs and lizards but mostly made leaves, which they didn't want.

One day Alicia, an Aboriginal woman married to an Italian outcast, took possession of a small empty shop on the highway through the little town. The cyclone-fenced train line ran behind the shop, and on the other side was their house. Alicia, filled with hopes and dreams, was granted the use of the shop by the town council. The cast-off crafts of others were collected, reworked and recreated by Alicia and myself and put on sale. I, her mentor, guarantor on paper.

Together we would sit on cold winter mornings, at the hearth of an open fire, in the cottage by the railway line, where we would make clay beads and animal shapes, throwing them into the hot coals to bake in the ashes.

Macramé string curtains were threaded with the burnt leather leaves, and frogs, shells and tree nuts, baked clay beads, bleached bones and feathers appeared. The nameless shop, soon baptised Nidja Craft, attracted scant visitors. Undeterred, the beaming Noongar woman, with her long pink fingernails covering her mouth when she chuckled, stood there behind the counter with her hopes and dreams. The gap where her front tooth once stood replaced by her dazzling fuchsia-lacquered fingertips as she proudly told of her intention to forge a better life for her adopted Noongar children. Our efforts, built together like this, made mentor and pupil interchangeable and then made us the friends we were.

I had started this work while in cohabitation with the leather craftsman who doubled as the duck farmer. I had learned many skills and had won a prize for a painted leather garment I made and entered into "Crafts in Gear". The garment became the feature tabard over my plain coarse-weave wedding dress, when I did not marry the duck farmer but instead married the lamb butcher.

I had written my first letter to Uncle Raymond back in April, without really revealing too much, only loosely telling him of his yet-to-be-claimed family in Western Australia, but the story must have captured him.

The creative spirit residing in us and all Moult descendants lay in wait. His first letter, having arrived at my parents' house, had seen me slowly deciphering the arrangements of the alphabet all marching in forward motion, stepping over misplaced full stops, with important capitals suddenly appearing out of nowhere.

I stood in the doorway of my parents' kitchen reading this first letter aloud to my mother. I needed to pause, to take a breather. The letter was certainly newsy and I was struggling to read his writing.

My mother was in the vestibule next to me and was midway through the ironing. She took advantage of the pause and disappeared down the passage, gone to hang my father's shirts in the wardrobe.

The ironing board was set up with a view through the open glass doors to the TV, which was blaring away in the lounge room. From where I was in the kitchen doorway, I saw my mother enter the lounge and stand in front of the screen. I read on silently.

You are like a beam of light to me. I do believe in Reincarnation. And UFOs are my special subject. I am fortunate to have seen one at close hand. and was not a bit perturbed. I felt an affinity.

UFOs? At last, I felt the potential of support, although no more was said of it. I, at age fourteen, and locked away in a country boarding school, had been gazing out of the dormitory window one night after lights out with two other girls, when our eyes locked upon a huge, magnificent cigar-shaped glowing form. It came out of nowhere, glowed a brilliant white light but curiously did not light up its surrounds. We three were kneeling on our beds in an enclosed verandah on the second storey and could clearly see the dam in the horse paddock, over which the massive long object appeared, hovered and disappeared, neither radiating light nor reflecting it. No one makes that stuff up.

You didn't mention your marital status or your age. But that may be asking too much. I have enclosed copy of a painting and a short resume of my P.O.W. days of the Burma Railway. I have been back a couple of times. and Changi. But that's enough.

A folded magazine article lay on the kitchen table with the opened envelope, presumably where the painting and résumé resided. I would look at that later.

A little further into the letter, I again paused to contemplate the content. It was full of seemingly random thoughts listed but without being listed. Written like dot points without the dots, the words instead leapfrogging full stops that had no reason to be where they were. Never a dull moment in this mind, I thought. Reading on, I saw that he, without so much as a blink, like a salesman on the job, revealed his own status and my position within that.

> *My wife died nearly three years ago. No children. (officially) (boy and girl). I am now back on the ISLAND with a Female friend who is looking after the cooking and the cleaning. I thought I was close to John's daughter PENELOPE. But it seems I am much closer to you. Whoever you are.*

Such a claim. Whatever I had written to him in that single letter seemed to have had the effect of catching him, hook, line and sinker. I wished I had kept a copy, but I hadn't and, with the months that had passed between our correspondence, it was difficult to remember. I looked down at his letter again. Not a paragraph in sight, it took ages to find my place again, after I had looked up to ponder.

> *"GYPSIES". Once in England I bought 2 'GEORGE MORELAND' paintings. Both of GYPSYIES. And always had a leaning towards them. I have a lot of things that might interest you. Family photographs. Mementos.*

I called out to my mother, "And he is like you and your mother. He likes the idea of being connected to gypsies." My mind wrapped itself around the image captured in a painting my grandmother had done of a group of gypsies gathered around a campfire. As a child I loved looking at that painting. But the small painting of a Native American girl kneeling by a stream was my favourite. I could feel the water as it passed over her cupped hand. It was real to me.

> *And as you say. this longing to own land. I had 8 properties on this Island. And now down to this one. Am INVESTING IN GOLD. As my surplus cash is affecting my War Pension. So I shall dispense with it. And get a M16 with 5000 rounds of AMMO. And hope for the best.*

What was he telling me? Five thousand rounds of ammo and an M16 to protect his gold! Is he saying he had translated eight properties into pure gold so that he gets a meagre war pension? Absurd! I start to see him like some kind of weird movie character. Both intrigued and compelled, I follow my finger to its tip and read on. But with each rush of his pen's contact with the page something vastly different is presented.

> *I have a photograph of MOULTS ANTIQUE shop in London and his three spinster sisters were dressmakers to the Royal family. How about that. And the antiques at WARWICK. Came from the DUKE of BEDFORD's estate. Carved oak side board, marble credenza. Queen Anne bed. Admiral sea chest. etc. and here it is nearly a month since you wrote. I feel so guilty. I am rushing though a few lines to make it up. Will be more thorough next time.*

More thorough? My God, reading this letter is a bombardment, an assault on the imagination. I took a deep breath and followed my finger again.

Ah, the stage, art and dance – that is certainly a family trait on my mother's side. Both she and I could also speak of such experiences and were well ensconced in the world of theatre and costume construction. I called this out to her as she headed back to the ironing board. I followed my finger again and began to read out loud.

Had a farm, bank. Post office, hardware. Groceries. Newsagent. Been around the world about 4 times. Worked for WALT DISNEY in HOLLYWOOD could be taken and have been taken for LEE MARVIN. Have broken horses in California. extra on movie set.

My mother and I looked at each other, both blurting out our astonishment wrapped up in a single questioning word: "What?"

Now it all comes together. "GYPSY". I like it. I do own the two properties. Plus 'old masters' wood carving and "FOUND OBJECTS" driftwood rocks etc. love making collages ... But please reply. And thank you for all the work you have put into this. I was beginning to think. What a waste of. A whole goddam life gone down the shoot. And no one to share it with. Or pass onto.

We two were battling to comprehend all that he had written. My mother was trying to figure out if he really was a long-lost relative.

My sister LINDA died three years ago and brother JOHN. Is in England. Very smart. Can do anything. Has a caravan. Goes all over the place: and it was just chance that he mentioned the family in WA. And as I said I called into the house when I was there. And no one at home. So it's all beginning to gel. And I am very grateful you took the trouble to answer and have such an interest in the family. I hear sounds in the kitchen. She is cleaning out the fridge. As WALTER MATHAU would say. SHE IS NOT PRIMITIVE she's FERAL. But I get fed and no stupid ideas about marriage. Lets work something out I'll visit

THE FIRST LETTER

you or vice versa. You'd be very welcome. Much love too. Ray xxx

The letter, a maze of false starts and dead ends, gave me some kind of unexplained anticipatory sense of hope, a connection pre-emptive of a future I could not explain. My mother, on the other hand, had resisted him and his words, and was busy attempting to fault his belonging.

With so much revealed, I had to read through the letter again and again. His excitement shot darts of recognition into me. I understood him, but why? I saw his story like he had summarised a lifetime into billboards for sideshows and circus acts. My imagination did the rest.

With his correspondence arriving in the same year I was to marry, on impulse I invited the cryptic Raymond to my wedding. It was next to impossible to verify his family connection as it had soon come to light that he had been with seven foster families since the age of two. His memories of family were scant and seemed unreliable, but I nevertheless somehow knew and believed he belonged.

The problem of verification of his claimed identity occurred because the two Western Australian Moult descendants of immigrant parents no longer had connections with the family in the UK.

All they had was a sketchy family tree on their grandmother's side. Both remembered seeing it on a scrap of paper at various times but no one knew where it was.

The frustration lingered until, in a timely fashion, it did emerge, found in its hiding place safely tucked inside the old Moult family Bible.

Once discovered, the Bible's sweet, musky smell and its secreted information wafted from the fragile, soft tissue paper. The slight scent of printer's ink stamped into tight black letters front and back of each sheet still lingered. The delicate pages were enclosed in a worn, pitted, black leather cover with fragments of gold quietly twinkling in the corners of the embossing, the glistening signalling hope.

In turn, the tattered, folded paper, containing the remnants of a family tree, was like a precious jewel, time-worn by the hands of ancestors long since transferred to the great unknown. An examination of its antiquity, its mystery, its perfection, its flaws, disclosed handwritten information that had somehow slipped inside the very fibres of the paper. The name Norman Moult sat at the top – no dates, no mention of a wife, but two sons stretched out from him, Tom on the left and Jack on the right. All eyes fell heavily onto Jack's line.

It could be seen that Jack Moult married Phoebe and from this pair came eleven children, with only two adult children claiming marriage, the others just seeming to fade away, their names receding into the paper and difficult to read.

The two deemed married were son John Thomas Moult (Raymond's father) and daughter Ann Moult (my great-grandmother). Each had four children. Ann Moult and her four children had moved to Western Australia from the UK in 1920. Of John Thomas Moult's four children, the story was a little more complex. However, written for all to see was the name of his youngest child, Raymond. The evidence was in and, with the wedding looming, both Western Australian-born descendants were now convinced Raymond belonged.

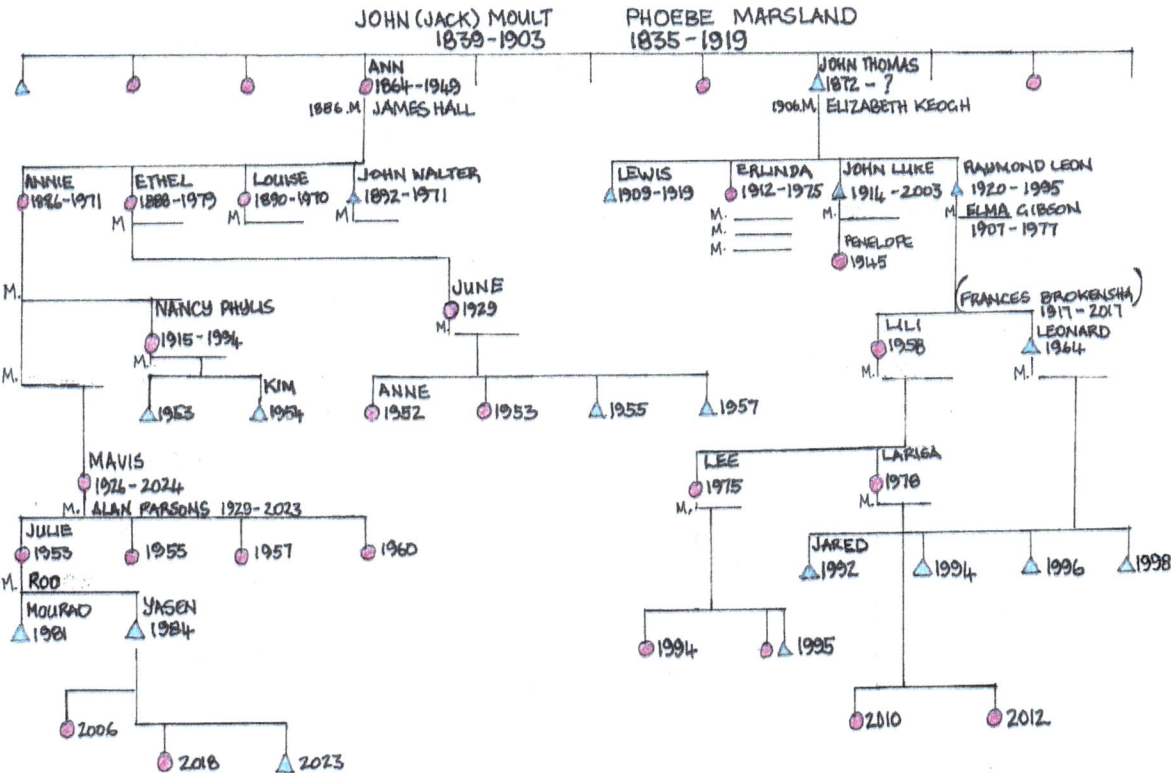

ABOVE Family tree, showing key people mentioned in this book

Dear family from the SWAMP.
IT's true I live on a ridge in the middle of a SWAMP.
And this morning when venturing out I found two
carpet snakes mating under the Lantana bush. ...

Raymond Moult-Spiers, 1980

2
The wedding guest

Time marched on and I made my wedding invitations and slipped them into handmade leather wallets. I told my guests not to wear pointy heels. Not to wash the car. And if they were at the wildlife park they had gone too far. I sent one to my newly found Great-Uncle Raymond, a stranger to his Western Australian family.

Perhaps it was the handpainted leather wallet or the whacky invitation that secured his flight to Western Australia, or was it perhaps the echoes of things so dear that drew him? We shall never know. I had mentioned a "Swamp Dusk Thing" to be held after the wedding, a mystery in itself, and as he loved his swamp he may have felt the immediacy affinity affords.

Certain that he belonged to us, Uncle Raymond then flew across Australia with a large, wet painting, his wedding gift. Through fear of it being damaged, he had carried it with him into the aircraft's cabin. It surely would have been dripping with its thick collage of found objects set into layers of soft malleable house paint. How he managed his meagre luggage while juggling the painting must have been a source of bewilderment to onlookers, likely drawn in and soon to be a party to his excitable shenanigans.

Arriving at Perth airport, in the middle of nowhere as it was, challenged most back then. There was no direct airport-to-city public transport to speak of, so into a taxi he clambered for the long drive to the Perth Railway Station. Here he took the train to Bunbury. Still juggling the boldly framed hardboard, he arrived on "the day" and was collected at the station by my parents, who were compelled to take charge of this stranger, now deemed a long-lost relative destined to be reunited with his kin at their daughter's wedding.

He had come from afar, this sacred ceremony also his welcome back into the fold, his return to the tribe and with an exchange of gifts. Such a welcoming.

FRAGMENTS OF THE SKY

ABOVE Raymond Moult-Spiers with the bride and groom, Aug 1980

In keeping with who I was then, though unbeknown to Raymond, was the painting he gifted. It was called The Rainmaker, inspired by the stories told to him by the First Nations women on the island where he lived. Evidently, the women would throw crystals and plumage of native birds into the air in a ceremony said to bring the rains. He, however, had thrown smashed windscreen glass and old duster feathers into the air, allowing the whole arrangement to fall, randomly embedding into the wet house paint. Other objects were arranged for good measure. The energy in the work was apparent and filled some who viewed it with silent awe, but rendered others simply speechless. My husband-to-be had come without the trappings of a close family. They, from whom he had escaped, lived across the border and beyond. His resistance to integration into family, any family, was yet unknown to me.

I had made him a handpainted leather belt to match my feathered leather tabard. The outlined simple triangular design, carefully burned into the leather, was filled with blocks of turquoise, red, yellow and white, so bold on the brown leather, supplied to me by the duck farmer.

With complementary leather, we were a match, my husband-to-be and me. Back there on the dairy farm where we rented a cottage, I fell pregnant a week before the ring was put on my finger. Not knowing, you see; still concealed from me.

Oh yes, that ring, my grandmother's gypsy silver band of crescent moons dancing in a circle. My grandmother, Uncle Raymond's cousin, provided me with the right of passage to travel the blood-tie river with Raymond Moult-Spiers a while.

But what of those cows, some aborting their unborn? Those cows eating the grass along the poisoned irrigation channels, sprayed by the two men? And me drinking the milk from the dairy?

But let us not ponder such things with a wedding to be enjoyed.

On Mr and Mrs Rabbit Ears' farm was where we were. The one at the end of our road. These Rabbit Ears played their part as music-makers in the bush band called the same.

Once guests were positioned on the property, transport was the horse and buggy trotting along the winding track, surpassed only by the tractor toting a trailer-load of hay-bale seating supporting teetering select guests hurled up there by Mr Rabbit Ears himself. Told to perch on these bales, their street best and stockings caught in the straw, all sat where they landed for the journey down the winding bush track to where the river meets the swamp, and trepidation joined anticipation.

On the little bridge we stood. He in moleskins tucked into drover's boots, woven cloth and painted belt. I in leather and feathers. Such a pair, with their commitments committed to paper and turned to words floating through the air. Nothing done by tradition, it was all made up with flair, like children playing.

Who told those costumed folks, those filmic extras to come along dressed so? Who said wear hats and boots? But there they were – a Moroccan princess, a red, white and blue baton-throwing band leader, a safari hunter, an Edwardian golf champion, the Queen of Spades – all mad hatters, all wedding tea-party attendees.

No one knew how to be at this wedding they could not hear and scarcely see. Bride and groom up on a distant bridge, a river passing underneath, bride clutching a bouquet of cascading emu feathers later worn on her head. No throwing the bouquet for the single girls to dream on. No garters, no something borrowed, something blue.

And this husband of mine changed the script and surprised me with his own. Heartfelt and tender it was, and only I could hear. After which two rings took their places on fingers so that others would know what we had done.

All the while, Raymond, with his conjured connection to Canada and the Native Americans there, saw a different wedding. As told in letters yet to come, he saw a wedding of many kindred souls, a union, a reunion. Souls thrown together in the air like the crystal shards that landed in a painting. Electric charges firing as they hit one another falling to the earthed surface. The significance of being married in feathers and leather over running water was not lost on him, him and Grey Cloud, his Native American spirit guide. Him and his belief in the disincarnate entity here to guide us. Then we, husband and wife, and our select few guests ventured back to the Rabbit Ears' farmhouse for music, nonsense and a jolly good wedding feast.

The two tables were at right angles, following the line of the L-shaped living area, husband at the end of one, wife at the end of the other, sitting together at the outside corner, the place where the tables aptly joined. High, fan-backed peacock chairs for we two, a prince and a princess.

The pottery tableware was all handmade especially for the Rabbit Ears' spread. Bowls, plates, goblets and platters, with motifs from the First Nations culture so dear to me, set upon kangaroo-print cloth, curtains matching.

A toast was made by Tina, my theatrical sister, with scarcely a mention of the two now joined. Goblets like cement pillars were raised to bride and groom, all the rest balderdash and absurdities delivered by the family dramaturge. Goblets drained, gorging began on rustic homemade bread and soup served from a pumpkin for fun, a banquet of roasted meats and baked veg. Apple crumble and custard to finish the spread.

With feasting done, then came the wandering performers, artisans, minstrels, all set free, igniting laughter and flights of fancy on the way back to the bridge across the river, on the way to the swamp to romp.

Uncle Raymond – where was Raymond? Ah, there he was, sitting with his two cousins, all new to him, Mavis and June, all the same age, their blood matching his. Like a moth to the flame flew the family dramaturge as she and he could outdo most with their animated witticisms, sparring against one another to entertain. More proof he belonged.

ABOVE Raymond Moult-Spiers with cousins, Mavis & June, Aug 1980

THE WEDDING GUEST

ABOVE The wedding gift. Ray Moult-Spiers, *The Rainmaker*, 1980, collage of mixed materials on board, 60x50cm. Private collection. Inspired by the ritual created by Quandamooka people on Minjerribah (North Stradbroke Island).

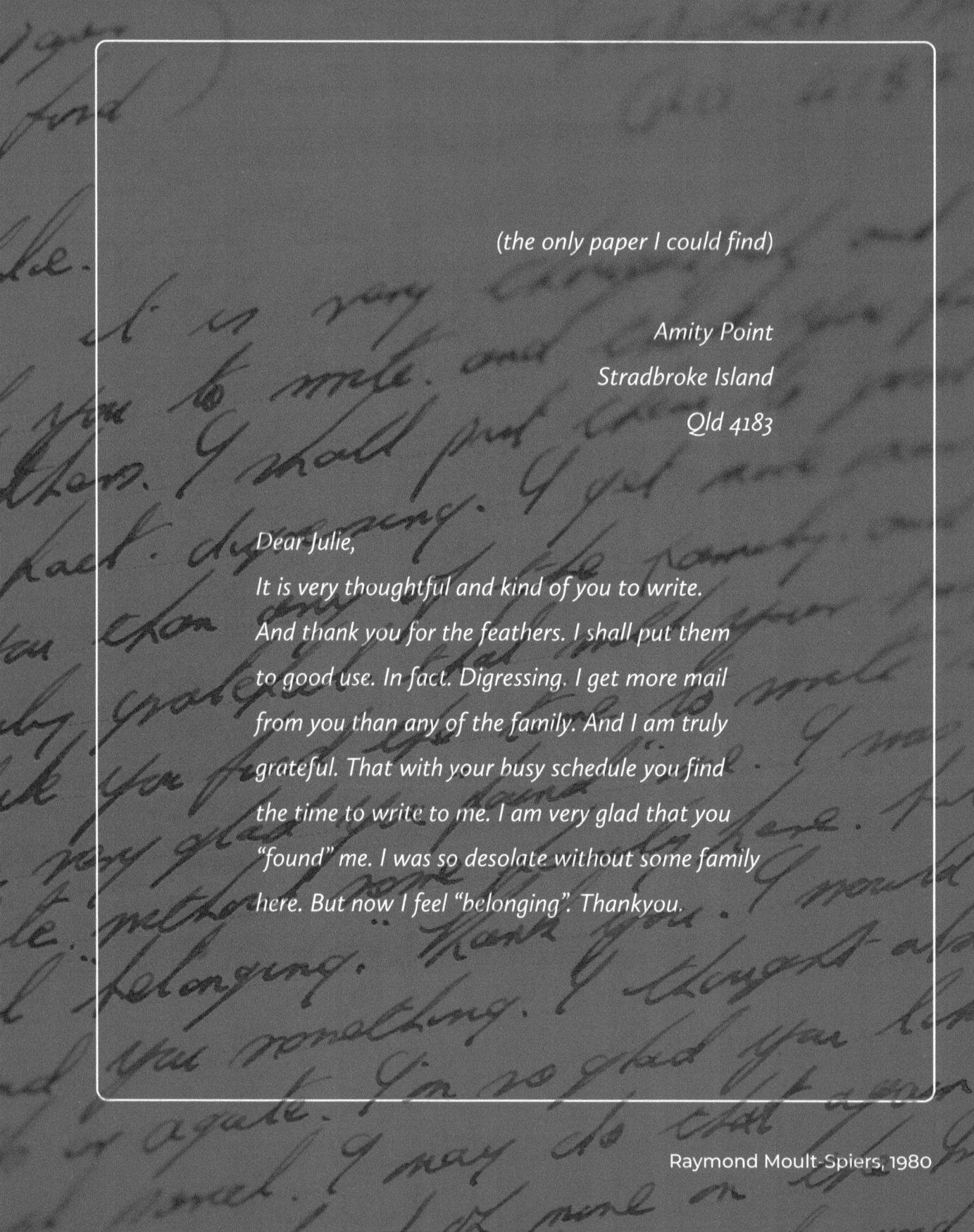

(the only paper I could find)

Amity Point
Stradbroke Island
Qld 4183

Dear Julie,

It is very thoughtful and kind of you to write. And thank you for the feathers. I shall put them to good use. In fact. Digressing. I get more mail from you than any of the family. And I am truly grateful. That with your busy schedule you find the time to write to me. I am very glad that you "found" me. I was so desolate without some family here. But now I feel "belonging". Thankyou.

Raymond Moult-Spiers, 1980

3
The next letter

It was the opening sentences of this letter that intrigued me. How is it he was orphaned and bought up in several foster homes, yet refers to his family? How had he found his brother John and his niece Penelope? This question would stay with me for decades.

At the wedding, blood kin all three, all the same age, even though Raymond was a generation apart, were meeting for the first time – Raymond, Mavis and June. And him with a photograph of Mavis and June's grandmother, saying she was his mother.

"Impossible!" the cousins cried. "She was already in Australia the year you were born." A shamble of misinformation and identities never known to a child aged two, thrust into an orphanage. And here he is aged sixty, gripping that photograph of his father's sister, calling her his mother, hearts going out to him. Stories shared, laughs galore, warmth, connection, and future visits planned. For the bride, none of that. Distracted with her wedding, it was a mere brush with her Great-Uncle Raymond, both still strangers, penpals waiting to meet.

With a honeymoon abroad pending, husband and I left the wedding party and drove to Perth, where we caught the ferry for the thirty-minute trip overseas to Rottnest Island, a very affordable honeymoon. A strange mirror image of the island off Brisbane where Raymond came from.

A few days in and the nausea made its appearance. Try as I might, I could not avoid it implicating its way into our enjoyment. My husband, disappointed and appalled, asserted his anger about things not going the way he wanted. Although chastised, I could not fathom why, let alone make the nausea go away. Unable to change a thing, I did my best around the queasiness.

The failed honeymoon over, we discovered the reason for the nausea – I was pregnant – I had taken our baby to our wedding.

Back home, thankyou notes on handmade paper were made, folded and sealed with hot red wax, and sent out. Far too primitive. I was yet to realise

LEFT Ann Hall (nee Moult) 1864-1949, c. 1910, Raymond's aunt and my mother's & June's grandmother.

the full hidden meaning of sealing wax, yet to understand the role of the seal to Raymond's lot.

Straight into the hayfever season we were … this time it was my loving husband who was incapacitated and unable to change how his body responded. His hayfever provoked an anger that flared into a violent outburst one night, until unborn baby and I surrendered to his stranglehold on the situation, we three now encapsulated in silent trauma. The vehement incident lay set like a trap we all knew to give a wide berth to.

That aside, we moved forward with plans and dreams of a build on the bush block amid the tall timbers of Pemberton. Hopes for a cabin, a hut, a home uniquely fashioned by our own hands, with only one book to inspire this imagined alternative abode. The handwritten, hand-drawn pages set and printed in black and white on large-scale pages of rough paper was called Shelter, a manual for unskilled builders with dreams of their own. And yet the arrival of another publication was sheer delight. *Handmade Houses: A Guide to the Woodbutcher's Art* built visions and filled us with inspired possibilities.

Uncle Raymond somehow understood us and had sent us this volume, which held a gorgeous collection of images of the most unique creative constructions we had ever seen. He sent this along with indications of collected items used in his collages that might also be suitable to include in the build.

Good luck with the sculptured house. Perhaps the book will help. Let me know if I can assist have plenty of dolls eyes. Pens' heads. Railway tunnels. Boot laces. Hair pins. Dogs collars. Shirt studs and stained-glass windows.

He also wrote of his other interests, such as botany, specifying a huge collection of plants at his country seat in Warwick, along with mentions of the acquisition of some strange, or perhaps weird and wonderful, antique and exotic collectables. This man had some broad interests and a mind to match. At just twenty-seven years of age, I doubted I had much to offer, save some kind of alignment in our DNA.

Deeper into the letter he referred to Kath Walker (known as Oodjeroo Noonuccal from 1987), a Quandamooka woman of the Noonuccal clan, whose brother Eddie, like Raymond, had been a prisoner of war on the Burma Railway.

Kath Walker. The Aboriginal poetess lives not far from me. In fact, we have quite a large tribe here. I get oysters and fish from them. But like you. I would like to see more of their arts and crafts. I hope the "RAINMAKER" is working. According to the weather charts. You should have received rain by now.

Leaving that topic, the coincidence of my using sealing wax on my wedding invitations and thankyou notes was revealed when he claimed to have received a royal seal among some of his English family's relics.

The sealing wax was dribbled over Raymond's envelope, which bore the imprint of the said seal, and the letter was duly delivered to our country estate in Western Australia. Reading on, I noticed he had begun to underline headings:

FAMILY

LUKE. LINDA. RAYMOND. LEON FATHER JOHN LUKE. Was the first man to transport Irish horses to America. He had three spinster sisters who were dressmakers to the Royal Family. IDA. ADA and EVA. Very strange perhaps that's where the seal came from. I have seven foster parents. And never lived with the others after mother died. The name was Elizabeth Keogh so there's a bit of Oirish in there ...

INTERESTS

Art. Antiques. Afghan rugs. Agriculture. Anti-Socialism. (ADAMSKI. UFOs) And ANNEXES. Mad about shelves. And the brief glimpse I had of your place inspired me to build an "ARBOUR" on the back lawn. JASMINE and all kinds of creepers and ferns and gourds. I have seven plants four planted out and three still in the tub. So as soon as it rains. Which should be tonight: I shall plant the rest out: A house full of antiques at Warwick. Which will be the next home for a while. Probably stay there until after Christmas. When all the "tourists" have gone home.

His alphabetically inspired interests written amid a mix of capitals and plantings and then news of his impending escape to his country seat. His list of interests starting with "A" implying or threatening that the rest of the alphabet is yet to follow!

Such mental agility.

Saw the first carpet snake last week – asleep on a tree branch. But he slipped away during the night: like the tip.toeing mangroves. Fortunately, the whole island is a sanctuary. But the sand miners play havoc wherever they operate. Luckily well away from here. Saw some exhibitions in Brisbane last week and was inspired by the Japanese wrapping show …

What? Inspired by the Japanese wrapping show? After years being their POW, how very forgiving he must be.

DOINGS.
Apart from building the studio from scrap timber from the mill. I am now building a PATIO out front. It will have benches made for all kinds of ferns and creepers. And shade the house at the same time. Last week I saw an orange wallaby and I had a witness. So I asked the local wild life expert. And he says. YES. it's a golden wallaby. Very rare. And called a Wellsby. After the local who first saw them. So when I go bush now. I will take the camera. In case I get close enough …
THE ORNAMENTAL GOURDS are thriving. And will make a good addition to my shelves. I have a MANIA for Shelves. For paintings, pottery. Driftwood. Also I shall try and get you a GREEN sea snail shell there are a few about. But not a lot. A good collection of bronzes …

This man's expansion exploits and interests are surely never shelved! They appear so plentiful that a vision of never-ending, half-finished projects spill out from his property into the surrounding swamp, where endangered species lurk, watching.

Unfortunately, I only had a few shots left in my camera at the wedding. But a good one of you. Your mother and me. And a couple of you by yourself. (change of ink) love your handmade paper on the thank you letter. I shall treasure it. Sounds of summer. Crickets. Frogs. And sea hawks. And bush fires. But luckily this place is a bit like the everglades it's in a swamp … Also, if you or any of the family would like to visit. I will make the home available. I have a separate flat I can use. But I must fix the water pump first. Sincerely hope all is well with you. And kind regards to the family and thank you again for inviting me to the wedding. It was beautiful and you did a terrific job. Much love Ray

And now added to the list, a water pump to fix before anyone can visit. The invitation to his home thwarted while it is contemplated. Arms held open, the watergate closed for repair.

Meanwhile, my own waters were preparing to break, although much too early. First responder, husband Roo, was caught on the hop.

ABOVE The author in her wedding tabard with emu feather headdress, 1980. Winner of the regional Crafts in Gear, Award for Excellence, 1979.

SUMMER QUARTERS.ONLY
55 Forde St
Allora
QLD 4362
Feb 1981

Dear Jooly, Androo and MOURAD,
I am glad to report everything is alright. I have had a word with the people upstairs. And they assure me no harm shall come to his lordship.

Raymond Moult-Spiers, 1981

4
new life

On Australia day 1981, just six months from the day when Roo and I had stood on the bridge over running water to vow we loved one another enough to make our own tribe, our little papoose began wanting to get out ... in somewhat of a hurry.

Barely showing my baby bump and contractions in full gear, a rush was made to the local regional hospital. The contractions were held back with drugs and by restricting me to a hospital bed, all of which lasted scarcely one night, before we two, mother and still-encapsulated bub were flown by the Flying Doctor to Perth. Then, with siren whirring, we were raced through the city streets to dock at our new port in Emergency at King Edward Maternity Hospital.

With a difference of opinion between husband and me about when a foetus can be saved, and consequently no husband by my side, Eleanor, my sister in Perth, came instead. As a professional computer executive, she was ill-prepared when, to her horror, she witnessed it all. She witnessed the rawness of birthing and the clinical life-saving doctors who swooped on the twenty-four-week-gestation foetus scarcely within the limits of being able to be saved in 1981.

They wrapped him in cotton wool and aluminium foil and pumped oxygen into his non-functioning lungs. They took him away and gave me a photo of a half-baked red-skinned foetus being inflated by a breathing machine.

My husband came after all, literally after it all. He watched in stony silence as a doctor stitched up the long cut they had made in my vagina to stop any contractions damaging our baby's head.

Our difference of opinion stood between us, both right in our stance, but a living baby to prove one wrong. With the unknowns vast, the confusion enormous and a pure miracle fighting his battle for life, we both stood firm in our corners.

Baby knew it was safer out than in and was willing to take the risk. Father thought "out" meant something was wrong, some horrid unknown flaw that might show itself as imperfection. Father feared this potential. Eventually we learned it was the poisons sprayed on the channels to kill the grass so the water could flow to the pasture that fed the cows whose milk I drank that did it.

Exhausted, I was taken, nurturing the photograph of my new baby, to a ward full of new life held close by doting mothers, each enquiring as to the whereabouts of my own. It was then that I broke. Such a thoughtless thing to do, young mothers and me all now traumatised. A brave mother stepped forward and compassionately asked that I be moved to a childless space.

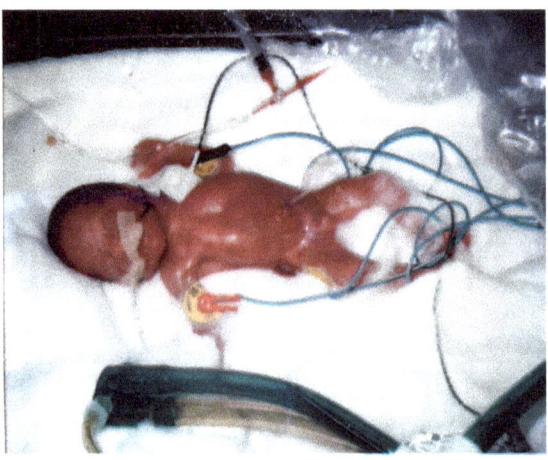

ABOVE Baby Mourad - one hour old.
Born 24.5 weeks gestation, weighing 810g.

A young, perhaps too young, social worker appeared at my new lodging's door. Terrified, she did not enter but spoke to me from the safety of the corridor. She told me there was a support group for the parents of premature babies and a phone number down in the special nursery. I reasoned these parents were already suffering their own experience and shrank back into myself.

A young paediatrician advised returning to my life as quickly as possible. I left the hospital immediately. Harsh as it sounded, this advice gave me back to my husband.

Scheduled in the first week of "Born Too Soon's" life was open-heart surgery. I, as a first-time new mum, could scarcely fathom what was asked but I did not refuse their request for consent to carry it out. My job was to stay with "Born Too Soon" and travel in the ambulance filled with life support equipment to which he was connected. We were transported to the children's hospital where the operation was to take place. I was to keep him calm by sitting by his crib. Awkward, troubled and in the way of "those who knew", I eventually felt confused and anxious, so I left my sleeping baby and disappeared into the suburbs. The inevitable surgery set a valve in his tiny heart to enable his lungs to function.

My new mission in life was expressing milk every three to four hours. Mrs Rabbit Ears from the dairy farm where we were wed, knew a thing or two about milking and so 'twas she who taught me how to express my milk. I drove back and forth to the hospital in the city to see "Born Too Soon" and deliver my milk, now frozen in little breast-sized plastic bags. This gesture was not lost on all the premature babies who were also fed my milk. Perhaps expressing milk was an elusive art for other sudden mothers. The hospital set me the task of telling my ways to these sudden mums. Just how was I able to keep up my milk supply? But Mrs Rabbit Ears' country ideas were too radical for these city girls. These girls who reeled at the idea of extracting milk from their own breasts, or of having their own partners help to maintain a strong milk supply, their compassion for their fragile babies thwarted by their own self-conscious judgement. These city girls who reeled at the thought of various women all over the world who chose to breastfeed another's vulnerable child. Some New Guinea highland women are known to breastfeed their much-valued pigs for the benefit of the whole tribe. Shock and horror on the faces of the city girls, and we all carried on as before.

Raymond's next letter arrived soon after "Born Too Soon" was announced as delivered.

His bold words with the people upstairs and their resulting assurance provided me with an inner strength and sense of knowing I otherwise would not have accessed … deaf and numb as I was to the many spoken words.

I drove back and forth because the doctors said I needed to return to work at the job I had in another city, that I must keep my life as normal as possible "in case baby does not make it". None of this was normal but the head paediatrician said one thing that enabled me to hold the reins steady.

"If your baby were a racehorse, I would bet on him."

Mrs Rabbit Ears sometimes came with me on these hospital trips, where together we tackled the then-unheard-of skin-to-skin contact. But my confidence was shaken on a solo trip when I had peeled my garments away to place my baby near my heart and on my skin and the head nurse, a bloated foreboding creature, stood over me and said in no uncertain terms that what I was doing was disgusting and that I must desist immediately. Her nursery, her rules.

Heartbroken, I covered myself. I waited instead for the time when I was allowed to bathe my baby.

Meanwhile, a virus took "Born Too Soon" into solitary confinement and I was left to paw at the glass around his entombment in the isolation chamber for two weeks.

But Uncle Raymond was there, his spirit hovering, protecting, pulling in the forces, his letters pouring out assurances. But "Born Too Soon", now named Mourad, seemed to inspire some other surprising responses.

I am glad you utilised the MOU as in MOULT.
And the RA as in RAY. So when I open
my new account to avoid the TAX MAN.
I shall be grateful for your permission to
use MOURAD. As the Christian name.

But as time went on further insights arrived.

25 March 1981
55 Forde St
Allora
Qld 4362
Dear fabulous Family,
Thank you for your letter of late and how is the "little buggar". I sincerely hope all is well. It should be. I have offered up alms. Done penance. Fasted in the wilderness. And God knows what if. so he should weigh at least 10 lbs and have a STRAWBERRY ON HIS LEFT SHOULDER. Please don't disappoint me. (but don't hesitate if funds... private ... are urgently needed ... private).

At first, I read his words with a mixed heart. There was my baby embedded in a Special Nursery in a hospital two hours away and me expressing milk and driving it to that city to feed not only my baby but, as it turned out, many of the babies whose mothers could not.

Reading his letter again, I was surprised by the reference to the strawberry mark on the left shoulder. Mourad did not have a strawberry mark on his left shoulder, nor was this further explained (it is, however, my second son who bears that exact mark).

As I read on, to my surprise, news of Raymond's life with a mysterious lady in among the antiques at his country seat of Warwick, began to be explained ... more through what was missing than what he had written. She was never named:

I want to return to the "Island". But this ambitious woman has got herself a job with the local solicitor. And will be leaving her LIVE. IN job in TOOWOOMBA. And living here. My god. Is nothing sacred. No studio. No beach. No roos. No koalas. And most of all. No fishing or privacy. Must have that. So I may form a monastery.

In time I learned his country estates, first at Warwick, then in Allora, Queensland (near Toowomba), were not only stuffed with extraordinary antiques, but also hidden among them was a woman, a wife replacement gone wrong. He had taken up with this independent young woman who had ideas all of her own. She still worked and intended to maintain this status. But she wanted far more than Mr Moult-Spiers anticipated, and he was caught. He liked her being around but did not expect to get so entangled with her financially. And she came with a ready-made fully grown daughter, his own children still believing another to be their father.

In the same letter, I learned of his sentiment for the struggles of imprisoned cattle. Perhaps the POW in him screamed out at the injustice.

I am appalled at the way cattle are left in the sale yard here. Since last Thurs with no feed or water. I tried to let them out. Appealed to the council. The RSPCA. But all to no avail. The auctioneers say it's the responsibility of the owners. So now I am a vegetarian. And when I get back here will get a couple of geese to keep the grass down.

That subject covered, he was mentally at work constructing a second imaginary studio at his country seat. I am not sure why, as he appeared to enjoy his much-needed escapes to his Stradbroke Island studio.

Also, I am trying to beat the system by "MAKING" a studio. it's absolutely no good if you get an orthodox building. The artist has to make it. Then the products will be that much better. I am thinking of poles (not BLUE). And making an A frame type of dwelling. But one has to be wary of local councils. it's a sub rural area. And I may get dobbed in. Alternatively, I could apply for a grant to establish an "art gallery". But the yokals here wouldn't want to know.

He wrote of his passion for big old American cars, particularly his Buicks. Finally, I read he was back in the film business, or at least the business of attempting to be cast in a film that was never to be made.

Have applied for Film extra as Lee MARVIN's stand in. making VOSS by PATRICK WHITE. And filmed S.A. film corp. Marvin plays JUDD. I'll be lucky to play the horse. BUT. If it works out. I will come and visit – then I can see you all again and MIRACLE MOURAD keep the firewood dry. Love all everybody Ray. Who else?

With a month to go before his real due date, Mourad required twice-daily surveillance by the eye doctor as his retinas had begun to quiver, threatening him with blindness. Now convinced he was a sure bet, I took my leave from my job and drove straight to his side, where I stayed for a month until he was released from hospital in May.

That same month, Uncle Raymond sent my first and only Mother's Day card ... a twee 1960s card showing a grinning woman in a jerkin and sensible shoes pushing an oversized pram. This image was about as far away from my reality as you could get.

Four months had passed since Mourad's birth, but he was home and I was managing to breastfeed him, the reality of the situation just showing itself. Thrush was everywhere, eating away at his flesh and insides; breathing could not be taken for granted. I slept with him on my tummy to make sure he was alive. Another four months and into town we moved, the hospital now required more often than was anticipated.

Rabbits, rabbits, rabbits. The man I married proceeded to dig his way through all this. On weekends he went to the hills, where he dug into rabbit warrens to steal kittens from their families for our family. He dug up the back yard too, turned the soil over and over, finally planting vegies. Then we sold our pristine forest acreage, which enabled us to purchase our rented digs from my father. Still digging, my husband dug down to the water table and let the swamp water ooze up to make a pond. The real swamp outside the back gate became our horse paddock. Our two horses grazed there, cows gone and goats brought in for milk and meat. Chooks for eggs, cats for mice, rabbits for pie and dogs for guards. All in the middle of the city surrounding what was called the Big Swamp.

A job at the Agriculture Department on the outskirts of town, and on his horse he went. He dug there too. For me, a job teaching art in the centre of town, and on my rusty bike I went, skirts and straw hat flying.

Mrs Nextdoor was a big sixty-year-old Polish woman hidden under a hairpiece, with a big heart and a big voice to match. Mr Nextdoor, a little Polish man hidden behind a smokescreen of endless cigarettes, with a muffled voice and heart to match. Chooks, ducks and a cocky yelling from its cage, Mrs Nextdoor yelling from the fence, and into the fold we went, mother and son. She took charge of us and we did what she said. Just like when she and her five children moved to a hut in the remote wheatbelt when her husband got a job on the railway, and a snake wriggled in. She told all her five children to get on the table and to stay there. And they did, staying there for most of the day, while she with no English went for help in the nearby town.

Uncle Raymond's letters came filled with treasures in words and pictures. I was always excited to receive them, but with his writing difficult to read and words easily misread, other stories got made up and mixed in. The result often confused me until I realised it was the energy I felt that was the thing. Some letters were funny, some were sad, but they all reached in and took me away from myself, from my worries. It was an energy that arrived and swam about me for days. Those responding words of mine enveloped and sent to the island.

Amity Point

Sept 27th

Dear Julie Roo

Mourad

Please forgive this needy reply. [Change to black pen] but I am so emotionally disturbed about Mourad. That I felt I must COMMUNICATE AT ONCE.

Raymond Moult-Spiers, 1982

5
G-spotting and the rattlesnake

That was all that was said about the urgency. Judging from the date, Mourad was sure to have been struggling with the spring pollens, asthma and resulting hospitalisation. Raymond's letter went on:

thank you for your generosity. photographs. letter, JADE etc. I once had 10 pieces of the best but my wife didn't approve. so I hide them in the STUDIO where some got broke. so decided to sell the lot before total disaster and concentrate on BRONZE of which I have several pieces including a suspicious "RODIN DECENT FROM THE CROSS".

"A suspicious Rodin" sounded very suspicious.

IF this be love. play on. but my sometime girlfriend prefers to fritter her spare time away going to classical concerts or strange journeys on steam trains. also she suffers from verbal DYSENTRY. no wonder her boss is forever taking many trips into the bush but its been going on four years now. and she is desirous of sharing or stealing my privacy. she wants to reduce me to a pumpkin and listen to Bach and Beethoven all day and half the night. But I found a way to shut her up temporarily. I discovered her G.SPOT. named after ERNST GRAFENBURG in the 1950s. of course Masters and Johnsons laughed it off. saying it didn't exist. so being on neighbourly terms with Dr DAVID CILENTO BROTHER OF DIANNE. he confirmed the G SPOT did exist. Located in the vestibule bean shaped. well I found it and gave it hell. she was so exhausted after 2 hours and 24 orgasms later she fell into a deep sleep. so I stole her vibrator. (what a bloody insult.).

The female anatomy lesson was very unexpected.

Glad to hear you are COMING to Brisbane. [Change to texta] in January. you shall cross the BAY to this TROPICAL PARADISE. AND I SHALL SLEEP IN THE STUDIO FLAT. DOWN TOWN

At this point our planned trip to Melbourne with Mourad to meet Roo's family was very much on the cards, so taking the extra step to Brisbane seemed completely possible. We got to Melbourne alright. In the mix I recall going to see Roo's old girlfriend, who, despite being shacked up with her new fella and having been through a couple of other blokes prior, still had Roo's underpants neatly folded on a shelf in her cupboard! Roo was only interested in retrieving his stereo and Joan Baez records, which she also still had. Why I will never know, as I don't recall him ever being a Joan Baez fan. The underpants were told to stay.

The intensity of events in Melbourne shaped a hasty return home. Caring for a fragile one-year-old child and Roo's sensitivity around his family complicated things, and retreat seemed the sensible option.

But sentences in Raymond's letters like the one following, went soaring over my head at the time. And our retreat back to Western Australia saddened him … temporarily.

I COULDN'T BELIEVE YOU EXISTED. UNTIL I SAW YOU. TOUCHED YOU. WROTE YOU. IT'S UNREAL YOU ARE LIKE MY REFLECTION IN A GLASS DARKLY

Darkly? Perhaps because I had brown eyes and hair, the opposite to his blond hair and blue eyes. Or is it a reference to obscuring reality as referred to by Paul the Apostle, when he used the phrase to explain that we do not see clearly now, but that we will do so at the end of time? In which case Raymond obscured.

I WISH TO ELEVATE EXTEND THE LOUNGE STUDIO ROOM ELEVATE THE STUDIO. UP. UP ABOVE THE SWAMP. WHERE I CAN OBSERVE ALL THE WILD LIFE. CURRENTLY A PHEASANT IS NESTING OUT FRONT. A LACE MONITOR IS UP A TREE. PHOTO ENCLOSED. AND KERMIT IS SINGING. "DON'T BRING YOUR SONS UP TO BE COWBOYS"

His love of the wildlife was beautiful, but frogs singing rhythmic country and western? Hilarious and a little too easy to conjure but it is what he did with frog carcasses that completely astounded me. I learned he painted some frog carcasses and glued them onto vases, which he positioned in pride of place inside his house.

SAW MY OLE RANCH ON T.V. YESTERDAY. IN A 1953 FILM CALLED. "MONEY FROM HOME" "WITH DEAN MARTIN & JERRY LEWIS. EVEN THE SHED – ROW. WITH MY BUNKHOUSE INCLUDING RATTLESNAKE. WHICH WAS UNDER THE BLANKET. HOW WAS I TO KNOW IT WAS ALREADY DEAD? IT'S A FORM OF WELCOME THEY HAVE IN CALIFORNIA. IT'S HARD TO STOP THE TEARS. PERHAPS I AM ALONE TOO MUCH. I GET PLENTY OFFERS BUT I REALLY DON'T CARE FOR ONE NIGHT STANDS.

After what Raymond has been through during the war, I was surprised he found the rattlesnake in his bed a form of welcome, but I went on humming or rather croaking, "Don't bring your sons up to be cowboys".

I WENT BESERK LAST WEEK AND ACQUIRED SOME REPRODUCTIONS FROM THE "LOUVRE" 'WINGED VICTORY' AS ON ROLLS ROYCE. ASHANTI DOLL. LADY TYE ETC. CATALOGUE ENCLOSED.

Raymond's love of beautiful things seemed to lead him to make sudden purchases, but an African fertility doll? I rather thought that ship had sailed.

Meanwhile, my mother and father were on an

across-Australia road trip in a campervan and had stayed on the island for the first time, even though Raymond had business elsewhere, placating the loss of my own visit.

> LOVE YOU ALL THANK DAD FOR WATERING THE GARDEN. I WAS GOING TO ASK HIM TO. WHEN HE RANG. IT'S JUST I'VE GOT THIS THING ABOUT BAMBOO. THERE'S A CLUMP SNUNK THROUGH THE FRONT FENCE. AND LAST TIME THE ROTTEN COUNCIL CUT IT DOWN. SO I put them on notice. NOTICE READS.
> "KEEP OFF. SACRED SITE. DEPT OF BAMBOO PERMIT NO 497682. 394511 EXT 46. OFFICIAL." WHAT A LOVELY A PERSON YOU ARE. I HOPE TO LIVE LIKE GEORGIA O'KEEFE TO 99. AND SEE MOURAD WIN THE 3 MIN MILE ENCLOSED SMALL CONTRIBUTION FOR THE TRIP [return to biro] SPECIAL LOVE RAY

Raymond had hoped I would still come to the island but I returned the $50 contribution immediately. Prior to this letter, a parcel had arrived. Its contents were bewildering to say the least. Enclosed was an August 1981 copy of Playboy in its entirety!

Raymond had written an obscure note saying that he was threatened with a paternity claim if he didn't marry the claimant. In this instance he said he was going to plead insanity if that went ahead. As I had not heard any more about it, I was left to ponder.

He went on to mention Allan Moult, an aviation writer and photographer who was published in the Playboy and who he believed to be a relative. He also mentioned a Keogh cousin (on his mother's side) turning up, a chap who works on a London newspaper.

I later learned poor Allan Moult had also been previously pursued by my Tasmanian cousin, Kim, when Allan was giving a talk at my cousin's school in Burnie, back in the 1960s. Noting Allan's surname, Kim had pegged him for a long-lost relative and somehow managed to convince him to visit their home for interrogation by his mother, Nancy. Being interrogated by Nancy, my mother's half-sister, was not something you survived without a memory of it forever. She was foreboding to say the least. The sound of her advancing footfall would visibly send shop assistants into a tizzy. She demanded a certain interaction from anyone in service.

Being born on 4 July had some bearing in Nancy's case. She, crowned with her flaming red hair swirled into a bun and pinned down with a diamanté clasp, presented as a dynamo of opinions. Allan Moult didn't stand a chance. Proof of belonging was never found. Regardless, Raymond now had him in his sights.

This was Raymond's third letter of the year. It had arrived in a large envelope and was an artform all its own, written on a metre of waxy backing paper. The backing paper from a length of adhesive contact used for lining cupboards in the 1970s. The thing was scribed in permanent texta and written in marching capital letters, halted by misplaced full stops set like prickles on a path.

55 Forde St
ALLORA. QLD. 4362
29 January 1984

Dear Darling Julie.

I am writing to you personally. As I feel we both come from the same mould. Are both subject to extremes of feeling. Either love or despair. As Robert Frost would say.

"Many promises I must keep.
Miles to go before I sleep."

Raymond Moult-Spiers, 1984

6

Straddling Straddie

We certainly are from the same Moult, so why not the same mould? Although most of his letters came from the swamp, this letter came from Allora. And, though I personally responded to all his letters, he always addressed his replies to the whole shebang. This letter was different. It was addressed just to me.

Mourad had just turned three, his little body still struggling with one respiratory-tract infection after another and a constant array of decongestants and antibiotics. This little boy was getting sicker, not better. I had tried to breastfeed him for as long as I could but, as a new pregnancy progressed safely, away from the poisons in the dairy country, so did his intolerance of the changes in my milk. Weaning him was extremely difficult for both of us. Without the benefits of my immunity, he was now on his own. He looked strong initially but, as the months progressed, he grew thin and weak. He had fought meningitis and won but it was the slow progression of near-deadly asthma attacks that were the most difficult. He and I lay awake in the early hours as he struggled with every breath, with bolts to Emergency when he just couldn't breathe by himself anymore, his struggles with colds and flu, of mouth breathing and hearing loss as congestion moved in permanently. His eyes, too, were still being watched for possible retinal detachment. Finally, the medical fraternity booked him in for an operation to remove his adenoids and tonsils and to put grommets in his ears. This was to happen a couple of weeks after the birth of baby number two.

Feeling swamped took on a new meaning. Being on opposite sides of the country, Raymond and my communication continued to be enclosed in stamped, addressed envelopes, my little family living at the edge of a swamp, him living at the edge of a swamp; both with snakes, ours poisonous, his beautiful pythons; both with rabbits in copious supply, one legal, the other illegal. My husband playfully suggested he run something he called "Swamp Enterprises".

With baby number two on the way, so came my urge to renovate, to build out and up. The decision was made to go "up", due to the constant digging, which had led to much of the back yard being taken over with the results – vegetable gardens, pond and burrows.

I drew up plans and employed Cyril, a one-man building company. I located vintage building discards and recycled doors, windows, floorboards, a staircase and anything else that took my fancy. My vision and industriousness proving too much, my husband stepped back as the house and the baby in my belly grew. Studios for both of us at last—our reward!

The January letter arrived on the day baby number two was suddenly born.

I scarcely had time to read it, what with the sewing machine running hot, me running hot and the summer running hot, all of which combined to create a huge hot patchwork. I stitched faster and faster, driven by some kind of mad pre-birthing maternity. In the end I squatted and strained over the hot-off-the-press fabric collage and out popped baby at around ten in the evening. Unexpectedly, but fully baked, on the lounge room floor. Him with the strawberry birthmark on his left shoulder. What did this mean? A question that was never answered.

But Uncle Raymond had made sure he was there in one way or another, if only to bear witness to his predicted mark on the wrong baby. His letter continued with reminiscences of love, albeit a mixed bag of truths, similes, comparisons and lack.

Love first hit me in the form of an Indian girl in Malaya. Who had a twin sister. And shared everything including me. Plus a son by the first girl. She would not marry me as her family had a husband already picked out for her. Love is like crushing your hand in a ringer. And not yelling for help. But having the sense to reverse the machine. Love is changing and cleaning a disabled girl. And not expecting any rewards. Love is winning TWO ART prizes and the championship.
And in one day. Love is knowing you. Knowing you are there. And sufficiently interested in me to write. But most of all. Love is a painful experience. It starves the body and soul. I am a skeleton for love. Naked bones and all. The waiting. Listening. Hoping and there is no let. Up. It keeps gnawing away. Until I am like a stunted BONSAI. But that is as it should be. Like the beggars of BENGAL. Hoping for anything but getting nothing but grief.

His first love, her twin apparently sharing the experience, and a son by Raymond. This must have taken place during the first part of the war, when he was posted there.

I have a son and daughter in Australia from a previous love. But she flew away. And I see MY children occasionally.

This was my first realisation as to the complexity of the man. He was listing his most impacting love affairs, both of which produced children. His former wife, and current relationship with the lady hidden in among the antiques, were simply not included. I later learned that, when his Australian children visited him during most of the second half of the 1980s, they did not know they were visiting their birth father.

Love is what I felt when I met that huge family in WA. It is comforting to know that you know. Edna St Vincent Millay [an American poet] knew about love. If. I find a copy. I will send it to you. She said at 85 that although life had been brutal to her. She had known LOVE. So that made everything else worth-while. At present I have no love. But who knows? Suddenly it happens. And one is smitten. If it's reciprocated IT'S OK. But loving someone from a distance is cruelty in the extreme. If it would help. I would sell up here. And come to WA but perhaps the comfort of knowing someone who cares. Counts for a lot.

Although the letter itself has no paragraphs and words are randomly isolated by full stops, his next sentence, expressing hope of not being narcissistic, may belong to his discourse on love and not his studio work, but we will never know.

I hope I am not NARCISSITIC? but I do have some of my paintings and collages. The latest is "DIONNE WARWICK AT WOLF TRAP" which will win the $1,250 prize at TOOWOOMBA. Because it is an inspired work. Three days and nights of toil. Sweat blood and tears. Because before it was dry. Two HOONS broke into the house and STUDIO at Amity Point. And nearly wrecked it. Apart from beating me up. And nearly making off with the TV and valuables.

What? Two *hoons* breaking in and beating him up mentioned in passing? Did he not count this event as impacting? (This was the first of a number of reports in which he was robbed and sometimes bashed.)

Have just returned from there after the tourists had left and to COLLECT the Mangoes. But the flying foxes get in for their chop during the night. Also took the PYTHON back and released him. Or her. And just missed the start of the first cyclone of the season. Was disturbed that you may have been involved in the floods of WA but hoped you were not.

I was not caught in any floods. But was struck that both my husband and Raymond were happy handling pythons. Roo had suggested I send Raymond a book. He saw something of a fringedweller in Raymond and had wanted Raymond to read his then-favourite book, a kind of mourning of the failure of the counter-culture movement in 1970s USA. It was not my thing at all. The author advocated weapons and drugs, and it was indeed written in a very self-oriented, journalistic style. But Fear and Loathing in Las Vegas, by Hunter S. Thompson, was Roo's bible in the late 1970s.

and "THANK YOU" for the book. I hope you read it first. As noting his philosophy. Everyman for himself. And never ask for help. Perhaps he should have been P.O.W. because we had to help each other to survive. With food. And Malaria and Cholera etc. no sign of it so far this year. The book is great. In that it shows a one man. Crusade against the establishment. And winning. I agree with him that there is so much bullshit. About insurance and rates and concessions. It's pathetic.
Well, I hope I have some of his caliber. Not that I would want to insult people in public or urinate in their pot plants. But. He gives some valuable advice about how to survive on your own. I have been in this situation for

a long time. Since my wife died. And all the pressures to get married again, fall on deaf ears. Anyway, she may be getting another job soon. So, I will have even more privacy.

Raymond's fear and loathing seemed to be centred on the partnership he had with a woman he only ever reveals by not saying anything good or concrete about her.

2 DAYS LATER
I can't even write a letter unless I tell her who it is to. So, here's hoping she does get a job. And I can get back to the island and STUDIO. Applied for job as CONSERVATOR at NATIONAL GALLERY in Sydney. But it was a No. No. but there is still the possibility for stand in for LEE when he stars as JUD IN Patrick Whites books. VOSS. Am selling a few paintings privately. And hoping to collect at the local show this weekend.

And the wonderful aspirations of a man long retired actively pursuing his dream of being a Lee Marvin stand-in or holding a job at the National Gallery.

Thank you for your letter and consideration.
A lovely photograph of Mourad and Roo.
Two father xmas's in the one family.
Thank you for your friendship and love.
As you say Love of the special Kind
Love Ray
Xxx
Thanks again for the book.

With Yasen, baby number two in tow and baby number one still struggling with ill-health, I began to question allopathic medicine. Following Yasen's homebirth and my midwife providing an introduction to homeopathy, I slowly changed my view on healing approaches. But not before Mourad took a turn in the children's hospital in Perth. My poor three-year-old, now stripped of his defences and still unwell, was diagnosed as an asthmatic requiring drugs every four hours for the rest of his life. Still having his retinas monitored with frequent trips to the eye doctor in Perth, a mere bump on the head threatened to take out his vision.

Ever so slowly I made a turn towards homeopathy. Added to this was the blessing of discovering a doctor from South Africa who had seen healing occur in unexpected ways and who allowed the homeopathic medicine to work side by side with allopathic medicine. My doctor even asked the hospital to administer the homeopathy during the nights, as I was not permitted to stay there when Mourad was hospitalised with life-threatening asthma attacks. The doctor was keen to try this approach in preference to cortisone. Slowly but surely Mourad's local hospital visits reduced.

Meanwhile, if my husband couldn't live in the forest, then a makeshift forest came to us. The house in town had succumbed to being surrounded by a high fence, imagined and built entirely by Roo. It was constructed from upright bush poles filled in with rough lengths of first-sawn planks still showing the outer face of the tree, bark and all. The view out and the view in, now obscured by the tall timber clad with horizontal slats, allowed him to bring the livestock into the front yard.

Yes, we had horses, goats and dogs too. These and the fenced-in yard attracted the colourful elderly lady from up the street. She who wore a kind of conglomeration of national dress and spoke no English. Donned in a patterned head scarf tied tight around her beautiful wide face and wearing a brightly patterned skirt covered in a soiled apron, she frequently set herself in motion down the middle of the road, stopping opposite our house. With her wide feet clad in sloppy socks that slumped around her wide ankles and pooled in her wide slippers, she stood firm to make a parcel hurl.

She would not accept that we did not want her to do this. She would waddle down shouting all the way and then hurl her paper-wrapped bundles of used soup bones into our yard. No amount of reasoning and gestures stopped this activity.

That was until Roo, in his wisdom, had fixed a bull's horn to a kind of Darth Vader helmet I had made and mounted the artefact on a long post at the gate, thrusting it high into the air. This effectively stopped her Latvian feet proceeding beyond her own yard, too far to effect a decent throw. The helmeted gargoyle spoke her language and halted all parcels of cooked bones being hurled our way.

Mourad & Roo with the finished front fence before the installation of the effigy. 1984

THE SWAMP

25 march 1987

Dear Family,
For years it is in hibernation. Then BOOM – cop that young Harry. I was so glad to hear from you. Not that I have not been in touch – I have. I was even at the births of YASEN and MOURAD. Just to make sure everything went alright ... with MOURAD well it nearly didn't – and him being so small but my friend assured me all would be right in the end. NOW look at him. Marvellous Mother and Father. In fact my Indian (RED) is so good. he can predict when a certain party has arrived home in Allora. She still doesn't understand it.

Raymond Moult-Spiers, 1987

7

The cat, the rabbit and the python

The Stradbroke Island mineral sands mining industry had been sifting through the precious sand since the 1950s.

But when they got close to Ray's beloved swamp, it was war, and into action he went. Their intention was to fill in the swamp with the mining industry's radioactive tailings, so that a housing development could be opened up.

Ray singlehandedly managed to stop the infill for twelve months. His cherished swamp was then out the back. Ray the warrior sent the minister for the environment photographs of Aboriginal bones he had found in the swamp. The investigation did the rest.

It was finally discovered the supposed burial bones were random old bones and the development went ahead, flipping the back of his house to face its new frontage. The street's road was asphalted into place, with all that side of the street's back yards now front yards. Astoundingly the new houses were built facing a row of back yards.

The back of Raymond's house was appalling – and it stayed that way.

At the end of my maternity leave for Yasen, and faced with the decision to resign or return to my position as art lecturer, a surprise turn of events occurred when my husband pleaded to be the home person. In 1985, I returned to full-time work and learned too late that my husband could not get up to children at night. With our often-unwell first born and still breastfeeding our second, I moved us all into one room, where I had covered the whole floor in mattresses so that it was a bedroom. I could attend to the night-time needs of each just by rolling this way or that.

Despite rolling this way and that, I also learned that without a good night's sleep my day-time performance was slowly gathering a level of stress. As stress built, so I and both my children were faced with being mildly unwell more and more frequently. These were often strange afflictions that we chipped away at with homeopathy.

Then, like to a distant lantern in the dark, I was drawn in and inspired to be part of the emergence of a group of women who met once a month on Sunday evenings in accordance with the cycles of the moon. We called ourselves Women's Spirit. The circle brought energy, wisdom, support and understanding, all of which were rejuvenating. We took it in turns to lead the gatherings, which were always hosted at locations where menfolk were absent. Without this energising group, I would not have been able to step up to the pressures and joys my life held.

Through the group and inspired by the most honourable of intentions, I was led to learn from my own spontaneous and intuitive responses, from my insights and extemporaneous body movements, all connected to the highest intent held by both myself and the women with whom I sat. All of us from diverse walks of life had come together to support one another. Under this protective umbrella, I began to enter into and explore the mysterious worlds of the unseen.

It emerged Raymond, too, was led by unseen forces. Just mere mentions shared between us implied this was so. Being new to these things, I felt unable to translate the experiences into words. What I was doing did not use language. Even now, making words shape the experience is of little use. Suffice to say both of us were conscious of the other's immersion in it.

Meanwhile, with all the homemaking, working and raising children, letter writing had fallen to the bottom of the pile for a year or so, but all was quiet on the Raymond front too.

After nearly two years as the home person, and haircuts given by his own hand, Roo had lost his way and resolved to return to work. He took a position working shifts with a company connected to the mineral sands industry and I dropped my hours right back.

Western Australia's mineral sands industry started at about the same time as Stradbroke Island's. My childhood memories of two huge pyramids of ilmenite at one end of the quiet waters of Koombana Bay, a family beach, stand firm. The dark metallic sand blew all over the pretty bay, darkening its calm waters. Thirty years later, Roo had a job in the laboratories of the company that converted the dark-grey sparkling sands to the white titanium used in the manufacture of plastic and paint.

With things beginning to settle and space emerging in my life, I wrote to Uncle Raymond for the first time in nearly two years and soon received a reply.

Raymond's reference to his Native American friend fascinated me immediately, what with my own interest in Women's Spirit thriving and leading me to seek understanding of the knowledge of Native American medicinewomen, I was immediately enthralled.

Congratulations on the great work you are doing but I think it's about time you graduated to more SPIRITUAL subjects.

Taking this advice was easy.
I was already teetering.

Hope for MY "CREATION SERIES". 45 paintings mostly all sold. But I am keeping the best.

Huge numbers of paintings are often referred to but where were they going? Who was managing or arranging where the work was shown and sold? He never wrote about this part of the process.

Time was limited when your parents were here. They did come to the house – hovel – HABITATE. So I asked your Mother what you would like. So I can make the necessary arrangements. I do not want any of Madame's family to have my treasures. They will be divided between my boy and girl and you. The other Boy – Indian – is in MALAYA and unable to accept me as his mother was already promised to another man.

My parents certainly talked about their second visit, but I gather they had a hard time tracking and placing all the information he was giving them and that, combined with what they saw, gave them a very unreal "hard to hold onto" experience. Neither did they meet his madame.

I expect to be arrested any day now. As I AM UTTERLY FED UP with BUREAUCRATIC BUNGLING, so I am now driving two cars. One unregistered. Also did your father receive the $100 money I sent $100 he paid the deposit on the GOLD Pontiac. He must have. It was great to see them again Alan said I looked well fuller in the face.

His passion for big American cars reached out and involved my father, who was asked to look over the said Pontiac on their drive back to Western Australia. As it was in good condition my father had put a deposit down on Raymond's behalf.

THIS ETHEREAL BEING advised me last year that a friend of mine was ill in SYDNEY. He had been a RADIO ANNOUNCER, he saw me recognised me and died the next day.

Raymond's reference to the energy of this ethereal being indicates he had invested a strong belief in the spirit world and its resulting manifestation of companions.

Enclosed Betty Churcher you probably know her but why the MS? IT's stupid. why not like you. A straight out JULIE.

Strange but true, not long after this Betty Churcher actually turned up in Western Australia as the new director of the Art Gallery of WA and came to our regional gallery for an event. I introduced myself and asked her if she knew the work of my uncle, Queensland artist, Raymond Moult-Spiers. She was lovely and looked at me imploringly. Clearly she had no idea who I was talking about. She began questioning me as to his location, galleries, exhibitions, artists he mixed with. I could not answer any of her queries and began to wonder if what Raymond wrote was true or if perhaps the mysterious Sydney gallery he claimed to sell through had a complete monopoly. I was shocked into acknowledging all was not as I thought.

My pet python ate my pet rabbit and cat. So I had to kill him to spare the cat only just in time. One baby rabbit died of fright. And the rabbit he ate was completely asphyxiated. 30 feet long. Of course rabbits are VERBOTEN IN QLD. IF Caught $6,000 fine. Just over the border in NSW they are breeding them for the WHITE MEAT MARKET.

Good Lordie, with the python at an estimated nine metres long, one must wonder why Raymond himself wasn't consumed.

Meanwhile, in Western Australia the rabbits on the western front were becoming a thing of the past for us. Roo's acquisition of five acres of horse paddock with its own rabbits, snakes and goannas, as well as Aboriginal artefacts, replaced nearly all of his suburban breeding programs. Roo had found his mistress in this acreage and digging became an even more serious pastime. First, a well of sorts, but the water was too salty. Then he began digging down into the only high spot on the property. He dug and he dug until he was standing deep inside a wide pit surrounded by the rest of the hill. Then he laid a floor and walled in the sides to keep the sand from falling in. Then he made a roof with a hole for a chimney attached to a potbelly stove inside. Then he put in steps from above, down to a sunken porch with a door and little window leading to a single room. Behold, he had himself a kind of bomb shelter. This, as well as a mega-pond, slowly moulded from a dam he had started to dig by hand. Fortunately, realising the enormity of hand-digging a whole dam, it was finished aided and abetted by an excavator. Roo was set. He could cook and sleep peacefully after his nightshifts without the hassle of family life around him.

Roo's bomb shelter, c. 1990, family photograph collection.

A new TOWN PLAN was presented last week for AMITY 5. Point 5 = 10 (Street number At ALLORA was 55. Street Number of AMITY 55) FILL in SWAMP with RADIO-ACTIVE SAND. BUILD CONDOMINIUM HOTEL. MOTELS ALL PAID BY JAPS 40 million in 3 mths. I can't ever forgive or forget. to think I died IN BURMA (5) Was resurrected.

A preoccupation with numerology was emerging, although his method, seemingly using a combination of multiplication and addition, is obscure to say the least. Finding the number five hidden in many words describing the places that were important to him included Burma. It was here he says he died and rose again, only to be topped with the recent news of the loss of his beloved swamp and further intrusive plans by the Japanese now on Stradbroke.

And won't buy anything JAP. I can still feel the blood on all they possess or touch. I've hit a few I've spotted in BRISBANE but no response. In a restaurant I walked out without paying. After a JAP came in. I kicked his chair over. Broke his glasses. Now they want to take over the Island. Well. They've got a shock coming.

When I first read about his response to seeing a Japanese person, I was astounded. In 1987 I only had the teeniest inkling of what he had been through. Actually, in 1987 I had no idea.

Thank your father for putting the deposit on Pontiac. The one I have is packing up and to make it road worthy would cost a fortune ... 5 P.M. time for breakfast. That way I can live on 2 meals a day. NO I am not floating off this mortal coil. Till I am 99 = 81 = 9.

PICASSO 98. Georgia O'Keefe 96. Painters live longer than ordinary people.

And now he instills the belief that he aims to live for a very long time. His frequent referencing of his living to a ripe old age had me totally believing it. I even imagined that, once the kids had grown, I would go to visit with him a while. After all, he was going to be around well into the new century.

This letter is just the start. I am trying to think of how I can thank you for writing to me and sending all those photographs. if the JAPS do take over I might sell up and get a HOMEABILE 10 feet long and come to Perth (5) and would you believe the street in ALLORA Forde (5). I am not into politics. But I do believe poor JOH is grossly overacting. As Stan Freberg put him on a 497. I was saddened to hear the MUSIC MAN ROBERT PRESTON 76 trombones has died.

And there it ended far too suddenly, only to be picked up a few days later. I liked the idea of him travelling about in a mobile home. I loved caravanning as a child, with the thrill of a new location every afternoon.

Continued on 2 April 1987
Sorry there's been a delay. But my cat has been shot at!!! Not dead. But very close. And an "ABSININON BLUE", also I have hurt my neck. Which I feel I need a brace for. Never mind all is well ...
Glad then you have a good housemaid there is a lot of it about. Lately. The husband doing the housework while the wife brings home the bacon who can afford BACON. I am down to 2 meals a day. And have not seen meat for months. Anyway it's all in the mind. As the

experts tell us. Hope all is well with you and all the family. Thank you for the photographs. You're doing very well. Love to all Ray

By then Roo was no longer the home person and was back to bacon hunting. But exactly why Raymond was only eating two meals a day was a mystery. Was he trying to save money for his long life? Had he forgotten where he secreted his gold?

In December a twee Christmas card arrived from Raymond telling me he had either fallen in love with an idea and was missing his paintings in his latest show or that he had a brief dalliance.

"left his heart at his current exhibition in Sydney. Large pockets, large houses, large paintings 5ft x 4ft" ALSO EDNA O'BRIEN. BUT TOO MUCH CATHOLIC YUK"

Edna O'Brien was a novelist whose work explored the struggles of women in finding their place alongside the implications of Catholicism and moral values. Her novels were so sexually explicit they were banned in Ireland.

Raymond Moult-Spiers with pythons. c. 1970.

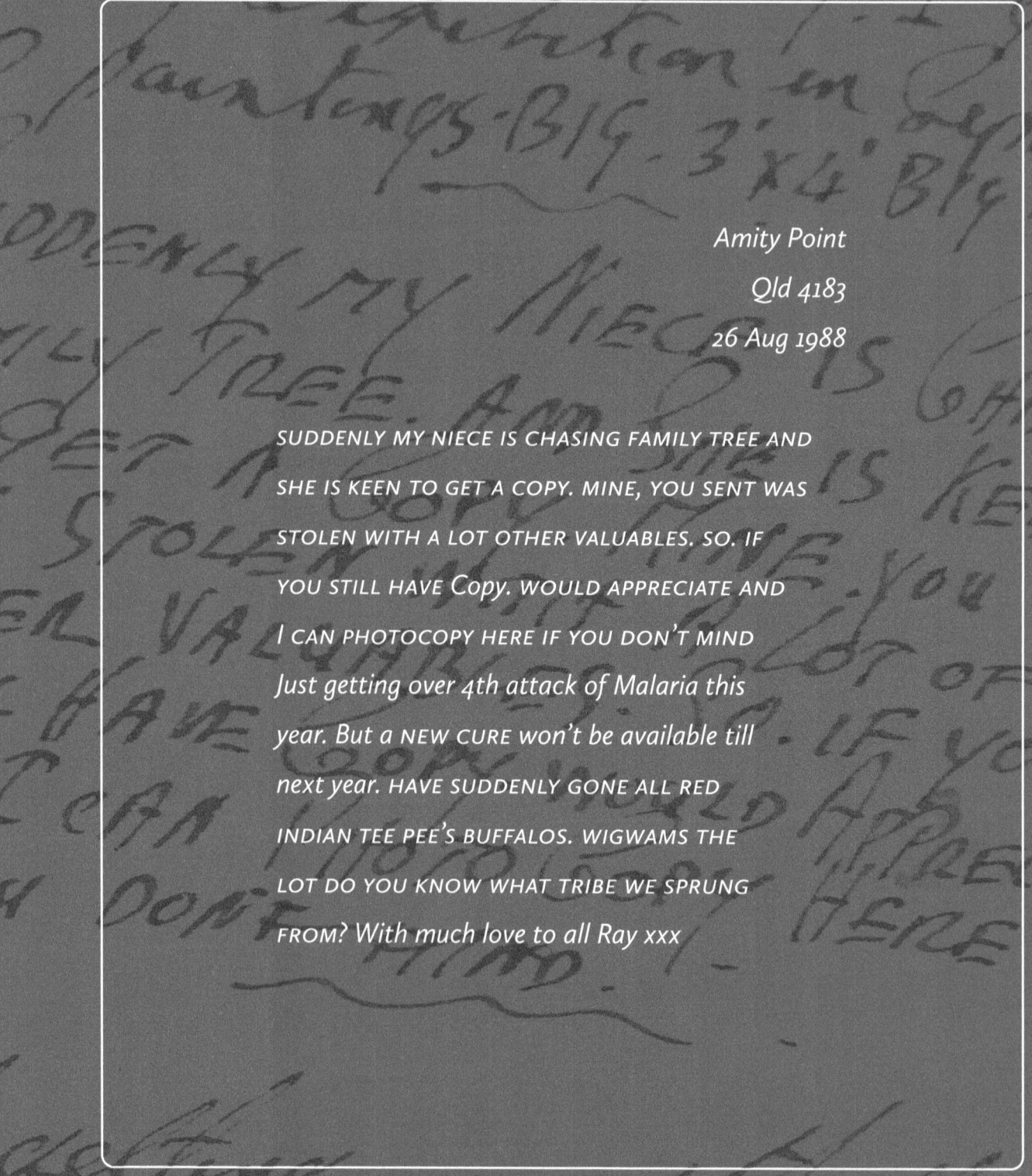

Amity Point
Qld 4183
26 Aug 1988

SUDDENLY MY NIECE IS CHASING FAMILY TREE AND SHE IS KEEN TO GET A COPY. MINE, YOU SENT WAS STOLEN WITH A LOT OTHER VALUABLES. SO. IF YOU STILL HAVE Copy. WOULD APPRECIATE AND I CAN PHOTOCOPY HERE IF YOU DON'T MIND Just getting over 4th attack of Malaria this year. But a NEW CURE won't be available till next year. HAVE SUDDENLY GONE ALL RED INDIAN TEE PEE'S BUFFALOS. WIGWAMS THE LOT DO YOU KNOW WHAT TRIBE WE SPRUNG FROM? With much love to all Ray xxx

Raymond Moult-Spiers, 1988

8

The crocodile boots

"Suddenly gone all Red Indian" was nonsensical but perhaps it was the inclusion of the word "all" that made the difference. Unbeknown to me at the time, in mid-1988 Raymond's unclaimed daughter, Lili Brokensha, had realised that he was not just a longtime family friend but her birth father. Later that year Lili bravely went to visit him on Stradbroke, for the first time as his daughter.

The revelation had come about when Raymond had enlisted the help of the "daughter who did not know". She was living in Sydney at the time. She went about fulfilling his request, arranging to have a pair of crocodile boots made to wear to a Gough Whitlam function on board a boat on Sydney Harbour. On taking delivery of said boots Raymond's true identity emerged through a "nosey" observation made by this "daughter who did not know". Sitting next to him in the car she noticed they had the same noses. Prior to this it had occurred to her that her brother Leonard bore more resemblance to Raymond than he did to his own (presumed) father. The pieces were falling into plain view now.

With a pair of crocodile boots between them, the penny had dropped and Raymond instantly knew she knew. To be sure, Lili waited for him to own the recognition by speaking the truth, which he did. With the cat out of the bag and with confused feelings, she later told Priscilla, her now "half" elder sister, who fainted!

The girls confronted their mother and a pact was made. The news was never to be shared with the menfolk in the family. Lili's brother and "father" remained in the dark (or so it was believed), while the women accustomed themselves to the harsh light of day.

A couple of months later, a letter arrived for me, written on 26 August, a date I now know to be Lili's birthday. It was written on a torn piece of perforated computer printout of the time, a recent discard from the judicial system, although how he happened to have such a thing is beyond my understanding.

From this great position called hindsight, I observe now the synchronicity family ties may bring. Although unknown to each other, it appears his niece, Penelope Moult-Spiers, in the UK and his daughter, Lili, were simultaneously reaching out to find more about their family connections, albeit in totally different ways.

He in turn, as Lili's father, visited her in Sydney. Lili had taken up with a bonza bloke called Bazza, who, being a finely sculpted specimen, paraded confidently about the house in his racy budgie-smuggling Speedos. It was the late 1980s and budgie smugglers were the choice of "real" men's swimwear at the time.

Australian men not only wore them at the beach but also when mowing lawns, drinking beer and tinkering with their cars. Bazza, for good reason, was a leading proponent of this trend. Spotting this craze, Raymond, now sixty-eight, took up the challenge, got himself a pair and arrived at Lili's house ready to sport his wares. Strutting his stuff created amusement, but only just, as Lili and her daughters, Lee and Larisa, discreetly sniggered behind closed doors.

Meanwhile, back in Western Australia, baby number two had grown into a four-year-old and had a friend no one could see. A "jungle keeper", we were told. Our four-year-old's favourite colour was black, slowly turning green. Given Raymond's sheer survival and loss of mates in the jungles of Malaya and Burma during World War Two, I can't help but wonder about this connection.

Especially when linked with Ray knowing about the strawberry birthmark on Yasen's shoulder. There is no way a conclusion can be drawn from this wonderment.

Raymond's letters often described his ongoing battles with his jungle-acquired malaria and, in the letter below, he began to add other problems.

The Island
12 Dec [1988?]
Dear Family,
Please forgive the 12 months I have been incapacitated. back. SCLEROSIS. BLOOD IN LEGS. NO MONEY. A CROOKED GOVT and. stupid old JOE. Hope he goes to JAIL. Hope all is well with you all. must not let this happen again. but if I get my $25,000 from the JAPS. I'll be able to visit, wedding or not. Had a card from June and Brian. My conscience got to me. so I hope you'll forgive me. I had not forgotten my favourite family. Just hoping someone will buy some new paintings. Gone all impressionist Monet especially
Love Ray

It would seem the financial situation was moving towards challenging, but at that stage there was naught I could do about it, other than read his glorious mail. Negotiations were, in fact, being made with Japan for compensation to surviving prisoners of war, but they were never realised. This last letter didn't exactly say but rather implied sales were slow at his Sydney gallery.

With his capacity to jump from topic to topic over a never-ending supply of subjects, the thought of being in his actual physical presence overwhelmed me.

La Swamp
Dec 20 888 =24+20=44=8
Dear Family, What a joy to get
your letter. card. Photos ...

I am glad you are in your 6½ HEAVEN. The 7th comes later. but to speed things along. get the train moving call Stan FREEBURG (author song writer etc). get closer to NATURE. it's all there. you don't need Dr Spock or Dr Who. it's all in YOU welcome to the club. I thought there must have been more to you than just ART ...

Stare as I might at his baffling approach to numerology displayed at the top of this letter, the logic of it never once showed itself to me. The letter continued.

I'm glad you've elevated to your present state, each one gets better. until you reach the 7 stages of MAN. and become a complete whole person. My GURU told me I had visited thrice already and only two more to go. Each a lesson in survival. you must be a survivor? You sound very happy in your NEW MODE. it suits you. It's meant to. now prepare for the next upwardly MOBILE ....
YOU SHOULD WRITE SOME BOOKS
YOU STILL HAVE THE LOOKS
AND THE TALENT TO CHALLENGE CAPOTE
SO GET ON YOUR BIKE AND START TO TYPE
THEN MAYBE YOU'LL OUT SELL JACOBI

Rereading this small rhyme in the twenty-first century stopped me in my tracks. I didn't know either author mentioned back in 1988 let alone why he may have chosen these two, aside from the rhyme! I now know Capote's writing introduced a new form called narrative nonfiction and Jacobi wrote strange mystery horror stories stemming mostly from Malaysia.

I am not sure what to do with this information other than see it like some kind of signpost.

Back in 1988, after four years in my purpose-built studio, my new work was all done at speed in the scarce time available to me. I would begin with a kind of energetic frantic scribbling until the image began to appear. I never knew what I was working on until it emerged or its definition made itself known. Mixed media were applied randomly on heavy paper but always with an excitement of meeting something or someone new. I felt a deep form of communication of sorts. I began to demonstrate views of myself playing with energy or travelling the spiritual path. My work went out to numerous exhibitions. I was also involved with the local arts festivals and theatre productions, and sat on various arts committees. The local press began to turn up, recording my various creative activities, not because my work was deserving of merit but more because of the human-interest aspect. A public profile had begun to grow whether I wanted it or not.

Along with this expansion of self, the children and I began to face yet another period of managing ongoing, mild and often obscure sickness. Although I was highly energised and functioning well, something else was going on. I noticed at certain places in the house my now decidedly sensitised hands would tingle. After first exploring my children's unwellness by unsuccessfully going the traditional and alternative medical routes, I decided to approach these health issues from a different angle.

I contacted a radiesthesist (dowser) by post, a man who had worked for the navy during the war, locating the position of submarines. He now worked dowsing geopathic stress and underground waterways, divining over maps, possibly with a crystal pendulum.

He located ley lines and some underground streams beneath our house, streaming away our health.

"Time to move," he said. "Seven years of this is all your bodies can take." This helped me understand the sensitivity in my hands in certain spots on our property.

We found a house on a hill on dry land but not too far from a river and estuary. The two-storey house started as a single storey at the top of the hill, then cascaded down. The rooms underneath held up what was a typical 1970s build at street level. Mission brown and apricot predominated. We moved in 1988, and our health did, in fact, quickly improve.

Here Roo ran a mouse-breeding program in a room with picture windows opening onto the downhill driveway under the house. It was soon clear it was to become a mouse restaurant for the carpet snake he put in there with the mice. The mice attracted Max the cat, who waited outside for endless hours, opportunist that he was. The snake would undress ready for spring, wanting to impress a passerby. None came. I reused the cast-off garment of scales in my work in the studio next to Snake-face's room. Pythons like to be involved with creative pursuits, it would seem, as Raymond's affinity also proved.

The snake was smart, watching the hands on the handle opening and closing the sliding glass door. Lost opportunities to mate seemed to be passing him by. Hugging that handle in hope, he wrapped around it looking for the magic "open sesame". A small push against the door frame and the door slid open, just enough for a snake, and into suburbia he did slide. Two weeks away and found up an apple tree across the road, and why not?

With my children growing and my art practice growing, new courses of events were presenting. My work and dreams were decidedly more from spirit now, or so I chose to believe. I had scored a mammoth commission to create a major work on a feature wall at the International Training Centre at the local sandmining company, using their product. I went to the vast mine site with a geologist to collect samples of different coloured earths.

I intended to make my own paint from these, and did. While learning about the mine with the geologist, I could see aerial images on his computer of the radioactive earths and asked why they were so evenly dotted. He told me that it was early tailings used to build up housing blocks. Such was the practice on Stradbroke Island as well, it seems. The Western Australian mining company delivered a 3x6 metre solid marine-ply wall to my studio and I started work on my commission.

OPPOSITE *Imprint of the Soul*, 1988, mixed media on paper, 122x86cm. City of Bunbury collection.

ABOVE *Thread of Life*, 1989, acrylic paint on edge and thread, graphite, charcoal, collaged canvas on paper, 86x122cm. Private collection.

ABOVE *The Event of the Frog*, 1989, mixed media & leather frog made by artist, on paper, 73x60cm. Private collection.

FRAGMENTS OF THE SKY

ABOVE *Earthed Wisdom*, 1990, print, snake skin and mixed media on paper, 85x70cm. Private collection.

RIGHT *In the Face of Snakeface*, 1990, print, collaged drawing and mixed media on paper, 120x45cm. Private collection. The drawing shows Roo's jewellery-making, using teeth, painted bamboo and zamia palm seeds, hung on his carved skyhook gripped by Snakeface.

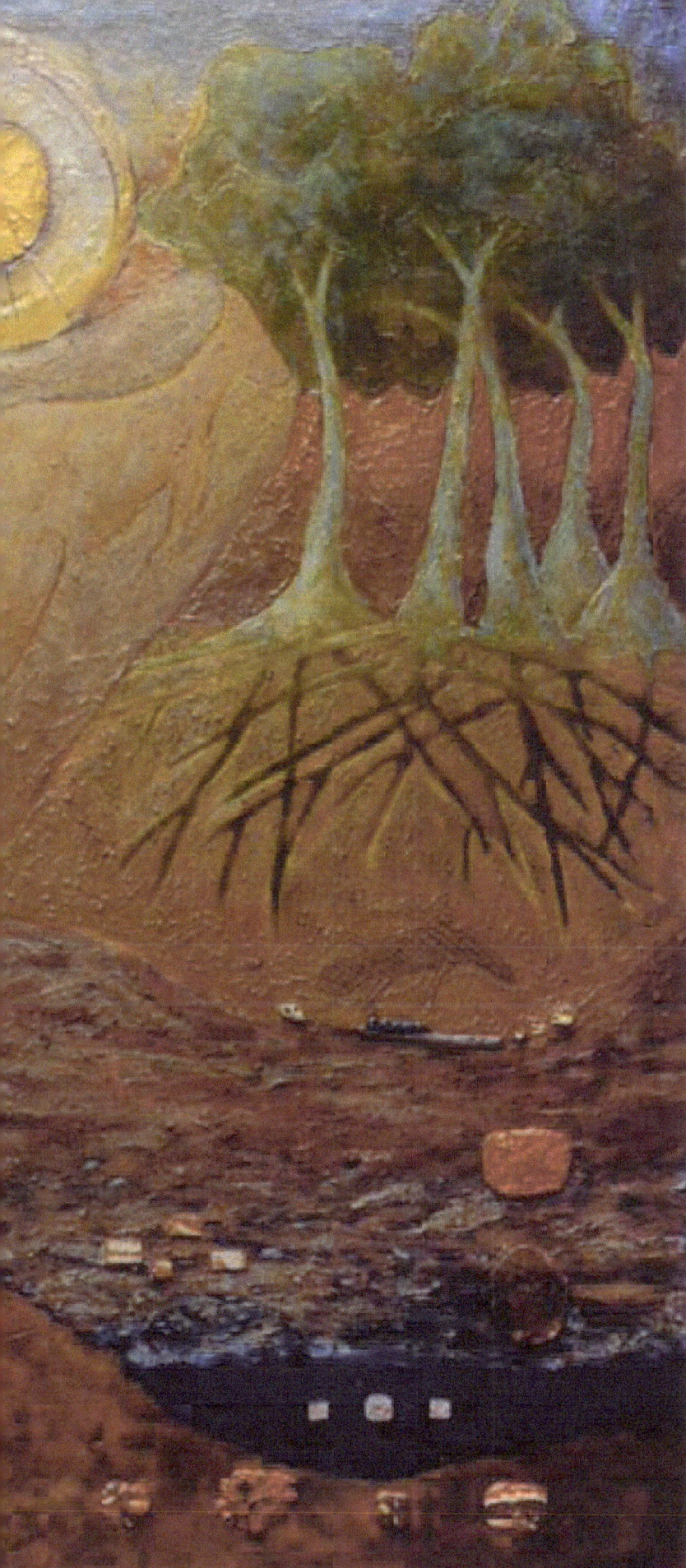

THE CROCODILE BOOTS

ABOVE *Sands of Time*, 1990, impasto with coloured earths, bones, teeth, collaged canvas, clay tablets, recreated Taap (Indigenous serrated knife unique to south-west of Western Australia made from wood, resin, quartz) & geologist rock pick on marine-ply timber panel 2.50x3.20m. Illuka Resources Art Collection.

20 DEC
1989
NORTH STRADBROKE ISLAND
AS THE JAPS HAVE THE SOUTH
Dearest Julie,
At last you have made it into the 4th DIMENSION. LOVELY STUFF ISNT IT? *Thank you for all your out pouring's. great to hear from you. just as I passed my medical. Doc says I'm as fit as a* BREWERY HORSE.? ... BUT MOSTLY GET SOME BOOKS BY RUDOLPH STEINER. CIRCLE BOOKSHOPS. HE IS THE INTERPLANETARY MAN. IE. COSMIC MEMORY. MY GYPSY TOLD ME *I* HAD MADE AT LEAST 10 TRIPS. I'M ALMOST READY TO BECOME AN ARCHANGEL ... ONE MORE TRIP SHOULD DO IT BUT *I* MAY HAVE TO WAIT 1000 YEARS ! OH WELL I'LL READ ARCHEMEDES PRINCIPAL BACKWARDS ...

Tracking back through my old journals written in the late 1980s, I can see I, too, was functioning on some strange levels and certainly struggling as I flipped from one level to another. My involvement with Women's Spirit gave me permission and support to explore things not normally accounted for in normal daily life. I had recorded a number of "other-worldly" experiences.

My descriptions of very real events, like the all-encompassing kundalini rising (spitial energy at the base of the spine, literally means 'coiled snake' in Sanskrit), cannot be overlooked, nor can the resulting visions and attempts to deepen my understanding of life. These experiences and more interloped with my daily grind and added to my relationship challenges, work expectations and joys of day-to-day family life. All voices demanding to be heard and responded to.

I WEAR SAFFRON ROBES. A PRAYER WHEEL AND A SARONG. MOST SUITABLE FOR TROPICS ... LOVE YOUR ART WORK. AND GLAD YOU HAVE FOUND YOUR FREEDOM. AIN'T IT GREAT? ...

Freedom ... really? Raymond appeared to be finding a different kind of freedom and was indeed feeling great. As explained in his next statement, Ray's availability was proving an attractive option for some women.

I'VE HAD 3 PROPOSALS THIS LAST 12 MONTHS. BUT THANKS AND NO THANKS. LATEST IS LAD/Y DIANE HAMILTON. SOME KIN TO HORATIO. FABULOUSLY RICH. MODELS AT ART SCHOOL. QUEENSLAND UNI. BUYING ME A GOLD WATCH FOR CHRISTMAS *I* HOPE ... TO MY FAVOURITE GIRL JULIE. LOVE RAY

ABOVE *Trap Ezed Artist*, 1988, mixed media on paper, 122x86cm. Private collection. This piece shows the force of energies around and within me turning the world upside down while demanding absolute trust.

FRAGMENTS OF THE SKY

ABOVE *Lady of Light*, 1989, mixed media on paper, 122x86cm. Private collection.
The drawing reflects a transition into an, "embrace with the unknown" as the powerful kundalini energy moves through, bringing with it a surrender to its visions, sounds, aromas and spontaneous movements.

ABOVE *To Vilify a Sibyl*, 1989, mixed media on paper, 122x86cm. Private collection.

THANK YOU FOR THINKING OF ME.

KEEP UP THE GOOD WORK! THE FAMILY
TREE IS THRIVING. NURTURE IT. AS I WILL
PRESERVE IT. TALK TO IT. LOVE IT.
YOU HAVE A GOOD MATE IN MAVIS. GIVE HER MY
LOVE and all the FAMILY AND MAY YOUR DAYS
BE SO LONG THAT I VISIT YOU SOMETIME. THIS
IS ONLY A STOP. GAP LETTER. MORE LOVE RAY

Raymond Moult-Spiers, 1992

9
The family fertility tree

I had begun to capture and organise my intrigue over the family lineage way back then. This next letter from Raymond points to his sudden interest in my mother's half-sister, Nancy Gray, who lived in Tasmania. She was some ten years older than my mother and five years older than Raymond. Like Raymond she was born in the UK. They communicated by phone more frequently than I knew.

The colourful character that was my Aunty Nancy, whose preoccupation with status would have got Raymond wondering, stood strong in her self-made, well-heeled shoes, her strength ever growing and widening over her generous bosom. Nancy liked to sip on a Pimm's in the early evenings. Her intense, sharp blue eyes constantly watching for social slip-ups. That aside, Nancy would have been equipped with snippets of family stories galore. Her ability to throw opinionated statements into the mix was never short on entertaining. I wish I could have heard the two of them communicating.

AMITY POINT
QLD 4183
SEPT 17 '92

Dear Julie,
I thank you very much for the enlarged Family Tree. Very interesting especially
NANCY GRAY. *and missing sister who I was told was Lucinda. making 5* FIVE
L's. *and also the poem Nancy Gray*
AS OFT I HEARD OF NANCY GRAY
AND WHEN SHE CROSSED THE WILD .
I CHANCED TO SEE AT BREAK=OF=DAY
THAT SOLITARY CHILD

BLUE WERE HER EYES AND HER GOLDEN FLAX
HER CHEEKS LIKE DAWN OF DAY
HER BOSOM BREASTS. LIKE
THE HAWTHORN BUDS
THAT OPTH IN MONTH OF MAY

Aunty Nancy did not have hawthorn buds; she was a buxom force to behold. Then suddenly I am to learn about his son, or rather his son's breeding program!

MY SON OR ONE OF THEM IS DUE TO BECOME A FATHER ANY MINUTE. BUT THE DOCTOR WARNED IT COULD BE QUADS, AS HIS WIFE IS OVERDUE 4 WEEKS. AND BIG AS A BUS. (DOUBLE DECKER).

These small snippets about his children were few and far between. It was difficult to understand how it all worked. He appeared to know some things about his children but didn't seem to enlarge on them or be engaged emotionally.

I believed his children still did not know he was their birth father in 1992, so I knew nothing then of the changed circumstances in regard to his relationship with his Australian daughter. This began back in 1989 for Lili, who already had her own dad in the man who had brought her up. I can't imagine what it must have been like to be pursued by a sixty-nine-year-old biological father who was ready to embrace fatherhood … of his thirty-one-year-old daughter. By then Lili had already started her own family and her two girls were now in their teenage years. Her eldest daughter, Lee, was set to start producing babies sooner than was realised. Life was intense and setting time aside for cementing a relationship with her birth father began to prove more and more difficult for Lili as his need to express his caring, coupled with his need for reciprocal attention, appeared to intensify.

This is Raymond's interpretation of his own immediate family tree, which reveals his six children. Albeit nearly thirty years since I saw it, it is still an unresolved conundrum.

ABOVE *Aunty Nancy with Husband, Pimm's and Dog*, 1985, watercolour, ink, pastels and coloured pencil on paper, 75x66cm. Artist's possession.

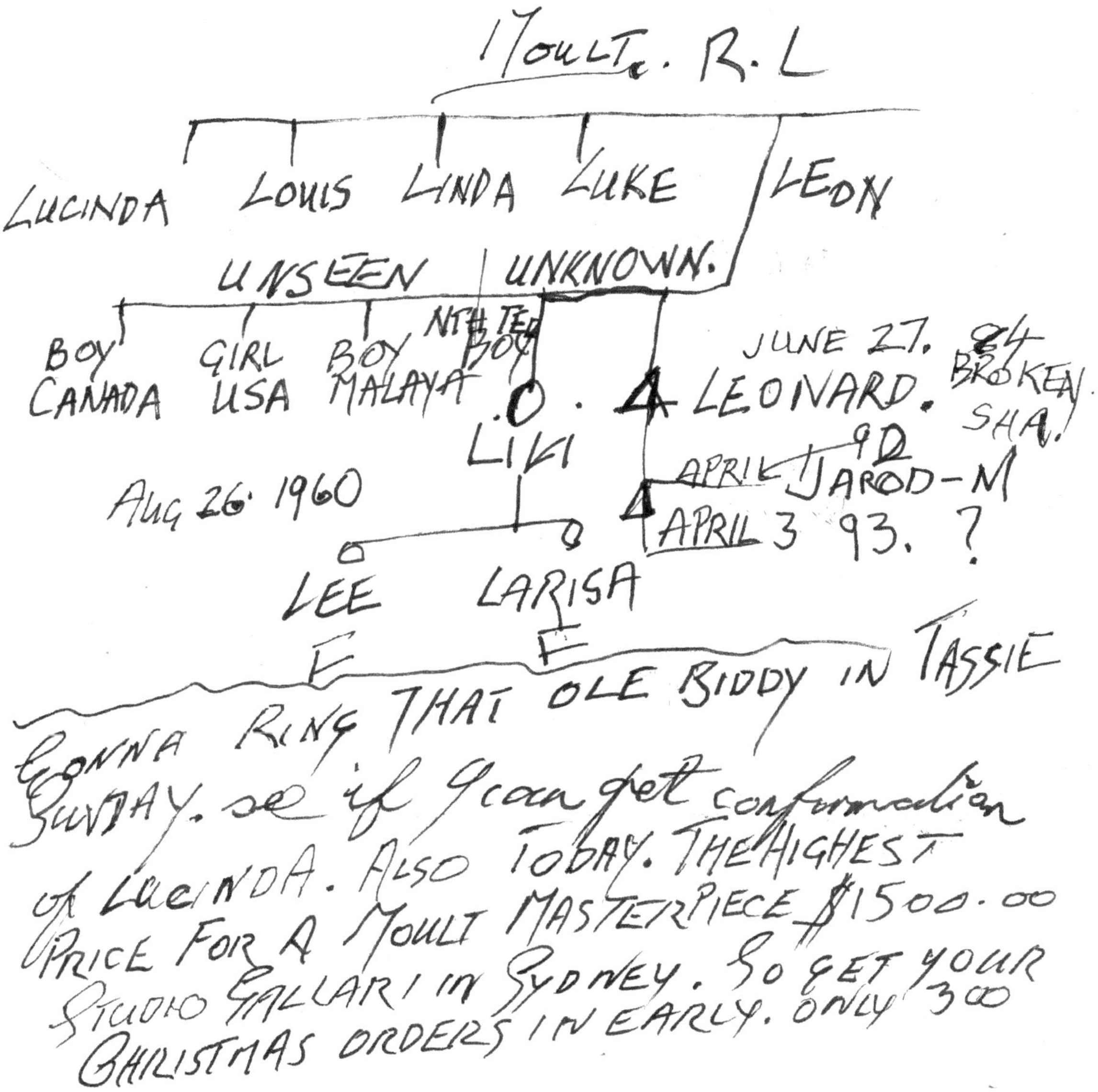

THE FAMILY FERTILITY TREE

Moult. R.L

- Lucinda
- Louis
- Linda
- Luke
- Leon

UNSEEN / UNKNOWN.

Boy Canada | Girl USA | Boy Malaya | NT'ILTED BOY | ○ △ LEONARD. | JUNE 27. 84 BROKEN SHA.

Aug 26. 1960

LIKI

LEE   LARISA

APRIL 9D / JAROD - M
APRIL 3 '93. ?

Gonna ring that ole biddy in Tassie Sunday. See if I can get confirmation of Lucinda. Also today. The highest price for a Moult masterpiece $1500.00 Studio Gallari in Sydney. So get your Christmas orders in early. Only '300

ABOVE. Raymond's letter with his version of his family tree, 1992.

The probability of Ray having these other children can only be verified by his word. Lili was introduced to the idea of a sister who may have also been conceived at Horsley Park and whose mother took her to live in the US. Astoundingly, Ray showed Lili a photograph of a young teenage girl who was blond, with light-coloured eyes not dissimilar to her own.

He had written briefly about his first-born boy in Malaya, but I didn't know about the Canadian boy or Northern Territory boy. I knew he had gone to the Territory to paint in Kakadu, just not when.

In another letter Ray had also referred to a son, the Canadian boy, and this caused the most confusion. Where was the evidence that he was ever in Canada? But maybe Miss Canada came to him. In attempting to understand why Raymond paradoxically and ostentatiously affected a Canadian persona as far back as World War Two is bewildering enough. Perhaps he spent part of his childhood in Canada.

What is known is that in November 1955 Raymond had applied for his birth to be registered in Manitoba (Red River), Canada, stating he was "born at sea" when his parents were en route to Canada. This is completely fabricated, although at the time he may have believed it to be true.

In February 1956 he penned a letter on note paper with the letterhead "Venn Terminal, New York, 215 West 34th Street" (indicating he was possibly at this location) to someone whose whereabouts were unstated but whom Raymond appeared to know, saying he needed some more help from them. He told them he needed to know in which town or village his father was in America. Without that information, Raymond said he could not proceed with what he intended. In lieu of not receiving a Canadian birth certificate perhaps he was attempting to apply for an American passport.

Raymond's son Leonard, who did not know Raymond was his birth father, went on to produce a small battalion of four strapping sons, but later separated from his wife. He was able to live on a pension due to spina bifida, in a small two-storey unit in a rural Queensland town. He had little contact with his family. I found him there surrounded by his own artwork, as well as a stash of Raymond's paintings, the majority of which were crammed into a wardrobe. Out on show was Raymond's abstract work and a small cluster of his former collectables, still precious to their new owner. Leonard's interests are uncannily similar to his birth father's, along with his sharp wit.

As the womenfolk in Leonard's family had elected to keep their menfolk in the dark concerning the genetic relationships with Raymond, this was where Leonard had remained, right up until his true birth father's passing. For Leonard, comprehending the concept took some doing and, at one point on the day of the funeral, the two siblings came to blows over Leonard's inability to grasp the punchline and embrace who Raymond really was.

Leonard and his first wife had cocooned their early life, initially living with the parents who had raised him. Even though he had visited the island and shared Raymond's interests and sense of humour, all this was a big shock to him. Punch or no punch, he eventually came to his senses, over the years, processing it all through his illustrative painting.

THE FAMILY FERTILITY TREE

You all take care now.

love Ray

Amity Blaze
2 April 1992

2 + 11 = 13
3 + 1 = 4
OK?

Dear Mad Moonshakers,
An earthquake just came through here in the form of Julie's missile – whosh – wot was that? Marvellous. Great Stuff Congratulations! A CONGRESSIONAL MEDAL OF HONOUR. NAME YOUR PRICE I WILL TAKE THE LOT. TOO HELL WITH THE SMALL CHANGE. WOT HAVE YOU BEEN ON? I HEAR RHUBARD WINE MIXED WITH VODKA. Will put hair n your ears. but LORDY ... you must let me have the RECIPE. POOR FAMILY. it's a wonder they haven't all committed HARRY CARRY? ... Stuff the JAPS. they still wont pay us. if they did I could come over as STAGE MANAGER. you could be TEA LADY and MAVIS sell PROGRAMS. LEAVE ROO ON THE DAM AND TELL HIM TO STOCK IT WITH CRAYFISH. ...
WHAT COAT FOR GOD? NOTHING. ...

Raymond Moult-Spiers, 1992

10

1992 Buckle your shoe

With the magic of Ray's numbers still hidden, I focused instead on his "What coat for God?" At the time, I had a number of projects on the go but added to them was a commission to design a coat for God and another for the Devil for a street performance showcasing the Easter Miracle plays, to be performed wandering through the city centre. Raymond was interested in the part of God alright.

> HE JUST APPEARS TO BE WEARING A ROBE. HE'S NOT. HE IS SEXLESS AND HAS NO REASON TO HIDE HIS NAKENESS. I HAVE LONG BLONDE HAIR. 6FT TALL MAKE A GOOD JESUS CHRIST. I CAN LOOK HOLY AT THE DROP OF A HALO. JUST NAME A PRICE. IT APPEARS WE DID COME FROM THE SAME MOULDT.

I smiled when I read his pitch for the role and laughed at the last line. In 1992 my studio and house were abuzz with creative quests. My children now eight and eleven and in good health, and my lecturing hours dropped, I slowly added more costume design to my pursuits. I had taken up Spanish dance a couple of years before and, as it was danced best by people with life experience, I had talked my mother (then in her late sixties), into coming to class with me. She was still involved with the South West Opera Company and together we worked on costumes for both.

The Spanish dance company was new to town and, like the opera company, we were part of its beginnings. There was much to explore in manifesting the foundations in costume. Meanwhile, Raymond was participating in theatre of a different kind. His stage production was set when he wrote:

> *Filling in the SWAMPS with RADIO ACTIVE CRAP from the mines (RUTILE) and SUBDIVIDING for HOUSING ESTATES. ...*

This had certainly happened in Western Australia as well but an individual stopping progress of this kind required a different approach. In this 1992 letter he wrote:

TWO YEARS FIGHTING FRIGGING FRIGHTENED FORTUNE TELLING COUNCILLORS. SAVE THE SACRED SIGHT OPPOSITE. SHOW US SOME PROOF? I DID. A BAG OF OLD ABORIGINAL BONES UTENSILS TOOLS EVEN A SECOND HAND ROLF HARRIS DIGGIREEDOO. ENGRAVED. ALL I SAVED WERE A FEW TREES. WHICH WERE IMMEDIATELY BULLDOZED BY FILTHY RICH AT $50,000 A BLOCK. PLUS HALF A MILLION DOLLAR HOUSES YUPPIES. ALL BMWs AND PORCHES SOME EVEN HAVE VERANDAHS AND ROCKING CHAIRS ye sons ...

Despite his heroic effort to stop the inevitable systematic destruction of the swampy bushlands with a supposed find of Aboriginal artefacts across the road from his studio home, he lost his battle. But I have to wonder however did these people sit on their porches in their rocking chairs looking across at his frightfully reckless back yard, now sporting a letterbox.

The "bones" of the matter came to both of us in diversely different ways but we were simultaneously reaching for bleached bones in the studio.

MORE POWER TO YOU SWEETHEART. I TOO HAVE MADE BOATS FROM BONES. CATTLE. DOGS. DINGOES. ROOS ...

I had told him of my use of animal fragments in my work. Roo was prone to bringing home road kill, which he then honoured by preserving their skins. Roo had also been making rabbit pouches from the skins of his much-loved rabbits and had even captured the skin of a road-killed cat to make a bag, and made me a pair of mouse-skin earrings, their little pelts stuffed with lavender. Bits of animal fur and bones from various critters – snakes, foxes and birds – were finding their way into my studio and I had begun to respond to this by integrating these things into my now very earthy paintings, drawings and sculptures. What must not be overlooked is that I, like Roo, had my hands in the earth, albeit with a different use in mind. I worked by circumnavigating my creations on the studio floor. The aerial view, breaking with traditional easel painting, provided a more cosmic opportunity.

I had already completed two artist's residencies, one at the regional gallery and another at the university. The coloured earths from the mining site were destined to be in my work and were always in use over the next ten years. I made my own pigmented paint from the very earths that science had created plastic and plastic paints from. My fascination with sounds from ancient instruments was being revived with the reawakening of world music and its ancient triggers. Sound had become part of my creative process. I was possessed by the magic that spun about in my studio, making each piece of work almost sacred.

A factor in this development was indeed Raymond's wedding gift; his spontaneous collage painting called the *The Rainmaker* was no doubt created in much the same way. Raymond's regular shows of appreciation of life appeared on the page with talk of a date with a lady, then another, and another.

I AM SO GLAD TO HAVE BEEN SPARED. TO REALLY LOVE LIFE. TO EAT DIRT. TALK TO THE TREES. AND THANK GOD EVERY TIME I FIND A LOST ARTICLE. LIKE GLASSES. CAR KEYS. EVEN THE CAR. THE DOG. ... I HAVE A DATE ON SUNDAY WITH A VERY

RICH WIDOW ONLY 51. A JAZZ FANATIC LIKE ME. THAT'S HOW WE MET. SHE KNOCKED ME DOWN WHILE DANCING TO FATS WALLER.

At sixty-two, his passion for Fats Waller was revealed to be lifelong, unlike the women who appeared to pass through his revolving door.

I NEARLY GOT LUCKY RECENTLY WITH A 26 YEAR OLD FELLOW AQUARIAN. SHE WRITES FROM MELBOURNE EVERY WEEK. AND RINGS UP CONSTANTLY. SHE LOST HER SON LAST WINTER IN A BOATING ACCIDENT. ON BRISBANE RIVER.

But he appeared to keep his curiosity about women balanced with the engagement of his intellect.

LATELY I HAVE BEEN ATTRACTED TO FEMALE AUTHORS. i.e. EDNA ST VINCENT MILLAY AND EDNA O'BRIEN. THEY SEE LIFE ENTIRELY DIFFERENTLY TO MEN.

His aloneness echoed loudly in his letters, written in the empty cave of his studio home.

I'VE BEEN DESPARATELY SEEKING SUSAN. but none measure up to my expectations or ideals. AND I KNOW THE RICH WIDOW ONLY WANTS FREE ART LESSONS AND A BIT OF THE OTHER. OTHERWISE I SHALL STAY SELLYBUTTE CELEBATE or whatever and wonder at the perfection of life. the sea. the fish. the pet frog.

So wonderful to read of his creative inspirations and that he still holds wonder for the simple things that appear in his world, but it was difficult to comprehend the level of his preoccupation with female companionship; his inconsistency confusing.

*I'M SORRY I EVER SOLD ALLORA WHERE YOUR PARENTS VISITED BUT IT WAS THAT CRAZY WOMAN. SHE DEMANDED I SELL IT. AS SHE HAD BEEN OFFERED A JOB IN SOLICITOR GENERALS OFFICE. SO NOW SHE HAS EXITED LEFT CENTRE. I DON'T MIND BEING ALONE. I CAN BE A COMPLETE SLOB AT MY OWN EXPENSE: AS QUENTIN CRISP SAYS AFTER FOUR YEARS THE DUST DOES NOT GET ANY THICKER. SO WHY KEEP BURNING OUT VACUME CLEANERS? SERIOUSLY, AS I INTEND TO LIVE TO 115. THERE IS PLENTY OF TIME.
IT'S IN THE MIND OF WHICH WE ONLY USE ONE TENTH. I BELIEVE IN REINCARNATION. REBIRTH. AND WE ONLY DIE BECAUSE WE EXPECT TO. PEOPLE HAVE TOLD US. ONE DAY YOU WILL DIE. WOT ROT. I DIED TWICE IN BURMA: PERHAPS I AM IN HEAVEN AND DON'T KNOW IT! BELIEVE IT OR NOT YOU ARE THE CLOSEST FRIEND I HAVE INCLUDING MY FAMILY. AS SOON AS I SAW YOU AT YOUR WEDDING. I KNEW WE WERE TWINS IN ANOTHER LIFE. THAT YOU HAD RETURNED AFTER A MILLENIUM OUT THERE. AND THOUGH IT MAY BE MONTHS BETWEEN DRINKS "HERES LOOKING AT YOU KID" DISTANCE IS NO OBJECT. I SEE YOU ALL THE TIME. NOW. WHEN I AM WORKING ON MINIMALISATION. I FEEL YOU ARE NEAR.*

It was and still is difficult to read this statement as I was living an intensely busy life and was only writing to Raymond a few times a year. Perhaps the exchange was fulfilling a need in Raymond to belong.

Towards the end of 1992 the boys and I went on a weekend trip with my parents. We returned to the farming community where I was born. I was excited to share this with my boys but unprepared for what else presented.

A former childhood sweetheart stepped forward to apologise for how badly he had treated me in my late teens. I was shocked and yet very pleased that he had gone out of his way to reframe events, which of course had been shaping the way I viewed myself for some time. He had flown for the Australian Air Force in Vietnam and gone on to become a commercial pilot, but was now back on the land with a family of his own.

It was easy for my childhood sweetheart to fill the gap Roo was leaving. Roo, with his new-found level of constant demands for "time to himself". Roo rarely participated in anything or came with me and the boys to anything anymore. He saw visitors, or our invitations, as opportunities he could excuse himself. He often asked for and got time alone in the house. On these occasions the boys and I would drive into the hills and find some kind of magic place to explore, often with a creek or the like. Many people actually thought I was a single parent.

Deeper and deeper I went, seduced by the pilot's written word, which he chose to send to my place of work. At that stage there were no sightings of this interloper. Come Easter of 1993, he invited me and the boys to go and stay on his farm, my old childhood holiday haunt. Lost in childish joys and sense of place, I agreed, believing his wife and children would all be there. But, when we arrived, they were not. There was only him and one of his daughters. His wife had taken the other two children to the city for Easter. Things moved quickly into an old familiarity of both him and place – far too quickly – and regret flooded in. Roo, who was working shifts back home, refused to answer my calls. Then my childhood love's wife suddenly returned, alerted by the daughter who had stayed behind. In the meantime, my sons were having a different experience on the farm. Mourad learned to drive, a confidence boost for a twelve-year-old towny largely ignored by his father.

Still on the farm, a drama of the highest level began to play out. I tried to speak with the honesty required. But it mattered not. I was a mere pawn in their already unstable relationship. His mother was called in. I found the whole misadventure overwhelmingly confusing. But most of all I found his mother's whispered insistence – that her eldest son and I were destined for this moment and that we could now choose to move ahead with our lives together – ridiculous, so ridiculous that I fled. I had a husband who was not a party to any of this. I wanted civil friendship nothing more, but as that was not to be it was finished, and Roo and I were left to face the consequences.

My guilt at having been a party to messing up so many people's lives, particularly Roo's and all the innocent children, manifested as a health affliction that could not be healed. The affliction did not allow things to return to normal. Fear of and for Roo now ruled.

A couple of weeks later I turned forty with mayhem on my shoulders.

OPPOSITE *A Peace of Time*, 1991, sands, ilmenite, plaster, stones and acrylic paint on canvas, 130x75cm, commissioned by Westralian Sands (the image perhaps foretelling of my, and their, future connection to Türkiye).

ABOVE. *Fishcake*, 1991, metal pieces, plaster cupcake, white clay, oxide, ochre, paint and charcoal on paper, 88x122cm. Private collection.

ABOVE *Earth Initiation*, 1992, snake skin, raw earth pigments, gravel, animal teeth, gold leaf and acrylic paint on canvas, 100x130cm. Private collection. The snake had grown (wise).

RIGHT *The Path of Medicine*, 1993, earth pigments, charcoals and acrylic paint on paper, 61x97cm. Private collection. For many years I often felt visited by Native American wisdom, which supported and guided me. From insight received in a dream I made a rattle full of crystal shards that, when shaken, would cause small electrical charges.

17 Aug 1994

FROM HALF BREED RUNABOUT

OUT BIBOU BAYOU

MISS SIPPY

CALAMITY POINT

QLD 4183

HE HAS DONE IT AGAIN

HE IS DOING HIS BLOCK

A LETTER FROM JULIE

IS GOD KNOWS WOT

Raymond Moult-Spiers, 1994

11
When love calls by

The letter burst into a rhyme in no time. It was an overexcited announcement of his intended change in circumstance, an envelope full of playful nonsense from a man aroused into action.

HE HAS LOST HER ADDRESS. HIS
NAME AND HIS SOCKS.
TIME HE WAS MANGLED AND PUT IN THE STOCKS.
THE SILLY OLE FOOL PUTS TEA IN THE CUP.
POURS THE HOT WATER ALL OVER THE PUP.
PUTS BLEACH ON THE CAT TO GIVE IT A LIFT.
SOMEONE IN CHARGE TO CAST HIM ADRIFT.
WITH SOME HARD TACK AND SOME SALT.
AS THEY FAREWELL OLE MOULT.
NOT BAD. BUT WENT STRANGE IN THE END.
FUNNY THAT.
COS HE NEVER WORE HAT.
BUT it's OBVIOUS HE IS CLEAR ROUND THE BEND.
HE NEEDS A GOOD WOMAN
THAT'S WOT THEY SAY.
COS IF HE DOESN'T SOON EAT
THERE ARE BE NO MORE RAY.
NO FUNNY HATS OR FREE DONKEY RIDES
AND NO ONE TO LAUGH AT XMAS GIBES.
BUT I AM SURE JULIE WILL WRITE AGAIN SOON.
FROM PEARL STREET OR WAS IT HALF-MOON?
I WOULDN'T DARE SHOW IT.
MIGHT CALL ME A POET
SO I'LL WAIT FOR THE 2ND OF JUNE.
ALL THIS FRANGIPANI FRACAS IS I HAVE FALLEN IN
LOVE WITH CRIPPLED OLD BLACK LADY. QUITE BY
ACCIDENT. ALL BECAUSE SHE WOULD NOT JOIN
IN ART GROUP. SO I MADE HER SIT NEXT TO ME.
MUCH TO THE ANNOYANCE OF THE FOLDERAL.
SHE IS SO KIND AND SWEET.
HARDLY ANY FEET.
AND RINGS ME UP THREE TIMES A DAY.
SAYS I MUST BE A SAINT.
AS SHE EVER AIN'T.
MET A PERSON SO KINDLY AS ME.
I DRIVE HER AROUND.
SHE BETS ON THE TAB.
AND LOSES AS MUCH AS SHE WINS.

> BUT SHE IS SO FULL OF LIFE
> MIGHT MAKE A GOOD WIFE
> BUT SHE HASN'T ASKED ME YET.
> LETS FACE IT. I NEED A HELPER. SHE NEEDS A
> MAN ABOUT THE HOUSE. ONLY 50 YEARS OLD.
> AND NOT BAD LOOKING. TO-DAY SHE GAVE
> ME A NEW RECORD PLAYER IN EXCHANGE FOR
> A BEAD CURTAIN. OF COURSE THERE WILL BE
> NO FANCY *Bits* GOING ON. SHE IS ALMOST
> PERFECT EXCEPT *she smokes a lot. Has ordered
> a painting. And another bead* CURTAIN. AND
> PROMISED A MEAL AT HER PLACE. I. DON'T
> WANT TO RUSH INTO THIS. BUT *I think we
> would be doing each other a* FAVOUR. SHE
> IS NOT NATÏVE OZ. CAJUN – FRENCH INDIAN.
> LOOKS LIKE NAOME CAMPBELL – WOOF WOOF.
> *Wont the natives be jealous.* LOOK AT
> HIM *thinks he is* KING FAROUK. *With one
> of his* HAREM. AS *I* DRIVE A MERCURY
> L.T.D. SHE MATCHES IT PERFECTLY AS IT
> IS BRONZE. COLOUR. WILL BE SENDING
> SMOKE SIGNALS ANY DAY NOW.

But, good lord, as I read on, I saw even with the excitement of this new love in tow he appeared to be casting his eye further afield. Perhaps this is how it works for some men.

> *My faithful* RAILWAY FRIEND *died last week of heart attack. And left a single sister behind. Perhaps I should go and console her.*
> *My life will probably end up as usual El Capitaino—pixo noxo. Nothing. But while theres* SNOW *on the* ROOF *the* FIRE *could still be alight. All my special love*
>   *– RAY*

The letter showed his optimism was out and about. He may not have thought himself lonely and looking for love but his jump-the-gun response was being shared with me.

Just like in the war years he wrote his poetry as if paper were scarce, never tempted to place it in lines or stanzas as I have here. Written in capitals and excited with hope, his love of art and poetry still eclipsing his love of a woman. Just, which woman? And how do you find just the right one? But when love calls by his response is immediate.

It was fifteen years since his wife, Elma, had suddenly died and the layers of the house on the island had just kept growing. In the 1980s his next long-term love escaped with half his worldly possessions. Through her he lost his country seat in Allora, near Warwick, and what was left was now all on Stradbroke.

Between his letters and my 2015 communication with some of the islanders and my imagination, lost in there behind the unruly garden, if it could be called a garden, was Raymond, a reclusive artist. Him sleeping with a crystal under his pillow, soup tins and books everywhere, the floor no longer visible. Tired old vegies and mouldy bread collected from the grocery store every few days, supposedly for the "lapin" (rabbits) and the chooks, but perhaps even for him. All of it hurled into the boot of the Pontiac for the two-minute drive home.

Him wandering around in a sarong, with a row of ducklings in pursuit, watching for a python with a gosling in a half nelson. Conflict with a neighbour about the state of Ray's overgrown garden and the neighbour poisoning his trees. Raymond putting a dead chook in their roof, the stench keeping the neighbour on the mainland for months. His house was a cryptic record of a lifetime of his interests and, according to the "Mrs Across the Way", "as fascinating as the generous man who lived there".

Unbeknown to me at the time, it turns out Raymond Moult-Spiers was "a man of letters". Sending passion via Australia Post was just one of his varied techniques in his search for love in the 1990s.

There was "Miss Pumpkin Lovely Lips", in Kuala Lumpur, to whom he had sent a china kingfisher, which had arrived smashed, with Ray insisting they were looking for drugs. There were letters written in 1994 to a Chinese lady called Judy Chan, filled with atrocious lies about his age. One look at him would have had the cat out of the bag. Love letters of a different kind, letters to and from his daughter Lili.

Added to his fatherly existence were the roles of grandfather and then great-grandfather. Lili already had two daughters, Lee and Larisa, and Lee was by now having children of her own. Raymond was now declared a great-grandfather. He was too young for such things and certainly was as far as his Chinese Judy knew.

His granddaughter Lee was given a gem of his wisdom when he wrote this to her:

Childhood is the Kingdom where nobody dies, that's why I refuse to grow up!

But having Lili now knowing he was her birth father made for some different complex feelings. In 1991 he wrote in a letter to her:

*You are so close spiritually
I can almost touch you.*

Ultimately, he gave up the quest for Miss Pumpkin. Lying in wait was the backstory, revealed in a letter written in June 1993 to a woman he had known for a very long time and whom he had never considered available, let alone that she had affection for him. It appears she had called him from Sydney and spoken at length about her feelings, or was it that her feelings were mixed with financial need? In response Ray had composed a draft letter in which he wrote about her being the only person who had shown consideration for him and how he had already begun making moves to alter his will in her favour.

In the same letter he talked about how her turning up expressing her feelings like this had created the impetus to cancel his trip to Canada to see his dying brother, who was in and out of a coma. He expressed his disappointment with his brother's lack of help over the years and was proud to have been able to save his $3000 airfare, to be put to better use. (What dying brother in Canada? I call out to him.) I thought his brother lived in the UK.

Discovered in 2019, in the kept boxes at Lili's, in among the mass of paperwork littering his life, was evidence that he had lent this love $8000 and mortgaged his property to do it. I am able to witness, like a ghost of the future lurking in his past, how he changed his will in her favour and worked really hard to help her reopen her antique and gallery business. He wrote that he had produced a new body of work ready for her opening. Raymond Moult-Spiers was back.

This new love was smart! She followed him up with his promises and had his new will (which left absolutely everything to her) witnessed. Of all the wills found floating about among his papers, this was the latest one made real, and it changed everything. As soon as she did this, it superseded the will held by the Public Trustee, which the mother of his two Australian children, Lili and Leonard, had secured only three months before.

Curiously, in his letters to Lili in 1993, he reported some avoidance behaviours of his new love. He questioned Lili as to whether or not it was normal to fear falling pregnant at fifty. In line with her needs, he also reported having a vasectomy at seventy-three. However, in the short time it took to secure his will, his financially needy new love appeared to have done her best to avoid intimacy.

This newly declared love affair seems to have lasted for as long as it took to reinvigorate her business. As we can see by his unsent letters to Chinese Judy in 1994, he was again looking around for a female companion.

ABOVE Ray with his London bus. His love-nest complete with costume wardrobe

OPPOSITE Ray's letter about his love life and vandals.

Let's face it. I need a helper. She needs a man about the house. Only 50 yrs old. And not bad looking. To-day she gave me a new record player in exchange for a bead curtain. Of course there will be no fancy bits going on. She is almost perfect except she smokes a lot. Has ordered a painting. and another bead curtain. And promised a meal at her place. I don't want to rush into this. But I think we would be doing each other a favour. She is not native. Cajun-French Indian. Looks like Naomi Campbell - woof woof. Won't the natives be jealous. Look at him. Blahs. He's King Farouk with one of his harem. As I drive a Mercury Ford LTD. She matches it perfectly. As it's bronze. Colour. Will be sending smoke signals any day now. Very busy down your way. Sorry about the missing mail. That is why I am selling everything of value. As the Vandals are rottening me blind. Must tell about the photo Nancy sent me p. Sunday to my eldest brother Louis. Who was killed at school. I just can't work it out. My faithful Railway friend died last week of heart attack. and left a single widow behind. Perhaps I should go and console her. But these meetings entirely end up? as usual be careful. XXXO OXO. Nothing but while storms snow on the roof the fire could still be alight.
All my special love Ray.

CALAMITY POINT

I am selling everything of value. So the VANDALS find nothing and STOP ROBBING ME BLIND. Must wait till I go out. The photo Nancy sent me is similar to my eldest brother Louis. Who was killed at school. I still can't work it out …

Raymond Moult-Spiers, 1991

12
The minister of bamboo

In this August letter, mention of the alternative bushdwellers on Stradbroke followed. These folks apparently often found it difficult to survive growing drugs, but this was not new.

According to the news of the day, the bush on the island was being used to grow and manufacture a healthy marijuana industry, which in turn supplied a hungry mainland. The hippies and druggies were harmless at first, and often struggled to make ends meet, but as the years went on so the grower's world changed into one of ruthless greed.

Raymond's recordings of his interactions with them in his letters were all written in capitals. His next letter, scarcely three weeks later, revealed far more.

3.9.1994

VANDALS. NOT AS BAD AS IT USED TO BE. BUT WITH ALL THE PROTECTION AND A WATCH DOG THEY HAVE GOT AWAY WITH 2 TVS. RECORD PLAYERS. ANTIQUES ETC. EVEN THE CARS HAVE TO BE HID IN THE BUSH. HAVE GUNS AT BOTH FRONT AND BACK DOORS – SHOOT FIRST. AN ELDERLY PERSON LIVING ALONE IS AN EASY TARGET. I HAVE NO NEIGHBOURS THANK GOD. EVEN STOLE PAINTING OF VINCENT FROM STUDIO.

For me, all the way over in Western Australia, these mentions of attacks revealed a fearsome situation; over the years he had referred to a few break-ins and robberies and finally a nasty bashing. This man was living in self-defence. He had adopted a holster for his Colts so that he was armed at all times. He had to be. The man, although once tall and strong, had succumbed to frequent attacks of malaria; surely he was now thin and brittle. Fear must have been eating away at him. He had survived the Burma Railway and prisoner-of-war camps (although probably not the memories). He knew what to do. Was this why he had turned to self-protection?

The real course of his life, like the ancient peat below the wetlands of Stradbroke Island, was hidden. The sandy surface of both man and island confused many as to the real richness below. He was unusually tall for an Englishman, with a Canadian accent. That, and his passion for big American cars, set him apart. So bewildered by him were the islanders that some folk even spun the absurd tale that he had murdered his wife. It is true his wife of many years had died suddenly, perhaps too suddenly for some of the people of Straddie to comprehend. This couple was outrageous from the start, but sympathy soon hatched for his wife, an older woman managing the endless antics of a younger husband.

The townsfolk who had known Raymond's wife reported that in the 1970s Mrs Moult-Spiers was the talk of Amity Point with her characteristic drive into town, mastered with nonexistent brakes. This was something the Straddie townsfolk learned to be wary of. However, after 1977, Elma's Mini Moke no longer made its way to the post office and general store to pick up the paper in the mornings. The locals missed seeing her long hair blowing in the open framework of the doorless buggy. Arriving as she did at the said location, she would usually circumnavigate its carpark, going around and around ... and around ... until her hair hung straight and her brakeless Mini Moke had stopped ... sometimes equally masterfully at the door of the shop.

The house on the island was now empty of Elma. Such a sudden event, her leaving home without a word like that! Everything of hers still there ... and his thinking around these left items, obscured and troublesome.

Although Elma had officially died of a heart attack, the feeling I got was one of "How dare she just up and leave". In my imagination this belief seemed to be layered in the gathering dust. But he had a way of adding things. Something every day appeared to be brought in and put down or strategically dropped or draped over her things, and soon all sign of Elma was lost in the layering. Dead and buried.

Some islanders, all fools they, dared to rumour she was electrocuted doing the washing and found on the front lawn, her hair all on end. Murderer, they said of Raymond Moult-Spiers. He should have fixed the electrics.

Raymond, home alone now, still angry at her for leaving him, or was he still angry at his mother leaving him in that same sudden way? Their burst aortas delivering their instant deaths – 1922 or 1977, it is all the same to him. Crying for his mother, crying for his wife.

While the complexities of Raymond's life shook me, there was a violation simultaneously dancing across the surface of my own family. It was being drawn towards us by a strong magnetic pull, behaving like a slowly forming tsunami, sucking at suppressed secrets pushed down beneath the surface.

The digger in my family had deserted his post as "involved father" way back, when he started working shifts and had bought himself his acreage, his mother of earth, his safe place, his roofed womb in her sands of time. He had finally dug down deep enough to root out those lifelong disturbances to his wellbeing.

For my part, as often lone parent, I was a fool for attention, but not just any attention. In 1993, when I too was drawn into a chasm all my own, with my former unresolved, unkind childhood love.

My brief but very real desertion through deception unravelled Roo and brought both our secrets crashing down on all of us. But, just as an incoming tsunami sucks back the ocean to reveal the seabed below, so the emotional tsunami revealed an insightful glimpse of Roo's boyhood ordeals.

His memories, like retrieved artefacts from the mud, were initially brought home and then together we carefully examined them one by one. Strangely, much of it was not news to me but already shown in my dark and unnerving dreams. These dreams, coupled with strange visions, had begun to manifest with odd regularity months before.

A vision seen of a car accident, the mirror image of the one I could not avoid four days later, taught me not to block but to pay attention to what was opening up, to go towards it, not away.

Marching towards emotionally laden situations was not easy, but doing this prevented further physical damage and allowed it all to play out, as frightening as it was. Nevertheless, the sighting of Roo's torment was but brief, before it all got submerged under the torrent of sea rushing back towards us again. The backwash of terror sat upon my shoulders thereafter.

With all my night-time busy-ness, some bees made a hive in the wall cavity next to my side of the bed, perhaps to remind me of the sweetness to come, but mostly to add volume to the frightening dreams I was having.

In keeping with the bees, the boys were busy with their own pursuits and mates, Roo was frequently at his five acres of wetlands and I was working on various creative ventures. Everyone was keenly doing their own thing and only coming together for meals.

The unresolved damage caused by the emotional tsunami saw Roo embrace the notion of rebuilding our lives with the move to a new house and a fresh start. Our letterbox again changed in early 1994, when we ultimately decided to move closer to Roo's shift work in the laboratories at a mineral sand refinery.

Like the queen bee and her workers, we swarmed, only to find that the gorgeous limestone abode already housed a hive of bees in the wall cavity of my new studio, the best studio I have ever had. This time my production of paintings increased to the hum of the bees and scent of their honey. Then, leaping from my dreaming and into my studio, was the kangaroo. He would visit me in the night and I would climb aboard and away we would bound, this way and that but never back again. The snake left and the kangaroo and I became interchangeable.

The new house gave us glimpses of an estuary with access to pockets of bushland and nearby rivers to explore. Yasen was now ten. He was a nature lover, and all over the new landscape, frequently returning home with bobtail goannas from which he removed ticks. He and his Davy Crockett mates often went crabbing in the estuary or fishing in the river. In time he set himself up with a surrogate family of boys across the road. Yasen was moving towards proving himself physically, with a heavy involvement in athletics and basketball, all of which were attended by his lone adoring mother. He was always a leader, right from his preschool days, when he was looked on like the company commander of an unusually male-dominated age group.

Although there was three years between my sons, being the same height saw them routinely

FRAGMENTS OF THE SKY

ABOVE *Roo United*, 1993, oil and wax on canvas, 68x88cm. Private collection.

mistaken for twins; even so, Mourad was a completely different operator. He and his mates were more inclined to produce creative innovations, such as soundscapes, which they might play over the phone or the like. Hours were also spent putting together sound grabs to make elaborate answering-machine responses, as well as tapes that were played in odd locations, such as the sound of someone falling down the stairs played near a staircase.

Another such recording, which included distant sounds of sirens blended with running and scuffling, was used over the phone to announce that their victim's house was surrounded by police and that they were to come out with their hands up. Very soon this talent was to be invested in by the local funeral director. He requested a soundscape designed for a street parade and service celebration of the long life but sad demise of Pat's Hamburger Bar, a place of notoriety frequented late into the night.

But for Mourad, after a computer had entered the house, that was the last we heard of his soundscapes. He moved quickly into images and graphics, with an impressive proficiency.

As I was now performing professionally, I would practise Spanish dancing regularly. If a big show was on, I would have to bring out the bata de cola skirt to rehearse operating in it, by kicking the long trailing flounces this way and that, twirling around and around, frequently with our small dog riding in the tiered frills as they swept across the floor. Flamenco guitar and laments lilted in the air, setting feet and castanets in motion to pound out the complex rhythms. Roo even joined the dance company for a time, which was fun until it wasn't. As well as working in my studio and lecturing, I continued to toil alongside my mother on costumes for opera productions. I had also begun to do costume commissions of my own. At various times the house would fill with racks of theatrical apparel.

But running tandem with Raymond's brush with intruders and thieves came our own experiences with break-in and theft. In my case it was the theft of a number of my large framed drawings, which were still stored in the unsold house we had just moved out of. The police were called and a report made. Dissatisfied with the inaction, Roo then took it on himself to investigate a set of tracks leading to the back fence. He followed them right up to a side entrance of a neighbouring house, where he could see into a room and spotted one of the drawings.

Together we went to the house and tapped on the back door. A woman answered and, while we were explaining our situation, she became concerned and invited us in. Our enquiry as to whether she had seen any suspicious activities had filled her with the fear of also being cased. From where I stood, I could see one of my picture frames and exclaimed that it was one of my lost works and asked where she found it.

She called in her nineteen-year-old son who swung us a walloping story, indicating he was not about to return my property. We left empty handed, his opportunity to come clean blown and our course of action made clear. Roo's successful investigating led the police to the lad's front door and the resolution of the world's smallest art heist.

Our boy's new bikes were then stolen from our new house. Yasen, not unlike Raymond, started a decoy collection of old bike parts, which oozed from my studio to its external surrounds.

Another yappy little dog was brought in. Meanwhile, Yasen creatively utilised the bike parts to build some very strange moving vehicles. He, for reasons unknown, had also begun to attract a vendetta of sorts. With no houses around us and no fences to protect us, some boys, on their way through the bush to the shopping centre below, began to target our property by throwing stones at regular intervals, occasionally actually breaking something. The police eventually caught them, interviewing the boys with their anxious parents, and quickly identified there was some kind of jealousy concerning Yasen at play. Thereafter, all flying objects ceased.

Meanwhile, on the island in 1994, the bamboo had become a thick, impenetrable barrier, a briar hiding Raymond's humble beach shack, studio and him – barbed wire was not required. Ever the survivor, he had plotted his way around the island via safe and unsafe areas and people. The Indigenous people were in his safe zone. According to some of the people who lived on Stradbroke at the time, this man never walked anywhere, even taking his huge car for the two-minute drive to pick up the paper. He never checked the oil in his cars, blowing up the gear box on one occasion. It is said he drove in veers, filling others on the road with the dread of encountering him. But many islanders thought he was a generous and funny man, in a hilarious kind of way, a larger-than-life character with hair all over the place and presenting a quirky sense of the ridiculous to brighten or spice their day.

According to old Charlie Flynn on the corner, "Ray used to wear a sarong with no undies to the store and when he bent over to get some potatoes all you could see was his potatoes!" This fella also quietly announced at the end of our chat that "Ray was a bit of a shagger". I wondered how he knew that! Towards the end of 1994 Raymond was getting ready for an exhibition, a two-person show on Stradbroke Island. This was unusual as I had never heard of him showing his work like this, and in Queensland what's more. He only ever spoke of selling and showing his work through a gallery in Sydney. Other works seemed to be sent off to group shows where prizes were involved. While I was very glad for him, I had no way of attending. The exhibition invitation looked good.

… Just having another SHOW but it's controlled by council. Which bugs me a lot. I am sure you are still forging ahead in all fields of art. it's hard to believe I am a great Grandfather. For I am too young. For what good it does me. Don't want to know. I am quite content with what I have. Best wishes to your large family and I hope you are all well and happy. With best wishes with love of the special kind Ray xxx

Enclosed in this letter was a catalogue for the Visitors Centre Art Gallery, Dunwich, North Stradbroke Island, continuing to 18 December 1994:

MOTHER MOON FATHER SUN
AN EXHIBITION BY
KIMBO WEBSTER AND RAY MOULTSPIERS

OPPOSITE Taken from the invitation to attend an exhibition of modern art by Kimbo Webster BVA and Ray Moultspiers

Mother Moon

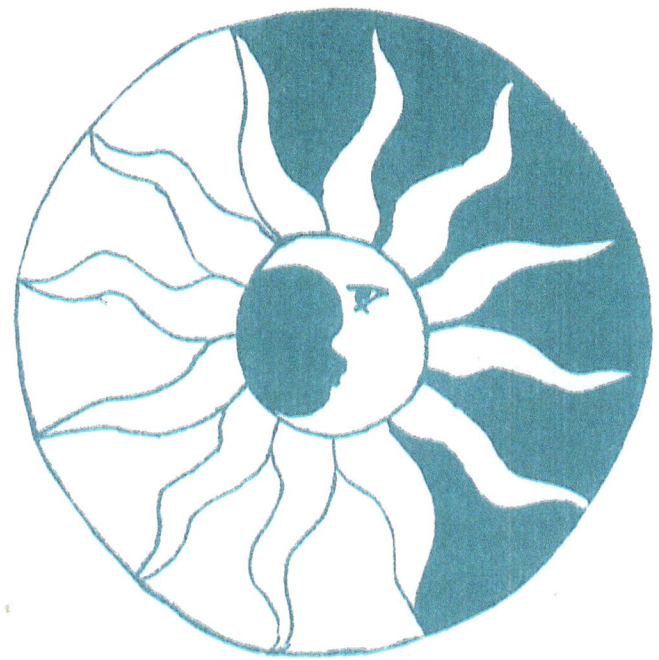

Father Sun

Ray Moultspiers from Stradbroke Island, Queensland, is a well-known artist, having been a member of the City of Parramatta Art Society for many years.

This exhibition consists of a collection of works painted in the artist's own style of abstract impressionism.

The artist's work has been acclaimed throughout the U.S.A., France, Fiji, Britain and Japan, notwithstanding the fame granted throughout the Commonwealth, emanated from receiving the winning prizes in several art competitions.

an exhibition of
sculptural assemblages and paintings
by
Kimbo Webster
& Ray Moultspiers
Exhibition to be opened
by Dawne Douglas, M.A.
(Lecturer at Q.C.A.),
Environmental Artist
Tuesday 13th December 2 p.m.
drinks and hors-d'oeuvres
at
The Visitors Centre Art Gallery
Junner Street, Dunwich
North Stradbroke Island
continuing until Sunday 18th December, 1994

*... Pity we live so far apart.
I feel I have missed a lot in life.
I feel so isolated here ...*

Raymond Moult-Spiers, 1994

13
Return to sender

"Return to sender" was stamped on the envelope. It was my 1995 Christmas card come all the way back to me from the other side of Australia. Nearing the end of January and there it was, weighted, containing a full-bodied letter asking about his wellbeing but describing and assessing my own during the past year. I held it a moment.

"There must be some mistake. Maybe Uncle Raymond has moved."

Time had passed and, with his birthday in early February, I had already posted a birthday card.

With Christmas long gone and no forwarding address, I decided to open the letter and, reading my own correspondence, I was immediately shocked by the truth of it. Its frank report on my life was so personal it read like a series of intimate diary entries.

I hid the appallingly frank Christmas letter under a woven mat on top of the fridge. If nothing else, I had always written to him about my circumstances with complete honesty. Exactly why that was remained a mystery. After all, I barely knew the man, save through his written words.

I contemplated why my letter might have been returned without explanation. I tried to believe that I may have let him down. I had not travelled across Australia to see his latest exhibition. But perhaps he no longer wished to communicate. Guilt is always such a desperate thing. Instead, I fell into the multitude of reasons and justifications I had for not jumping on a plane to cross the vast continent late in 1994 to attend the opening of his show.

Distracted, I reflected. My artistic endeavour was the weft being woven into and through the warp of my roles as wife, mother and lecturer. Like the strong weave of a cloth, I was woven into the fabric of my own tight existence.

The letter out of sight and my mind back on my own business, I forgot about the "return to sender" correspondence, until his birthday card was returned, stamped "DECEASED". The shock of that word, all alone on the envelope, set in. At that time there was no one to communicate with, no one I knew who knew him ... not a living soul. I just had to accept that one word ... that death sentence.

In Western Australia, in my professional woven cloak, weighed down by a busy family life, I was too embroiled to look into what had happened then. In fact, I knew nothing of the circumstances of his death for many years, so shrouded as it was for me, cut off from all knowing.

The only clue I had about Raymond's passing was my returned mail. He never once shared the full names or contacts of people close to him and, as no one ever got in touch, I presumed he did the same in relation to me. I had no idea what happened, so at the time there was naught I could do about it.

The year trotted on, busily filling with fanfare. Added to my part-time teaching was sessional work at the university up on the hill. Despite all income going to pay off our new home, my new appointment appeared to pose some kind of threat to Roo.

My studio work saw the production of a series of heart-stamped postcard pieces to myself from a holiday I desperately needed. I had compassion fatigue.

The Spanish dance company joined the opera company for their biggest production yet, Carmen, which included touring performances. I was appointed the costume designer for both companies. When the show finally opened at the city's entertainment centre, there were up to seventy performers on the stage at one time. Dressing all of them in the appropriate costume on a limited budget required unbelievable dexterity, which I soon discovered I had.

Working at the university brought new opportunities, one of which was an art tour of Turkey. Not to be missed, I borrowed the money from my parents, who in turn were excited to take the boys on a camping trip for the duration. I packed the boys' bags and they left for their adventure. I packed mine and left for Istanbul. I was immediately transported in the most unexpected ways. The intoxicating effect this country had on me was to lead me deeper into both dance and costume, all told through my work in visual arts.

The tactile response to working with nature's coloured earths had already changed my perspective to one of hovering above and entering a work through its layers, like a rich, textured universe. But, added to this, my subconscious mind was now more interesting to me than the outer world. Once back in the studio, traditional Turkish music distracted my busy day mind.

By the end of the year, marked by the receipt of Uncle Raymond's death notice, Roo and I had stepped off our "merry-go-round going nowhere". The marriage had become a debacle.

Yasen was just about to turn thirteen and was off to high school in the new year and in his capacity as leader of his pack now governed a vast territory across rivers and estuary. He knew every square inch of bushland and its secrets. Mourad was sixteen and skilfully managing any potentially threatening would-be's with his razor-sharp witticisms. With the entrance of the home computer he became the master of this world, discovering, developing and using numerous new skills. His self-taught abilities continually amazed me. The boys were teenagers keen to be making decisions of their own.

ABOVE Costume designs for *Abduction from the Seraglio*, 1996, acrylic gouache on paper, variations on 86x40cm. Private collections.

OVERLEAF *Turkish Coffee*, 1998, acrylic gouache and sands on paper, 80x70cm. Private collection.

By the new year Mourad wanted to start his own graphic design business and was busy with his new focus. He refused to go with me and Yasen on a short trip to Bali.

Once in tropical Bali, Yasen mastered his bartering skills while I tried to keep up with his bounty. He was a joy to travel with, so courageous and keen to understand any undercurrents, mapping his way through the streets in ways I could not grasp.

With our marriage ceased, it wasn't hard to see that Roo had been quietly moving out his possessions for some time. His final exit was done with a single laundry basket because everything else he wanted was already in his bomb shelter at his block.

Left alone with my longtime health affliction I began to wonder how things had worked out for my aviator childhood love, when news of him literally fell out of the sky, making the front page in all the papers. With a full-page spread, I read that he had been forced to bring down his engine-troubled water bomber in a suburban street, through power lines and housing, without injuring a soul, and stepped out unscathed. With such a clue given, I wrote to him to ask if he too had been afflicted with a consequence resulting from the betrayal. He wrote back telling me that, although he had lost so much, he was now happier than a pig in mud with a mate's former wife!

Being happier than a pig in mud was not exactly my experience. Roo was not only the love of my life, my husband and father of our children, he was my muse; with him out of the picture my studio work began to change dramatically, as survival slowly pointed me towards more cerebral conclusions.

At the start of the education year, I enrolled at a Perth university with the intention of researching the current re-emergence of public art in Western Australia. Simultaneously, however, I had begun to win public art commissions and was slowly finding a new area of expertise. This paid off, but increased my workload, so I was unable to follow through with the university course. Mourad's accumulating computer skills saw us working together to produce professionally finished graphics and projected imagery of my public art in situ, a collaboration we've continued all my working life. I focused on the variable commissions I won, both in theatre and public art, alongside part-time teaching and participation in statewide group exhibitions.

I was bowling along in fits and starts, sometimes under immense pressure and sometimes completely collapsed into myself, exhausted. For me, each public art submission required I meet, get to know and fall passionately in love with the project, while birthing my concept for it. If I won a submission, the real test of the relationship began. However, once the work was completed, my love would "drop" me. It was brutal.

In the meantime, following the "return to sender" theme and after four years on my own, I had managed to attract and get involved with two men. Both of them set about, although perhaps inadvertently, to deceive me with their secret dalliances with other women. If this was payback, then so be it. I took my punishment on the chin, at first.

On my discovering the extra woman of "deceiver number one", not quite a pilot, he wrote me letters sent in airmail envelopes, hoping to reacquire my interest. We bunny-hopped along for a while with "what goes around comes around" themes. Knitting ourselves together with wisdom and humour

ABOVE *Possum Paving*, 1998, cast concrete, brick paving, possum brick 30x30x9 cm. Commissioned by the Busselton Shire.

before Max, the family cat, who had been signalling his disapproval from the outset, unwittingly put an end to it all with an attempt to suffocate my "air male" as he slept.

Roo and I tried again but the damage to trust was as deep as our love. The terrifying tsunami, with its dangerous floodwaters of emotion, carried us away from each other once more. The sorrow never really goes away; we went through with the divorce in 2002.

The second deceiver, with his aeronautical name, had manoeuvred towards me back in 2000, but his neediness, reflected by the women he had hidden in the wings, ensured it didn't take off, but rather sank to the bottom of the sea.

With children and husband all flown the coop, I finally recognised I no longer needed to function in my former capacity. I focused entirely on my studio work, which had completely changed since Roo's departure. I needed it to be flexible in its earning capacity and accordingly secured a solo show in Melbourne and, with the bundle of new work, flew there.

As both Yasen and Mourad had long since left home, returning to our former family abode was no longer joyous. My alone times with the family's cats and dogs was just not the same anymore.

In the weaving of my life, my family was my mainstay, my warp, but, with its absence, the weft, my creative self, was falling in a heap.

The realisation that I was no longer the self-appointed curator of the family home, a museum to the relics of a family life long passed, began to set me free. So, in 2003, when the funding ran out, I deconstructed it all. I then struggled for ten long years, lost and without a home, my possessions dispersed.

At first I moved my studio into the city centre, taking over a former ceramic art workshop. It availed a gallery space and huge studio, which I managed to fill with my creative intentions.

By 2004 I had decided to leave town to do a postgrad in Perth. But I needed to top up my credentials. I chose to do this with a Design for Performance course. Next, I ruthlessly deconstructed my studio, keeping very little.

Yasen, who had taken the family's two cats, was already living and studying all things electrical in Perth. Mourad was well and truly running free after he won a short-film competition and had moved into film and television, and he too was living the city life.

I may have thought I was going back to study, but in reality I had entered a big production house where you learn on the job. Multiple shows opened every six weeks. Because of my background I was fast-tracked through the course. The pressure

ABOVE. *Air Male*, 1999, impasto, sand and plaster on timber, 43x96x5cm. Private collection.

to get designs done so they could be constructed from fastidiously measured plans was immense. If I thought I was under pressure before, I was wrong. This course was outrageous. There were many all-nighters.

At the end of that first intense year on productions and with nowhere to live, I had survived a series of house-minds, which extended to orchid management, fish feeding, bird custody, cat supervision and dog wardship. In between I stayed with my sister, Eleanor.

Then an actual tsunami sucked up the Indian Ocean and in mega thrusts spread it across fourteen countries. The devastation took me with it. Its effect was shattering. Every part of me was shattered. My empathy could not be contained. Like a spent marble column, I was still standing, shaking into my very foundations, but would I crumble?

Finally, with my empathic, shaky foundations, I considered my own situation and fortified myself in a bid to start anew.

Then my sister was diagnosed with cancer and suddenly had what seemed to be her whole second chakra removed. Fortunately, I was able to stay with her, whether it was a help or not is for her to say.

Instead of cleaning auras, I started to clean everywhere I stayed. I was unstoppable. Everything was cleaned and replaced, reordered anew.

As circumstances changed, I went to stay with our family cats in Mourad's room at Yasen's house. Mourad was headed for greener pastures over east. Fortunately, those long hours at the big production house prevented me realising I was, in fact, sharing the house with six youths, none of whom had ever cleaned the bathroom. The build-up of scum-ridden bum fluff was something to behold. I cleaned and showered simultaneously. When I did eventually do a head count, I wondered where Yasen was putting them all. Yasen was the king of that castle unchallenged, until in a funny twist – all because I needed a mailing address – the government

FRAGMENTS OF THE SKY

Police Complex Entry Statements, 2001, four bronze sculptures designed to evoke the lemon-scented gumnut and mounted on four glass-tiled columns, worked with Maree Norris Mohn, bronzes 50x50, columns 120x30cm. Bunbury Police Complex.

stopped his youth allowance because he was living with his mother! No one could see that it was the other way around. I needed to vamoose, not only because of this, but because I was not "cool" to have on site in conjunction with his cash-supplementation business in the laundry.

I relocated to a new temporary house-mind in the centre of Perth. Along the way and during the long semester breaks, I worked on shows in Melbourne, where I often shared living space with Mourad, who had moved there, employed to film and edit Noise TV and who was living with his girlfriend, a soon-to-be singer in a big band.

Then startlingly, back in Perth, an ill-prepared Yasen produced a daughter in a not-so-startling relationship that became a conflict zone. I became this much-loved, precious child's "go-between", her delivery service from one parent to the other, her minder during sickness. The cherished sleepovers, drop-offs and pick-ups were required no matter where I was housed.

Finally, that horrendous production house course finished and I started my postgrad. To supplement my income, I picked up costume design commissions and began part-time lecturing at the academy I had just left. Slowly my new love emerged as none better than the trickster, Harlequin. Not unlike Uncle Raymond, with his sudden appearances and disappearances, this shape-shifting, gender-bending nonsense figure had been materialising in my image repertoire for years, both making me laugh and cry with its "pull no punches" riposte attitude. My harlequinesque character had even wiggled its way into the hearts of many, as the year 2000 image on the state's International Women's Day postcard, acting the goat about the many roles women are expected to juggle.

ABOVE *If the Shoe Fits*, 2000, acrylic on paper, 66x86cm, State of Western Australia International Women's Day postcard. Original in private collection.

Accompanying me on various harlequined journeys was Pedro (from my flamenco dancing days). Together we went to Italy to flush out hidden remnants of the iconic costume. Then to Vietnam to seek the sources of exotic cloth used in the French stage version, which changed the harlequin's costume forever. Gradually I put the flawed geometric pieces together.

During the research period I returned to Melbourne, employed on another show. Again I stayed with Mourad and his girlfriend, this time in the Jewish sector, where I worked on my thesis at night.

Back in Perth at my "alive and well" sister's house, and during the last few months of concluding the written component of my thesis, I accepted a commission to illustrate a children's book required to be done in just three months. Although the illustration work was fulfilling, it was confounded by the finalising of my thesis. I somehow completed the commission in good time and the children's

FRAGMENTS OF THE SKY

OPPOSITE *The Trial*, realised set design, 2003, constructed and performed at the Western Australian Academy of Performing Arts, director Matt Lutton

ABOVE *The London Cuckolds*, 2005, costume commission for Western Australian Academy of Performing Arts, directed by Sydney's Aarne Neeme.

BELOW Costume designs for *Hairspray*, 2004, coloured pencil on black paper, 40x30cm. Artist's possession.

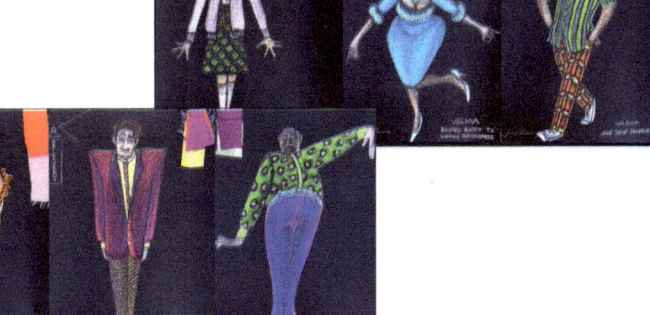

book was duly published. In the interim, Mourad completed his life in Melbourne and moved back to Perth.

Creative exhaustion hit, so I turned my skills to casual lecturing at both the academy and an inner-city art school. However, it was still not enough dependable or consistent income to allow me to safely rent a house but, even worse, with all the moving around I was doing, I didn't know where I belonged. I continued in the same manner, house-minding or helping others with their household chores in exchange for a bed. Nevertheless, the responsibility that came with Yasen's little daughter directed my choice of habitat more to south of the Swan River.

My harlequin thesis and a costume commission led me to work annually with the fanciful Fremantle Carnevale. A new man turned up adoring my peripatetic lifestyle; it was all masks, music and carnivalesque, with not a single connection to aeroplanes, but when the carnival was over, so were we.

Time passed and things changed again, this time through the help of my parents, and suddenly there I was housed aloft in a lofthouse, all my own; surrounded no less by many of my former possessions, once given and now returned to me one by one. The strange alchemy of "return to sender" was still at play.

My swansong in public art and costume design came in a neat package, with a brief to dress twenty-four trees for the iconic Kings Park Spring Festival. Included in my cherished construction team were my boys. Mourad worked to prepare the fabric designs for print and Yasen worked on creatively constructing the 10-metre costume design for the RoyalTREE, a majestic river gum planted by Queen Elizabeth II in 1954, the pinnacle of the temporal commission.

Then, out of the blue, in an act akin to being harlequinesque, the sender's mail returned to me. In 2015, in an innocent act skirting the mysterious, my father came across Raymond's mailings in the bottom of his filing cabinet, where they had been stored for safekeeping twenty years ago. Mysteriously yet, he uncannily delivered them to me on 9 February (Raymond's birthday)! The mail arrived on a particularly hot day entombed in an old briefcase. Inside were the dutifully kept letters and little paintings Uncle Raymond had sent me from 1980 to 1995, and my life changed again.

OPPOSITE LEFT *Palm Trees*, 2014, fabric design prepared by Mourad and printed in Melbourne, to dress the four palms at the top of Kings Park, Perth, overlooking the Swan River.

OPPOSITE RIGHT *RoyalTREE*, 2014, the 10-metre costume was built on site by Yasen from prefabricated elements including a conduit underskirt and 40 metres of netting, lycra sash and bodice with sequined trim and jewelled broach, topped with welded steel tiara with jewels. My design inspiration was taken from the traditional white gown, royal blue sash and tiara worn by the Queen in the 1960s.

"If you see a tree as blue, then make it blue."

– Paul Gauguin, artist 1848-1903

part two

THE HOUSE GUEST

> forgive me dear it's getting late
> I promised that I will wait
> till Kingdom come
> when that's all done
> I'll be loving you always.
> I am never Far away.
>
> Ray

Raymond Moult-Spiers
date unknown

14
Out of the blue

Twenty extraordinary years had passed since I received my returned letter with "DECEASED" stamped on the envelope. In that time, I was no closer to the truth. It had remained an earmarked, unfinished chapter in my life.

It was now 2015 and I was living alone near both the Port of Fremantle and the Swan River. As in 1995, it was again a commemorative year. Instead of fifty years, it was now seventy years since the end of World War Two, and as was the wont, images were dragged up of a raped and soured Singapore, a crushed and defeated exotic lady teetering on the edge of the Malay Peninsula.

Footage of war continually flashed across screens. Post offices brought out World War Two books and other potent knick-knacks, placing them close to their counters.

Aware of this peripheral play as I was, I was unprepared for my part in it.

As described, during the long hot Australian summer, my father delivered a timeworn leather briefcase full of old letters addressed to me. The timing of such a delivery can only be described as sacred scheduling, because exactly why they were delivered at all is one of those conundrums in life.

Strange these letters should find and make this small but significant rectangular briefcase their home. Like the letters, I too now occupied rectangular lodgings. But, after years of blowing in the wind, wandering alone from house-mind to house-share, I was housed in a home of my own and strangely ill-prepared for my new housemate.

When all was quiet and it was just me and the old leather briefcase, I ventured to make friends with it. Touching the rich leather, tracing my father's gold initials embossed between the clip-down locks, I felt real trepidation and, rather than unclip the locks, I physically stood up and stepped back.

Viewing it from a distance seemed safer somehow. After all, I knew what was in there, and I hadn't needed to revisit their contents for twenty years, so why now? I danced around it in more ways than one, asking questions of it, my reluctance constantly tapping me on the shoulder.

The briefcase, which sat mounted like a royal gift on an imported, embroidered and tasseled pouffe, continued to seduce my interest. It reeled me in, until finally I clasped it with both hands and unclipped the locks simultaneously.

Like a genie escaping from a bottle, so Great-Uncle Raymond leaped into the room. His vigour was undeniable. Whether I wanted it or not, I had company. He entered my thoughts and pulled me this way and that. He lured me with his mystery. I stared at the mound of letters, remembering how hard it was to read his writing the first time around. I picked up the top letter, gazing at it and then through it, back into my own life all those years ago.

Why did we correspond? We were complete strangers. I suddenly realised he was there for me throughout my entire lovely, but troubled, awkward marriage. He disappeared from my letterbox the Christmas before my marriage dissolved.

The idea of reading his eclectic scrawl allowed me to put the letter back and instead riffle through the chaotic contents. Barely able to remain cocooned in the cavity of the briefcase, the pile instead spilled out all over the floor. I tried to pick them up and put them back, reshaping the pile to fit. But I stopped, completely stunned, when that old 1981 Playboy magazine made a grab for my hand.

What is this doing in here?

I hauled it out in an effort to re-engage my mind with events of some considerable time past. Nothing emerged, so I began turning the pages from the back towards the front. Finally, I arrived at the contents page, which I scanned for a clue.

And then it jumped out. There, next to a small headshot supported by an article title, I saw the name Allan Moult, larger than it actually was, and remembered in an instant that Uncle Raymond claimed we were related to this man whose photographically documented article was embedded deep in this Playboy. Relief flooded in, as did the revelation as to why there was a Playboy among all the keepsakes. Allan had photographed aircraft not anatomy, balloons not bosoms. His photographs and article, titled "Ultralight Flight: It's a Breeze", really did cover custom-built craft, ballooning and hang-gliding of sorts.

I thumbed back into the magazine to find the article. The summer evening was still hot. I stared at the words and photos he had used and sat back, nested in my papasan chair, to let it all sink in.

The dusk slipped into a deeper hue, threatening to take me on its journey, but an idea was upon me. I sat bolt upright, stood, then motored to the other side of the room towards my laptop, grabbed it and returned to sink back into the circular nest.

The internet, scarcely a toddler back then in the 1990s, was now a know-it-all teen. I typed in Allan Moult and up came a website describing a nomadic photographer with the same birthdate as my own! His website was swimming in stunning landscapes. Certainly a professional. I buttoned my way to the contact page and wrote him an email. Did he know my uncle, a Raymond Moult-Spiers?

Having done that, I realised I could have a go at unravelling the Spiers part of Raymond's Moult heritage.

Ah, the internet! I typed in Raymond's full name and lo and behold there he was! He was immortalised on the internet. The first thing I found was a painting of his up for auction.

ABOVE Ray Moult-Spiers, *The Gully*, watercolour gouache, 39x49cm, 1950. Auction house

I stopped, content to stare at it, taking in its communications and thinking. His small paintings "lodging" in the sacred briefcase were nothing like this! The image on the screen was a masterful and considered landscape.

The foreground of this painting supported a lone but lofty, very central gum tree on a riverbank overlooking a fertile farming property. It was the distance that held me. The lone tree in the foreground immediately made me think it was like a portrayal of Raymond and his life, with everything just out of reach.

On the other side of the river stood another gum tree. This one is upright and elegant, almost feminine in nature. Yet the gum tree in the foreground, which I have now called Raymond, was tough but with its head in the clouds; it was teetering towards the other across the river (and all its potential possibilities).

Hi Allan,

I have just opened an old briefcase full of cherished letters, paintings and other small sent items from Raymond Moult-Spiers (b. 1920, d. 1995). They were sent between 1980 to the early 1990s (when all the communication ceased). He seemed to be estranged from his children, I think? I could never make sense of it. And no one knows where or why the "Spiers" got attached to the family's name of Moult.

I have no idea how he found us in Western Australia given his childhood in foster care, perhaps in the UK and Canada? However, he held dear a photograph of my great-grandmother, Ann Moult, whom he thought was his mother (but whom in reality was his aunt). His father was actually Ann Moult's brother, John Thomas Moult. Their father was also John but was known as Jack. Jack had eleven children, of whom only two survived to have children of their own. Jack's brother was Joseph Crampton Moult, known as Tom (who had four children, only one of whom had a child). Raymond always claimed you were related in some way but, as his letters to me were most often eclectic, I don't have much to go on.
I am somewhat down the line, born in the 1950s.

I believe my cousin is doing a researched Moult Family Tree, but as I haven't seen her for forty years, I will have to apply effort.
Anyway, if you don't have time for all this, don't worry about it.
The family tree I have is pretty sketchy. I only have names from about the mid-1800s. My cousin Anne may have much more by now. I was just urged to follow through with contacting you first.
By the way, your photographs are absolutely beautiful.

Good thoughts
Julie

"Just like Raymond," I thought, "and it leans into the future exactly like his writing."

My eyes watered, wandering through the image entering his very brush strokes until I began to lose myself in the magnificent brooding sky.

Lulled by the heat that evening, I lay back thinking of the magical ways Raymond painted his skies. Drifting into the sky-painting experience, I entered the realm of memory, asking: Just how do you paint the sky? It is not a solid surface onto which we peg birds, flying machines and clouds; it is infinite ... so how do you paint the sky?

But the real question was: Just how do I understand Uncle Raymond? He was never a solid surface onto which I could peg things.

And yet here he was, coming out of the blue as it were, into my lounge room. When did things change? When did the sky above change from that pure blue to the soft, misty silken hue that sits on the hemline joining the burlap earth? When did a pale, misty Raymond fold himself into this interfacing?

As I faced the luminosity of memory, I understood it was the foundation of a story, to be employed in the act of overlaying, tinting and applying washes of colour, each eddying against and into the other in a celebration, suggesting atmosphere ... suggesting Raymond.

He was here alright.

My mind swooped into and through that painterly atmospheric sky and found a thought floating there. Just how did he do it?

I had so long ago learned he had painted in a place where there was no brush, no paper, not even paint, and yet he painted, recording the beauty, emotion and horrors of the POW camp in each single telling stroke, each telling stroke like stamped, addressed envelopes. I saw what they recorded in their skies. I paused, remembering but not experiencing, just watching.

The next day, still filling with questions, I contacted my long-lost cousin to see what was turning up on their family tree search. I learned cousin Anne, a former medical scientist, volunteered in a library and in her spare time had been slowly chipping away at the family tree. She could access things I could not. We met and, with excitement, shared our findings. We ignited one another. But the gaps were huge, so we each set off on our separate quests to find answers.

Enclosed in Raymond's very first letter was a full-colour double-page spread of a feature article about his life and work, titled "Prison Camp Artist". It was written in 1953, the year I was born. The author, Herbert Hull, cited Raymond's war experiences and contributions to the Sydney art scene, including the establishment of the Parramatta Art Society. This article placed him not only as a Sydney artist but also as a survivor of the Burma Railway.

I then bravely set about rereading all Raymond's letters and noting down anything that referenced the family. I sent everything I found to cousin Anne. I also kept searching online and found a couple of books written by Changi survivor Geoff Bingham, which had included references to and even a whole story about Raymond during the war. Cousin Anne found that Raymond had sealed army files in the National Archives of Australia and had written asking to have them opened.

I tracked down his niece, Penelope Moult-Spiers, in the UK and called her at her Scarborough home. Although she was not keen to get involved, she was very helpful with the few facts she knew.

She did, however, strongly suggest that Raymond had committed suicide. This was because a war historian had also contacted her a few years before and shared his concerns and view that, during the 1995 commemorative year, Raymond was suffering the return of some really unpleasant war memories. She couldn't remember the name of his book but said it was a recent publication. She gave me the contact details of the historian's assistant.

I wrote to the email address provided and received a reply from his former assistant, telling me the author had himself also passed away (in 2011). However, she verified the belief that Raymond had suicided.

I contacted the RSL on Stradbroke but they were busy with their current commemorative duties. I eventually found my way to Barbed-Wire and Bamboo, a newsletter for World War Two veterans. I put in a notice looking for anyone who knew Raymond Moult-Spiers. The two amazing ladies running the newsletter found a few more clues, which helped me piece things together.

I also made contact with the North Stradbroke Island Museum in Dunwich, and found myself in the capable hands of Ms Gondwe from the Historical Society there. She followed up my query by kindly making a trip around Amity Point interviewing anyone who knew him and then provided me with a transcript.

In it I learned the islanders thought he was Canadian, dressed like a cowboy with a belt with a big American eagle and pouches and pockets where he kept his gold, that he was the stand-in for Lee Marvin in the film Cat Ballou, never paid for his cars, had an exhibition in Cabarita, which had supplied wine, wanted the church for a studio, was a dealer in gold and jade, and all in all was quite eccentric.

But one chap said it all when he reported, "He had a big American car and when he would drive it, everyone would say, 'Don't go to Dunwich today, Moult-Spiers is on the road!'"

With those descriptions from the islanders I could see Raymond was definitely a standout – something to be observed from afar. There was no mention of his character. But it was their other inference that disturbed me.

"The talk around Amity was that he killed his wife. They used to fight a lot. There was never any investigation."

None of this was true. Elma died from a heart attack in 1977.

The descriptions went on: "He had two silver revolvers, Colt 45s. He used to run around with his guns, shooting things. It was a bit scary. He went a bit crazy in the end, thinking he was still in the war. Towards the end he was a menace. He was found several days after he died. He had been eaten by goannas after he died. His belt and revolvers were missing. After he died somebody got into his house and ripped it apart, searching. A son turned up when he died."

These last pieces of information were not at all comforting and certainly not what I was expecting. The islanders not only had knowledge of what the flesh-eating lizards had done, they painted a very concerning picture of Raymond's death.

A couple of his letters had referred to the big monitor goannas and that he controlled their entry into his house by putting cactus plants on the window ledges. As awful as the state of his body was, why had his house been ripped apart? Where were his revolvers? Where now was his son? The whole story was unsettling.

I contacted the Queensland coroner's office. However, they advised me that, as the granddaughter of his cousin, I was not eligible to apply for any information about his death. They told me that I had to get an immediate family member to apply. With no idea of his children's surnames and with Penelope gone to ground, I gave up.

Through constant searching for Raymond online, I turned up five files stored by Austlit, an encyclopaedia of Australian writers and writing. The files contained a poem, some text, paintings done during World War Two and the biography written by the historian who had researched him. I wrote to Austlit to request access to his files, but they refused, also saying my being a granddaughter of his cousin was not close enough as a relative and that I needed to contact his children, despite Raymond being unable to legally claim them as his own.

These refusals to allow access to information set me on another tangent. How was I going to identify, let alone find, his children? None were ever officially declared his. I spent hours going through his letters again, looking for clues. I had the two Australian children's first names, but I didn't have their mother's name. It was hopeless. Raymond had written "BROKEN" next to Leonard's name, but it made no sense. Staring at this one day it suddenly dawned on me that the obscure "sha" written in lower case underneath "BROKEN" might be part of the word. I joined them then searched that surname.

This information became a central pivot in leading cousin Anne (who in the meantime had started looking through old electoral rolls in Horsley Park, the place Raymond had lived with his wife from 1946 to 1970) to tie that surname in with Moult-Spiers around the time of the conceptions of the two Australian children. It worked, and she quickly had names and dates of a Brokensha family who had lived in the area. We were able to track their moves to Queensland.

I soon found a published South African family tree online, showing Lili and a big sister. I now knew a little more about the man who raised her and her brother Leonard. But it was impossible to find anything further on Lili. I was able to find a phone number for Leonard. I called that number many times and manifested all kinds of reasons as to why he never picked up. Frustrated, I found Leonard on Facebook and I reluctantly joined the social media platform in order to message him.

On 9 August 2015 I sent my message.

Hi Leonard,
If you are related to my late Great-Uncle Raymond, as I suspect you are, I would love to make contact with you. I have been calling your landline for months but no one ever answers or returns my calls. Perhaps you are out of the country ... so I have joined FB but I am not sure if you are active here either. I am from the WA side of the family. Uncle Raymond wrote about you and your sister over a fifteen-year period. Despite my nomadic lifestyle over the last ten years, I have managed to keep all his letters and little paintings. I would love to get in touch.
Julie

FRAGMENTS OF THE SKY

Still no response. With more details and his address, I then wrote a letter addressed to him and his sister, explaining further. I sent them photographs, my address, phone number and email address. He responded with a text saying he didn't like to speak on phones. So we texted for a while before moving to email so that he could send me images of his drawings. Such a wonderful thing to find he, too, was an artist.

I soon figured out there was something fragile about him and that he lived a cocooned life. He told me he did not know Raymond was his birth father until Raymond's death. By way of working things out, the shock had prompted his rendering of a drawing of Raymond in the sky. He sent me a photograph of the image. Despite having four strapping sons of his own, he lived alone and had minimal communication with them and no communication with his sister. He told me he was born with spina bifida and had trouble with tasks and remembering things. I gave up thinking he would be in a position to consent to any research probes into Raymond's life. It was complicated because Leonard had to prove he was Raymond's son and there was no legitimate proof. His birth certificate stated Mr Colin Brokensha was his birth father. Somewhere along the line he gave me Lili's mobile number and married name. But eerily something told me not to contact her ... then.

My energy turned instead to investigating the Moult lineage who had arrived in Western Australia, and I drifted into writing a different story.

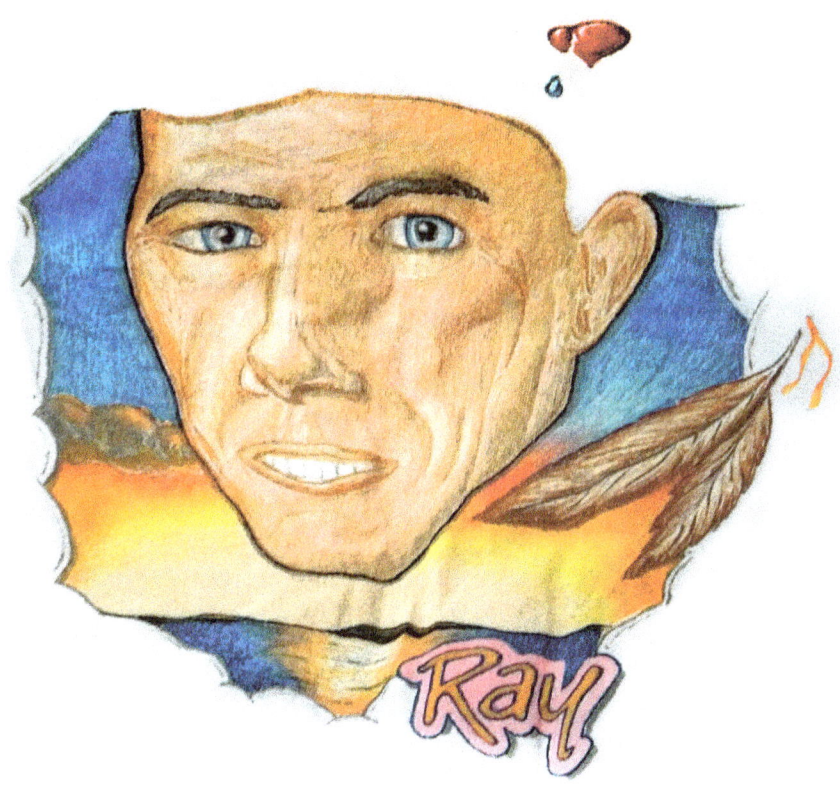

OPPOSITE Leonard Brokensha, untitled, paint on canvas, 2020.

ABOVE Leonard Brokensha, *Raymond in the Sky*, 1995, watercolour and coloured pencils on paper. Artist's possession.

**Amity Point
October 1980**

At long last obtained some sealing wax. And will use it on this letter. Strictly family. It is a royal coat of arms surrounded by a crown. The handle is CORNELIAN. *And it came with other family relics. See what you think.*

Raymond Moult-Spiers, 1980

15
Tailor made

Raymond's note about a "royal seal", which he had used several times during the 1980s to press into hot wax dropped on the envelopes, filled me with curiosity. I found it difficult to believe there was anything royal about it – it made no sense, despite his claim of aunts who were dressmakers to royalty.

In 2018, I finished my first manuscript and, with the assistance of Mourad, who designed and set the book's layout, we self-published the 300-page full-colour tome, which in part told the story of the arrival and survival of the Western Australian wing of the Moult lineage. The latter half of the year was then absorbed in caring for my parents for many months, during a challenging time with their health.

At the end of that year, Yasen and his lovely Italian counterpart produced a treasured baby daughter. As with Yasen and his first born, Anna Blossom, this daughter too was home-birthed. When Anna Blossom was growing up she and I embraced Artistic Swimming while daughter number two and I were to become companions when we joined a circus training troupe.

Early in 2019, while clasping two matching costume hats for my parents and running to attend my father's ninetieth birthday party, themed "At the Vat in a Hat", I suddenly found myself flying through the air and, despite the potential actuality of flight, I crashed down onto the unforgiving pavement. I couldn't move. I lay in the hot sun hearing a faint, faraway voice – "Are you alright?" – followed by the sound of a distant footfall getting closer. With good luck on my side, she who was running towards me was a nurse and so took control. I had bashed my head, twisted my ankle and broken a rib and a collarbone, so was carted away in an ambulance with Mourad by my side.

This is how Raymond got my attention in 2019. The call of "The Raymond" had come through the ether and reclaimed me that day. It was again 9 February – Raymond's birthday, not my father's;

his was three days away. Since then, Raymond has again been my companion.

The broken collar bone and rib required I stay still to allow healing, so I was once more held captive in my papasan chair. It became the cocoon where I spent my days transposed to another era, writing and researching Ray's story through the discovery of his heritage. Mourad and various others appeared at intervals to feed me. By April it was as if a portal had opened on Raymond's mother's life and information was pouring in from internet finds and her story written onto the page.

I wanted to know what circumstances led to Ray being left in foster homes at age two.

Running alongside this curiosity was cousin Anne's investigations. If there was a document to be discovered she had located and accessed it. Through her voluntary library position, she had visited census and electoral rolls, births and deaths, passenger lists and army records. She armed me with these factual findings so that I could then piece together Raymond's family's movements and lives. I had two addresses of where Raymond's birth family had resided. During my internet searches I came across his mother's family tree, detailing some of their history and showing a couple of photographs. With this new information Anne and I were able to cross-reference to establish Raymond's background.

Raymond's mother was born Elizabeth Mary Ann Keogh, in 1881, the first of nine children to Henry (James) and Ada Keogh. Henry Keogh came from a long line of journeyman tailors, having completed his apprenticeship. Although married life had started out in the slums of the West End of London, by the time Elizabeth was ten, according to the 1891 census, her father was working and staying at Kensington Palace in London while her mother and her siblings were located at Elizabeth's grandmother's house in Thame, Oxfordshire.

The family members were eventually reunited and soon established their home and place of work in London's bespoke tailoring district in Soho, once a working-class neighbourhood. The area was rapidly changing into the main entertainment locality in London, where it became fashionable for the risqué aristocracy to venture.

The family occupied premises in the now-famous Carnaby Street, close to the hive of the tailoring industry. Living in the area enabled them to work and raise their children in their three-storey terraced accommodation. As Elizabeth's father and grandfather were both journeyman tailors, who had taught their skills to some of their children, and, given Henry Keogh's work in Kensington palace, the Keogh lineage was extremely well positioned for their further incoming foray into garment construction for royalty.

OPPOSITE

TOP LEFT Ada Keogh (nee Bryant), 1859–1928, c. 1880, Raymond's grandmother.

TOP RIGHT Henry (James) Keogh, 1855–1936, c. 1920, Raymond's grandfather.

BOTTOM LEFT Sisters Ada and Lillian Keogh, c. early 1900s, Raymond's aunts.

BOTTOM RIGHT The royal seal with handle in Raymond's possession 1980s, photographer L. Brokensha.

This opened the way for two of Raymond's aunts, Ada and Lillian, both born in the 1890s and exceptional dressmakers, with clients stretching from aristocracy to royalty.

Finally, I began to understand how it was that a royal seal had found its way into Raymond's hands. Creating garments for royalty meant the tailors had received and were required to use a royal seal with all correspondence to the royal household. The hot melted wax was directed to fall across the point where the letter or parcel was closed and then the royal seal pressed into it, ensuring the palace that the last to close the envelope, had received the seal of approval!

The mystery of the royal seal solved, I went back to 1908, when Elizabeth married a mysterious man whose name was not his own. I found that, by the start of World War One, Elizabeth had borne this curious man three children, Lewis, Erlinda and John Luke, and after the war their fourth child, Raymond, by which time the family was living and working in Lowndes Court, not far down Carnaby Street from Elizabeth's family.

Tragically for all, but especially two-year-old Raymond, Elizabeth died on 14 April 1922. Her death certificate claims a burst aorta. Broken-hearted, perhaps – her eldest son, nine-year-old Lewis, had died tragically three years earlier, on 31 July 1919. Her husband, John Thomas, who was just home from the war, having survived the atrocities of the battlefield, was faced with the painful duty of signing his eldest son's death certificate. Lewis had died in a hospital from tuberculous meningitis.

All this was discovered and written up from the comfort of my universe in the papasan chair in 2019. By April that year the urge to contact Raymond's daughter for the first time had grown exponentially, so much so that I felt unable to resist doing just that. Glancing back at the dates I noticed a strange significance.

My first contact with Raymond's daughter, Lili, was made on 5 April. This auspicious event had occurred on the date of her grandmother's birth and communication continued to 14 April, the date her grandmother passed. It was as if Raymond or Elizabeth herself had reached in through a portal in time and made contact with first me and then Lili.

Raymond had impressed on Lili that his favourite number was five, either when a number's reduced to five or when number five featured. It was Lili's astute awareness that noted the exact time of my first text message was 5.55 pm. This clue allowed her to respond.

By August 2019, around the time of Raymond's passing in 1995, my cousin Anne and I had booked and travelled to Queensland to meet and stay with Lili. As if waiting for this event, Lili, back in August 1995, had swept her birth father's personal papers into a box and sealed it. She took it out of storage for us all to go through. For the next two weeks many answers and revelations flew into the light. But not all.

OPPOSITE Elizabeth and baby Lewis, c. 1909, Raymond's mother, whose interest in millinery is apparent!

...Am horse trading as usual. Pen tells me its in the genes. They are too tight. So I now wear saffron robes...

Raymond Moult-Spiers, 1988

16
Mr Moult or Mr Spiers

As revealed, in 1908, well before World War One had broken out, twenty-seven-year-old Elizabeth had fallen in love with and married Raymond's father. She was already five years past the average age of marriage for young women at that time. Perhaps she was focused on the Keogh family's tailoring business. Her husband, John Thomas, at thirty-six, was ten years older than the average bridegroom and, indeed, a man of the world, with an overseas trip under his belt. Yet some confusion as to his identity loomed. Elizabeth's marriage certificate states she married Mr John T. Spiers, but this was not his real name. This man was Mr John Thomas Moult.

While the origins of the invented name of Moult-Spiers continues to intrigue me, evidence shows Raymond's father initially used his family-of-origin surname of Moult, until sometime after 1902, when he swapped to using the surname Spiers. This shows in official matters like his marriage and World War One enlistment documents. He appeared to do this for around fifteen years.

Investigating why led me to the family myths about Raymond's father. First, of being a Canadian Mountie; second, of being responsible for taking the first Irish horse to Canada; and third, of being a horse rustler. These in turn led me to all kinds of possibilities as to why he operated under the pseudonym of Spiers during the early part of the 1900s. He certainly travelled to America, and very possibly did take horses onto the Canadian frontier from there.

At the age of thirty, in 1902, John Thomas Moult was recorded as being on board a ship that sailed from Liverpool, where he had worked as a groomsman, bound for New York. He was on board registered as "John Moult, cattle foreman" and was travelling with three others in their twenties, who were all calling themselves "cattlemen". Perhaps these cattlemen had a load of Irish horses bound for Toronto, the supply base for the North West Mounted Police, or perhaps they were out to make a quick buck.

The horse industry in Canada was rife with rogues making fast money through deceit. It is no secret that John Moult's hostler, or groomsman's, skills meant he could veil a horse's poor health by enhancing it until it appeared to be a much finer animal than it really was. But no one will ever know if this is what John Thomas Moult was doing, as proof of his taking horses into Canada has not been found.

I searched further in an effort to realise why horses were so needed in that part of the world and found that Canada was said to be "built on the back of the horse". But, more importantly, both hardy horses and courageous Mounties were in high demand. Attracting men and horses to Canada frequently required the call to go out to the British Isles.

John Thomas Moult was a highly trained hostler and had skills required by both the Mounties and the horse rustlers. In this respect he certainly fitted requirements.

Indeed, the terms of engagement for the North West Mounted Police requested an unmarried fellow being no shorter than 5 feet, 8 inches (173 cm), at least eighteen years of age, with a sound constitution, who was able to read and write English (or French), would show allegiance, be fearless and above all be an adept rider and well versed in the care and management of horses. While John Thomas may have possessed all the latter, his army records state he stood at 5 feet, 6 inches (168 cm). Nevertheless his joining the mounted police in some capacity can't be excluded, as the Canadian government often recruited young men from the British Isles. It was a tough recruitment and not for the fainthearted, with training and commitment to service lasting some three to five years at the

ABOVE John Thomas Moult, c. 1900s.

very least. The expectations of the gruelling and lengthy patrols demanded a steadfast prerequisite of extraordinary commitment. They required exceptional young men and exceptional steeds to face the life-and-death weather conditions alone. If a young recruit's commitment faltered, hefty prison sentences were handed out to deserters … if they were caught.

Either way, it appears that at some stage John Thomas Moult became John T. Spiers, a man possibly on the run from authorities.

It is evident that Mr John T. Spiers had joined the Keogh family and had lived together with them in the Keogh household for a short time. It is said he was a quiet, independent and mysterious man with his own ideas.

With the newlyweds' first child born in 1909 and Elizabeth's next pregnancy in 1911, John Thomas undertook to find a new home and premises within walking distance of the Keoghs' Carnaby Street property. Inside three years of marriage the little family had moved a few blocks away.

At Number 3 Lowndes Court, just off Carnaby Street, according to the census papers, John Thomas Moult hatched variations of the family name, finally deciding to hyphenate his alias, Spiers, with his birth name, Moult. With that, the family surname Moult-Spiers was born and eventually given to his children.

John Thomas may have continued his overseas business, between working as a private servant, a groom and a tailor, apparently all the while indulging his interest in antiques. With a pretty little shopfront on street level and the home above, things were shaping up, or were they? Unfortunately, and unbeknown to them, World War One was loitering in the wings and set to change everything.

Whatever else John T. Spiers did, he did his duty when he signed up in 1914. He was forty-three and his sound knowledge of horses ensured he was well placed in his area of expertise, the remount section of the army.

During the war it is probable that Elizabeth took in boarders or perhaps even let out part of the home to ensure some kind of income. It was known within the family that rooms were rented out in times of need.

But, as a consequence of going to war, John T. Spiers returned unwell with emphysema-like symptoms and was soon issued with a veteran's invalid pension.

Things were going very badly for the newly declared Moult-Spiers. After John Thomas's return, and the heartbreaking death of Lewis, two years later Raymond was born. Framing Raymond's birth but another two years on, Elizabeth's sudden and tragic death at the relatively young age of forty-one left all three of their remaining children in his care.

When Elizabeth Moult-Spiers died, Raymond's war-weary father was fifty and it emerged he was unable to care for the children, two-year-old Raymond (b. 1920), seven-year-old John Luke (b. 1914) and ten-year-old Erlinda (b. 1912).

It appears Raymond could only address his childhood in rhyme. But this poem says a great deal and must be read to comprehend the making of the man. The poem was found in a small handmade notepad devoted to the work, the size of which may explain the placement and arrangement of his words.

FRAGMENTS OF THE SKY

LEFT Lewis and Erlinda, 1914.
RIGHT John Luke and Lewis, c. 1916.
BELOW Baby Raymond, 1920.

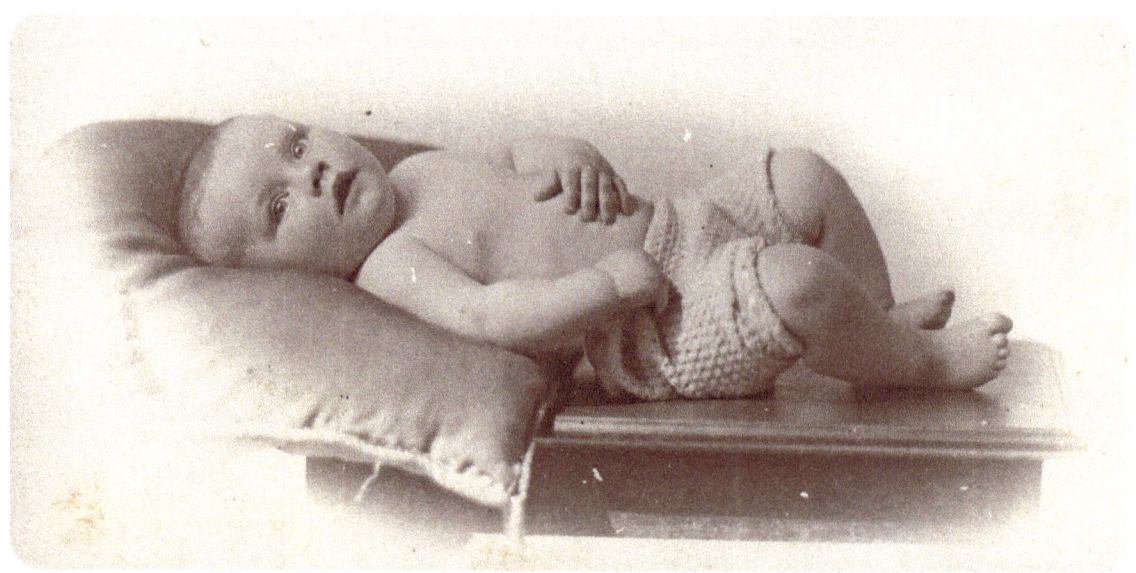

T'was only me when i was
Three in a red brick
House quiet as a mouse
The garden went to the top
Of the hill the rest of the
World was perfectly still
I'd sit in the sun get warm i
Me mother i called
Mrs burgess and me father
Called every now and then
In a pony and trap. He had two
But not for me
Cos i was an orphan you
He was so smart but
She did start when he came up
The hill and the world stood
I remember he wore a
Brown derby hat. But the pony
Stayed still tied to the trap.
I remember swinging on the gate
Looking in vain for a twist of
Fate hoping in vain for a
Glimpse of tucker cos he had a
Shop chock full of clutter

He mended shoes and had a lucky
Dip in a barrel of sawdust
Take your pick. Cherry blossom
On the wall oh
T'was a lovely time for all

Then i was moved when i
Was four to a house down a
Lane with a bright red door
And there again up and over
The hill the garden stretched
And probably still.
Twas another b name of bance
Had boy and girl and me in a
Trance cos mr bance came
Home at night i'd rush right
Out and hug him tight
Cos he was like a dad to me
Me mother dead at 43

I loved the garden up the hill
Could throw me voice come back
At will t'was wellington lane
At old ball hill

I was then moved up to
North end a long straight
Street with hardly a bend
From chapel to church was
Over a mile on the way one
Passed a broken style
a shortcut to the
Rectory house rabbits, hogs and
Several grouse. It must have
Been cold when i got bold.
Went to a fire very old wasn't
Lit so i rubbed me hands
Then i saw the plant stands
A castor oil plant. Now what's that
For? A frosted window in the door
To light the way two rooms upstairs
And a funny passageway of cares
i soon found out my previous life
Was heaven compared to all the
Strife was due to fall upon me now
Then two girls appeared sisters i vow
Maisie and dot stuck to the spot for
Mrs wise did not advise
no talking here
Be most unwise. Come out here and
Sit down there into a
kitchen almost bare

I don't want to dwell on
Those sad years. There was
No joy but only tears. Till
We was let out to take a
Walk the only time we had
To talk. But don't go back
Without some wood mushrooms
Cowslips as if we would to get
A box around the ears go to
Bed still more tears. And dying
Of thirst was even worse
Than being hungry all the curse.
Indeed it was a dreadful crime
To beg for more like oliver
Twist she'd break your wrist

The only comfort that we had was
We three together were not real bad
To take a drink or steal an apple
Oh what joy to go to chapel or
Wander down hazelbee lane not
Ever wanting to return again. It was
Maisie dot and brave little ray
i'm surprised we didn't run away

Raymond Moult-Spiers, c. 1960s

The shop of clutter was beneath the home where Raymond, Erlinda and John Luke had once lived. Although it was still there in the late 1920s and run by their father, the children had long gone, taken by the church and placed at separate locations as orphans.

John Thomas had to focus on getting and staying well enough to continue making a living. He no doubt deeply considered his situation and, with all the children born in the ancient Anglican precinct of St Martin-in-the-Fields, where each was christened, it appears he may have asked the church for advice.

The Soho area, including where they lived in Carnaby Street, was a strange eclectic mix of possibility, but eventually John Thomas Moult-Spiers doubtless reasoned that the church would know and do the best by his children. It was not uncommon in the day for a single parent to be forced to give their children up to be housed in an orphanage. Even with one parent still alive, the children were often referred to as orphans.

It ultimately eventuated that John Thomas Moult-Spiers sent his children into St Martin's Church foster care, but he tried to stay in touch. As told in the poem, for a while he would occasionally visit his children at their various locations when he could, bringing presents, but not the food and love so desperately needed.

Evidence shows John Thomas Moult-Spiers from Lowndes Court also worked with or for the antique dealers Agnew & Sons, which eventually led to him doing some on-selling for them. The timing of such a venture, with the slow demise of the economy, saw it colliding with the incoming 1930s depression. John Thomas Moult-Spiers must have felt the pinch before most. He and Agnew & Sons would have made losses because their line was a luxury people could no longer afford.

It is apparent he was locked in a financial struggle and perhaps battling with his lung issues, both of which likely contributed to his disappearance.

Around 1929, he left Lowndes Court without a trace. He was fifty-seven. Raymond was only nine, John Luke fourteen and Erlinda sixteen. The two eldest were technically off his hands, able to legally make their own way in life.

Did Raymond's father return to America or Canada? This man is a perpetual puzzle.

With little or no evidence to follow up, I looked to Erlinda. After the death of her mother when

ABOVE Raymond Moult-Spiers aged 9, c. 1929.

ABOVE Erlinda c. 1930. & her letter dated 1970,

she was ten, Erlinda Moult-Spiers may have even stayed with her grandmother for a short time. This may or may not be true and depended on Grandmother Ada's health. But her grandmother's death, when Erlinda was fifteen, would have put an end to that. Wishful thinking on my part perhaps, as I have found nothing but a single page of an embittered letter from Erlinda to Raymond, written in the 1970s.

From that single page of razor-sharp words, it is obvious she had an extremely difficult life. Her serrated handwriting was all over the place and full of irregular, sharp, pointy stabs into the paper, with lower-case or upper-case printing jammed into half-written words that do not follow lines all in the mix.

In her letter she wrote: "Dad had property, belonged to the banks."

And further down the page she added of herself, "… and being somebody instead of nobody I fought my first court case 30 years ago and won. Nobody shits on Linda." (Perhaps this is how she got her fortune.)

From the two surviving photos, I can see she was a very pretty child and beautiful young woman with a cheeky smile. However, her looks could not save her from the three difficult marriages to men whose menial jobs prevented her from returning to the status she had once known.

Erlinda's 1970 letter even mentions that their father, John Thomas Moult-Spiers, was found drowned. Perhaps he did drown or perhaps he drowned from pneumonia. Not an uncommon occurrence in those days. Erlinda fails to say how, when or where. With Erlinda's trail difficult to find, Lewis dead and Raymond and John Luke's reluctance to speak of their childhoods when living, much will remain unknown.

Many years later, when Raymond was able to reconnect with his older brother, he learned that John Luke escaped his foster home and lived for a time with a band of gypsies. Ultimately, he was sent to a navy cadet school by his father and the church authorities. This standard practice to rein in young boys was set to guide them to a life at sea. But perhaps this occurred the other way around. It might possibly be that John Luke escaped the navy cadets and lived with a band of gypsies. According to his daughter, Penelope, his adult life was not at sea but spent in part working to help children, inspiring them with inventive challenges to promote healthy minds.

A little article in an Arthur Mee children's newspaper about a Mr J. L. Moult-Spiers, describes him as being in charge of a boys home called St Catherine's Home, Hampstead Garden.

> *The boys at Catherine's Home, Hampstead Garden Suburb, have an aeroplane which glides across their playground on a wire 100 yards long. It was constructed out of a tub and tin (for the wings) by Mr J. L. Moult-Spiers, who is in charge of the Home.*

John Luke's only child, Penelope (b. 1945), is the single official offspring of all three siblings and the last to hold the surname Moult-Spiers. Penelope herself worked in care and never formally married, but has lived in a committed relationship all her adult life.

Penelope affirmed her father saying of her grandfather, John Thomas Moult-Spiers, "He was a strong but silent man, who sometimes made announcements at the dinner table. One such announcement was that he had been a Mountie." She added that he had an antique shop and was linked

ABOVE Penelope Moult-Spiers, c. 1980. The last in the linage

to Agnew's Auction House in London, but that he somehow lost a lot of money. Penelope was also told that the family had a large house (no doubt at 3 Lowndes Court) and that, depending on their financial state, they would let out either the whole house or part of it.

With next to nothing in Raymond's letters about his childhood, discovering his personal notebooks at Lili's allowed us some valuable insight. He also briefly wrote about a miniature log cabin given to him by his dad, which was filled with gold coins. He and another boy enjoyed playing with it that day but then it was suddenly and inexplicably ... lost? He wrote of one Christmas when he was about five years old, when his father brought him a train, but he only saw it once before it vanished. His not-so-caring foster mother had told his father that the house had been burgled. According to

Raymond, in reality, she had stolen the train and given it to her nephew.

It is interesting to observe that the career paths of not only John Luke but also of both Penelope and Lili, saw them all involved in the care of children. Even without a conscious connection to Raymond, Lili was led to work in child protection.

There is a massive gap between Raymond's early childhood memories and his arrival in rural Australia at age nineteen, when he claimed to have been still hungry.

We know he was brought up in seven foster homes in the UK and that he immigrated to Australia under a child immigration scheme and was placed on Captain Mercer's farm in Avoca, New South Wales. We also know he travelled to Australia from St Martins (Church) North End, East Woodhay, Newbury, Berkshire.

He sailed to Australia on the *Ormonde* (Orient Line), departing 25 March 1939, arriving at Fremantle, then eventually Sydney, where he and a number of other London boys went to the Church of England Migration Council in Millers Point, Sydney.

We may never know how Raymond came to have a Canadian accent or how he knew his sister's address in the UK and even named her as his next of kin when he joined up for the Australian war effort.

The lavatory wall
where we used to crawl.
In the Summer House.
Hide like a mouse.
Cringing in Fear
In case she was near.
But were lucky to be.
Still alive just we three.

OPPOSITE Raymond aged about sixteen, c. 1936.

"Blue has no dimensions: it is beyond dimensions."

--Yves Klein, artist 1928-1962

part three

THE SOLDIER

> I am the eighth soldier down.
> With ears blistering and noses expanded we lined
> up with our utensils in the boiling sun and believe
> it or not, it was a baked dinner on Wednesday.

Raymond Moult-Spiers, 1941
Notation on the back of photograph (opposite).

17
The new boy from the bush sails away

No stranger to years of starvation and thirst, when eighteen-year-old Raymond Moult-Spiers entered the children's migration scheme, like most of those children, he had believed he was going to learn Australian farming skills. He was lured with the promise that these skills would enable him to make his way towards a bright future. At the time he was considered a child. The hard labour and crude living conditions at Captain Mercer's farm at Avoca proved to teach him that he was little more than a serf.

During this ordeal, Raymond had teamed up with another young bloke. The two had been virtual slave labour in rural Australia at a time when having a young migrant Brit working and living in poor conditions, usually in a humpy, was the norm. A humpy, originally referring to an Aboriginal shelter, was a crude, temporary hut.

Coming up to the early 1940s, after World War Two had broken out, the two young mates, disillusioned with life on a farm out in the bush, stole

ABOVE Ray is the eighth man down, photographed in camp, 1941. Photographer unknown.

LEFT Ray Moult-Spiers, 1940 aged twenty, described in his war records at the completion of his training as having "a fair complexion and blue grey eyes, 6'1" tall and weighing 13 stone". Photographer unknown.

BELOW Rosemary Riley, 1941.

away and headed for the bright lights of Sydney. What money they had soon ran out and signing up quick smart was the next option.

Raymond had his sights set on being a wireless gunner in the Australian Air Force, but then so did every other young hopeful; the line was long and, as the lack of money grew, so did the urgency to sign up. At that stage the Australian Imperial Force (AIF) was only taking those aged twenty-one and older, so Raymond lied about his age and entered the AIF as an Australian citizen on 21 June 1940. He went straight in and began what looks to be six months of training (not the usual three months) as one of the earliest members of the 2/19th Battalion in the newly formed 8th Division, where he was fed well and trained well, and soon bulked up.

Most of 2/19th training took place in three areas west of Sydney. The first army training camp was Wallgrove, which was opened on 15 July specifically for the newly formed 2/19th Battalion. From here they went to Ingleburn, in Sydney, which provided barracks and basic training, followed by further specialised training in working together as a battalion.

Finally, at the conclusion of training, Raymond was stationed at Bathurst, a pretty little town and the oldest settlement in regional New South Wales. The town's buildings were heavily influenced by British architecture, providing Raymond with a kind of nostalgia. The Bathurst Infantry Training Centre, capable of housing thousands of troops, was located on a geographically isolated rural property. Raymond trained here during his second Australian summer, from 5 November into January 1941, after which he was appointed acting corporal. He took pre-embarkation leave from the end of December to 7 January and was sent to board the *Queen Mary* on 29 January, after which the ship left the harbour for the two-week voyage to Singapore.

Before their departure, Raymond and his absconding mate took their last shore leave in Sydney. Here they may have met up with a couple of brothers from Bega. These boys, Reginald and Ronald Riley, had hailed from a blacksmiths and dairy farm called "The Trees", in the Bega district. Their sister Rosemary Riley must have gone to Sydney to bid them farewell. Raymond states in his war diary that he only met her once and that he and Rosemary agreed to write but, by 31 March 1942, Raymond had her added to his service and casualty form as his fiancée. Rosemary, diligently and in good faith, went on to write to Raymond for four long years.

As the men were volunteers, their willingness to defend their country swelled. They were primarily from regional areas but mixed with a few city blokes and some Australians from New Guinea. The blokes from New Guinea and the rural boys knew things the city boys had no need of knowing. They knew how to tough out a situation, how to survive off the land, how to catch and grow food and how to help each other for the greater good of the community. Even their feet were tough. But the city boys were smart in other ways. Many were street-smart survivors of the 1930s Great Depression. This combination of men and their varied knowledge pool may have set them in good stead for what was to come.

Soon the fear of the Japanese threat exploded into reality for Australia, which was followed by a new urgency and change of destination for the 2/19th Battalion. Ready to roll, Raymond and many of the men were shipped out on 2 February,

Troops of the Provost Company, 8th Division assembled on the wharf after arriving in Singapore aboard the troop transport *Queen Mary*. Unknown Australian Official Photographer, Singapore, 18 February 1941 (photo courtesy of the Australian War Memorial, 005892).

heading to the Malay Peninsula to show the Japanese the Australian flag, or so they thought.

The plan was simple. Once they had halted any ideas the Japanese might have had of conquering Malaya, they were to be shipped out to the Middle East.

Throughout the war Raymond kept diaries and made small paintings. These remarkable records were not uncovered and transcribed until 2019.

The voyage over was hot and cramped, but made all the more exacting with the constant showing of war movies for entertainment. Midway during the voyage Raymond celebrated his coming into manhood with his twenty-first birthday and adventure on the high seas, thus leaving behind a cruel childhood to make his way in the world.

All the movies watched on board met a peculiar end, according to historian and biographer Ron Mumford, and a bewildered Raymond. Concerned army personnel bagged up all the Hollywood movies, weighted the bag and dropped them overboard, apparently out of fear the enemy would secure them! Heaven knows what threat to the war effort they may have presented if captured. It was 18 February when the men disembarked their sultry, uncomfortable ship in Singapore. The 2/19th Battalion was immediately moved 300 miles (480 kilometres) north to Seremban in southern Malaya for further training under tropical conditions. Here they teamed up with a detachment of British troops and were billeted at St Paul's School. This was where the talented Raymond honed in on and refined his latent creative flair, as he began to explore painting in his spare time.

ABOVE. Ray with his mate Bob, photographed in camp, 1941, photographer unknown.

During this period Raymond had also busied himself getting to know the locals. In time he had formed a relationship with a young Indian-Malay woman. This is the woman with the twin and who became pregnant. Although he loved her and wanted to marry her, her parents would not allow such a union, as they and their daughter were obliged to honour a promised family betrothal. Devastated, Raymond was forced to look on as the betrothal took place, his chance to form a loving family of his own dashed. (Years later he returned and met his son but was again requested to remain anonymous. Unable to reveal his identity as the child's father, Raymond was required to once more leave things be.)

Raymond's battalion was rotating between Seremban and Port Dickson on the coast but by mid-September they were based around the airfield at Kluang, Britain's administrative centre and an area through which many roads linked parts of Malaya, thereby making it a focal point for the Japanese army.

Contrary to the relaxed command of the British, the Japanese had appointed their top general, Tomoyuki Yamashita, who sent 25,000 Japanese troops into Malaya. They quickly overran every area they invaded.

Being "tops" at camouflage ensured Raymond was sent into central Malaya, where they were setting up and moving camouflaged camps designed to stall any hint of a Japanese advance. The Allies confused the Japanese alright. Eventually the Japanese were both in front of and behind the jungle-savvy Australian troops, one of whom was Raymond Moult-Spiers.

Meanwhile, back home, the *Australian Women's Weekly* produced propaganda articles to pump

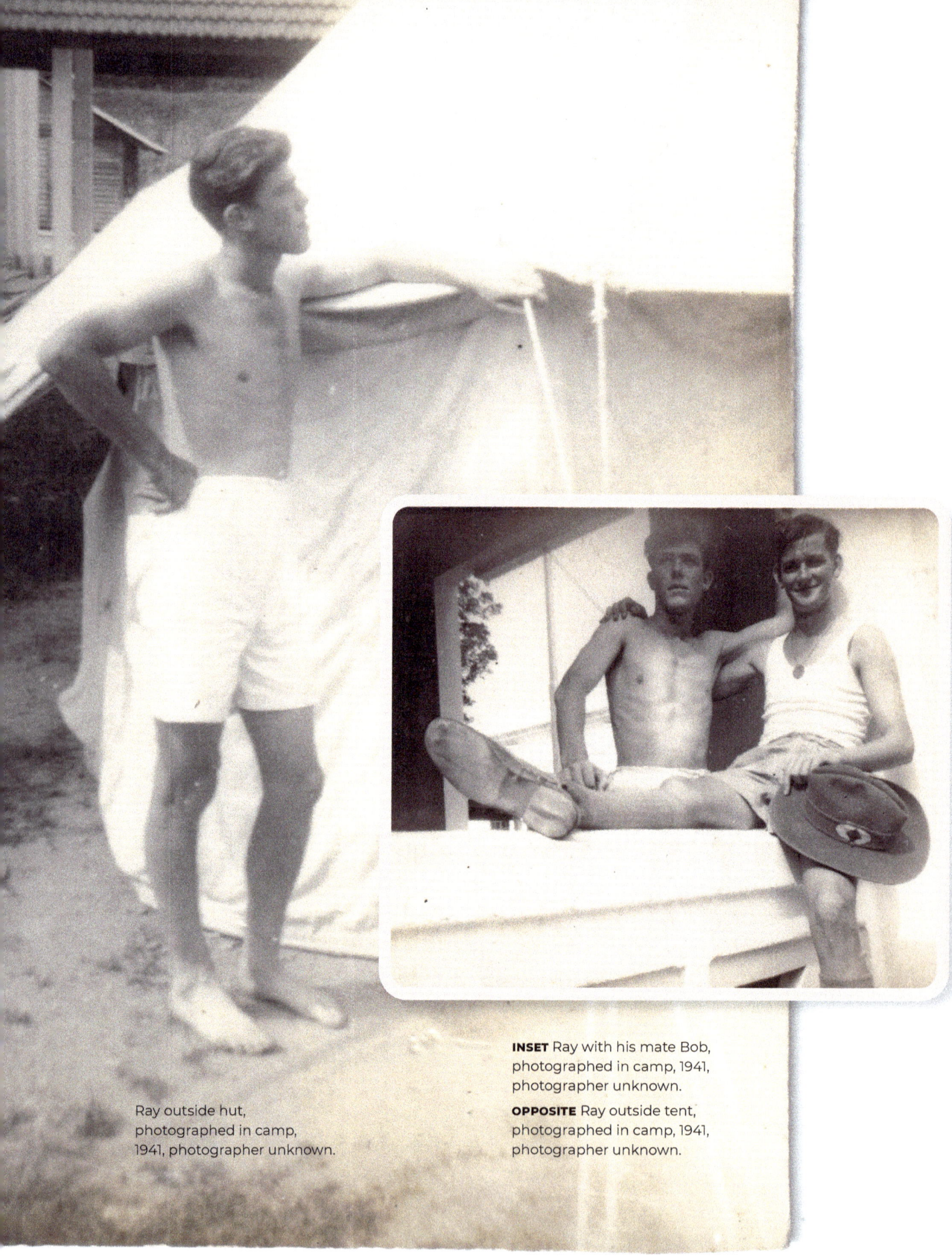

Ray outside hut, photographed in camp, 1941, photographer unknown.

INSET Ray with his mate Bob, photographed in camp, 1941, photographer unknown.

OPPOSITE Ray outside tent, photographed in camp, 1941, photographer unknown.

up enthusiasm and encourage more volunteers to sign up to defend Australia alongside the Brits and their colonies. The Weekly painted an exotic picture of soldiers in fabulously different cultures amid dance halls, clubs and beautiful women, all framed and protected by big, bronzed Aussie blokes.

Through these articles and other sources of misinformation, it was largely thought the Japanese were poor soldiers. Jokes pervaded about them being bespectacled, short-sighted dwarfs who were unable to see at night. As a result, the 20,000 Australian troops who found themselves Singapore-bound, believed they were headed to an impregnable British fortress, merely to dissuade any ideas of a Japanese advance into Malaya. A rude awakening was to come.

In southern Malaya, where Raymond was, news of the Japanese advance ebbed and flowed but concern was not apparent and mere speculation took centre stage. Instead, the troops did regular battle training in the tropical conditions. Here it emerged that the call of the day was to learn how to camouflage themselves and their heavy equipment in the jungle. Moult-Spiers, with his emerging colour sense and flair, was in his element. He was called on to assist others and found he was enjoying being genuinely useful, an important cog in the war machine. The drill was to head out into the jungle for three or four days and set up bivouacs, all the while practising manoeuvres, then back to St Paul's to recuperate. This pattern lasted seven long months.

I am 21 but I know nothing of life but despair, death, fear, ------, superficiality cast over an abys of sorrow. I see how people are set against one another and in silence unknowingly foolishly, obediently, innocently slay one another. Our knowledge of life is limited to death. What will happen afterwards? And what will become of us?

Unfortunately, Raymond's actual diary accounts from Feb 1941 to capitulation in Feb 1942 were lost in the early days of imprisonment. This is from his second (main) diary.

Raymond Moult-Spiers, 1942
Reflective diary entry

18
The run for Singapore

Raymond was one of the few Australians on the Malay Peninsula who was actually trained in Queensland's tropical conditions (albeit briefly). This deeper knowledge may have led to his placement in the overall Provost Corps, and assignment to this particular company. But understanding the full meaning of being in the Provost Corps, particularly in Malaya, was and still is shrouded in mystery. According to Glenn Wahlert's research of the Australian provost, there was scarcely an instruction manual.

At first, life in Malaya was very relaxed for the 100 members of the 8th Division Provost Company, in terms of their policing duties. Although the war was developing fast in the region, this was not immediately obvious. The Provost Company was loosely formed in a casual manner and lacked depth in their training and direction. They had no concept of what was to come, let alone how, as Military Police, they were supposed to support an infantry division.

To the Australians, the British MPs were simply too brutal and domineering. They always threw their weight around in an officious manner, which seemed to bring out the worst in some of the AIF men. Initially, on the Australian Provost's arrival in Singapore, they had watched this going on in the city and learned not to apply the British Red Caps' hard-handed approach.

As soon as the Japanese had hit Pearl Harbor in December 1941, their advance into Asia was swift. The distinctively uniformed but disgruntled British Indian Army initially took the brunt of the Japanese invasion of Malaya and were basically faced with annihilation (through captivity). So, when the Japanese gave them a choice, they were ripe to simply change sides!

Bombers headed for Singapore and Britain's promise to defend Australia began to immediately fail, revealing the British colonial masters could no longer keep the people safe.

When the frantic call came to move out and back

to Singapore, Raymond and the rest of the 2/19th Battalion realised they had to get across Singapore's sole entry point – the causeway, the only way in and out of Singapore – before the Japanese did, but equally they had been commanded to try to slow the Japanese down or, at best, stop them.

This unfortunately put his platoon well behind the enemy lines so, when the call came to get off the Malay Peninsula and over the causeway into Singapore, they were challenged.

As battle lines grew the provosts were advanced to security duties at the installations – control posts for stragglers, guarding various headquarters, managing traffic control for convoys, manning road blocks and so on. They were there but often invisible to the infantrymen. With no sign of the classic MP armband or red cap like the British, the Australian Provost Corps could only be distinguished by a small colour patch containing a white boomerang to denote their status as Military Police. To their credit it appears that, even though they lacked official training, the Provost Corps slowly grew into an increasingly complex and sophisticated unit earning and gaining respect from the men in the 8th Division for the job they were doing.

Australia was busy sending its partially trained young men to Singapore. The existing 8th Division still had the problem of getting either the time or the instructors to further train the incoming soldiers, many of whom appeared to be drawn from a younger cohort of enlisted boys.

As mentioned, Raymond's battalion had been in training with mild skirmishes on the peninsula for close on seven months before the Japanese absolutely made their intent known. By the time Ray and his mates made their horrific scramble and crossed the causeway, they were indeed among some of the last to do so.

But the Japanese were everywhere and the battalion took many hits, although not without giving as good as they got. Camouflage meant lying in wait, as still and as quiet as church mice, perhaps not exactly what Moult-Spiers had thought it was going to be. Still in Malaya, he and the others were ready for action, wound up and held tight in their anticipation for fear the enemy scouts would flush them out.

Each man knew his job. Each man was prepared to wait it out for as long as it took for the enemy to feel secure enough to cruise past. And cruise on past they did, many on stolen bicycles, no less. Hundreds of these were stolen from the locals. The Japanese had prior knowledge that the peninsula had a plentiful supply, as they had been selling bicycles to the Malays for many years before the war.

The last battle, called the Battle of Muar, began on 14 January 1942 with a series of extremely well-planned camouflaged ambushes around the area of Gemensah and the bridge, which crossed the Muar River on the mainland of Malaya.

The initial ambushes were very successful, with the Japanese taking huge losses, but the Japanese just kept coming. From 18 to 22 January, 2/19th commander, Lieutenant Colonel Charles Anderson, led his men, fighting their way from Bakri through one Japanese position after another, until they ran out of ammunition near Parit Sulong.

Travelling with their wounded took its toll on their efficiency in reaching the causeway before the main body of the Japanese infantry. The decision to leave approximately 150 wounded behind at Parit Sulong was tough, but the Australians believed they would be medically taken care of as prisoners of war. Sadly, not revealed to Anderson was the fact that the Japanese had not pledged any allegiance to the international conventions (at Geneva or the Hague) on the treatment of prisoners of war.

Raymond, a compassionate young man, faced leaving his wounded mates behind. The fit and able made whomever they could as comfortable as possible, placing them in a position of surrender and in plain sight of the enemy. Unbeknown to them at the time, all the wounded were brutally tortured and murdered by the advancing Japanese (This was known as the Parit Sulong Massacre).

Closer to Singapore and further down the road, the Allies had set an ambush and each Japanese soldier's fate was sealed as he passed the camouflaged men lying in the vegetation, in the mud, no doubt being eaten alive by mosquitoes – no swatting allowed, just being still – the carefully planned ambush beyond most men's comprehension. The tension held in the waiting was building. Some men in mud were scarcely hidden as the gentle rains washed them clean, still as a rock unseen.

Meanwhile, over the bridge they went, those men on bicycles, over the bridge with confidence. Then the order shouted loud and clear, "Fire", and out from the vegetation those camouflaged men came firing all the way, exploding that bridge in half. Bikes on one side and bikes on the other but still they came. Killing did not stop them. The Japanese continued to come; it was hopeless. Finally Major Anderson shouted the order, "Every man for himself."

After a fortnight of heavy fighting, of the 3000 or more men on their way to the causeway, only 500 made it. Encircled by the enemy at Muar River, Raymond and those who were left of 2/19th Battalion were told to make a break for it through the thick jungle. They were told to make sure to avoid the Japanese lines and attempt to reach the British lines at Yong Peng. It was a horrendous scramble, with not only impenetrable jungle but rivers and swamps to cross. It was certainly a case of every man for himself.

Back home in Australia, *The Argus* newspaper reported the battle, citing the 2/19th Battalion, in the 8th Division as, "the most deadly jungle fighters in the world". Corporal Raymond Moult-Spiers was right in among the best.

After the gruelling jungle retreat, Moult-Spiers and 270 men from 2/19th Battalion made it to the muster at Yong Peng and were withdrawn to Johor Bahru in Malaya (not far from Singapore), where on 26 January they were joined by 650 reinforcements fresh from Australia. With many untrained, the commanders began reorganisation and training immediately, but it was soon realised many of the reinforcements were far from battle-ready. Some unknowingly held defective weapons, while others had only joined up the week before departure. All headed for the causeway.

Following Moult-Spiers and those who made it safely across the causeway, came the Scots, last but not least, playing their formidable bagpipes, the shrill for all to hear. On 31 January the causeway was blown up by the Allies and rendered no longer an entry point to Singapore.

According to official historian Lionel Wigmore, several general references were made to the breakdown of discipline among the Australian forces after the Japanese landed in Singapore. Even the threat of being shot had no effect on the rate and number of Australian troops deserting their positions.

ABOVE *Chinaman Carrying a Coffin*, date unknown, water-soluble stain and ink on paper, 160x210mm. Painting from Ray's war diary.

As a provost, Raymond had his work cut out, as Wigmore's account [on Raymond's birthday] explains:

> By 0800 hours 9 February, hundreds of bedraggled Aussies were streaming down Bukit Timah Road on the way to the city. The Military Police (UK and AIF) attempted to check them but they were in no mood for homilies from "Red Caps".

Raymond may have been turning twenty-two that day but he was charged with rounding up the unruly men.

By 14 February the Japanese had complete control over Singapore's water supply and had captured ammunition and fuel depots. They were in the city and the following day, 15 February, Major Percival surrendered unconditionally. The 2/19th Battalion then surrendered on the outskirts of Singapore. This was both the worst British military disaster and the biggest British surrender in history.

The brutal loss of Singapore was inevitable and Raymond Moult-Spiers and others who survived were in turn rounded up and imprisoned in Changi.

Japan was now "supreme" and, in an unpredictable turn of events, was welcomed by the Malays as their liberator. This is because the British had brought with them Chinese and Indian citizens who had overrun the Malay people, all three ethnicities lording it over the Malay communities. Previously any Malayans who had tried to challenge British rule were imprisoned, considered communists or anything else unacceptable to the British. As far as the Malays were concerned it was "a wrong" waiting to be righted and they seized the day.

[Handwritten recipes on aged paper:]

Cream Puffs. ½ cup butter, 4 eggs, 1 cup boiling water, 1 cup flour, pinch salt. Put water and butter on to boil, add flour and stir quickly, until mixture sticks together, and leaves sides of pan. Remove from fire, cool, and add one egg at a time, beating all the while. After adding last egg beat vigorously for 5 min. Drop by tablespoons on greased tins, leaving a space between each puff. Bake in hot oven 25 to 30 mins. Fill with sweetened or flavoured cream; seasoned creamed chicken, whipped cream, strawberry ice cream, flavoured custard.

Shredded Mustard Salad. 1 cup chopped green mustard, ½ teaspoon minced onion, 2 teaspoons lemon juice, 3 drops olive oil, 5 teaspoons sugar, pinch salt. Mix sugar and salt, add lemon juice then olive oil, mixing thoroughly. Add mustard and onions, chopped and minced. Stir until greens are mixed well into liquid. Serve on meat.

Texas Hash. Cut cold roast beef or veal into cubes, cut same amount raw potatoes same size, put 4 tablespoons lard into iron skillet. When melted add 1 cup minced onion and garlic, fry golden brown. Stir in 2 tablespoons flour and add enough hot water to make medium thick gravy. Add meat and potatoes, season with salt and pepper, and cook covered until potatoes are tender.

But the Chinese, old enemies of the Japanese, were yet to experience the worst atrocities of all. It is believed the Japanese massacred some 50,000 Chinese Singaporeans.

Australia was now within the reach of the Japanese, who swung their line of fire towards Darwin and continued their bombardment. Darwin began to be pounded and, with these attacks from 19 February 1942, 250 Australian citizens were killed. But with the war effort and some sixty-five ships in the harbour the full death toll may never be accurately known. In all the confusion it is unclear exactly where Raymond was and how he had survived. But survive he did.

ABOVE Recipes on reverse of *Chinaman Carrying a Coffin* painting (opposite) – utilising paper Ray has written on the backs of his paintings – 160x210mm. From Ray's war diary.

OVERLEAF RIGHT Raymond's war diary, 1942–45, hardcover foolscap-size. Its cover is made of plywood and covered in timeworn army cloth (possibly an old shirt) hand stitched onto the thin plywood. The cover lists the twelve POW camps he was in.
Author, Raymond Moult-Spiers, 340x250x40mm. Private collection, Queensland. Photographer, Julie Parsons, 2020.

War Pays a Visit, date unknown, ink on paper, 200x260mm. Painting from Ray's war diary. Image held at www.austlit.edu.au, copyright Moult-Spiers' family.

Raymond reflected in his diary about his previous New Year, when 1941 transitioned to 1942. He had spent it in the grounds of the sultan's palace in west Malaya just prior to Singapore being lost. It appears Raymond's position in the gardens awaiting Japanese bombing raids would have been more secure than he realised at that time. But he didn't stay long.

The following diary entry was written after nearly a year in Changi.

Diary entry: 1942
I remember last New Year. We were in the
Sultan of Johor's palace garden waiting
for enemy bombers but we had to wait
till 2 a.m. when they appeared over
Singapore and the lights went up –
I feel very despondent this evening,
getting very moody probably thinking
about what might have been …
Wishing everyone and all old friends a
very happy and prosperous New Year …

SINGAPORE AND MALAYAN ROUGH DIARY FOR 1942

Showing the Hijra and Hindu Dates corresponding with the English or Christian Dates as given on each page of the Diary; also the Chinese Dates according to the Sixty Years' Cycle.

Printed and Published by
PRINTERS LIMITED
SINGAPORE

... when they marched into Alex Hospital after our boys retreated, they first bayonetted several boys who were lying wounded in bed, shot nearly all the doctors and orderlies, threw hand grenades into roomful of Chinese nurses and bayonetted the wounded man who was lying on the operating table. So you can just imagine our feelings towards these gentlemen especially when we get a public exhibition like today with the Chinese woman [who was bashed for receiving rice from the POWs].

Raymond Moult-Spiers
21 September 1942, Diary entry

19
Changi

Before the fall of Singapore, the beautiful gardens of Changi Peninsula were already being slowly replaced with barracks for the British military. Parts of the gardens were lost to the placement of defensive high-powered guns designed to defend the shores of Singapore.

In late February 1942, 15,000 Australian soldiers were herded into Selarang, a former British garrison for a mere 900 British soldiers, now serving as a prison camp. Selarang was part of the district called Changi, where Changi Gaol, village and several other camps were situated. Changi itself was an area of four hundred acres (25 square kilometres) on the peninsula at the east end of Singapore.

On the Changi Peninsula were eight major buildings and a dozen or so smaller buildings surrounded by beautiful gardens. Years before this Changi had risen up out of the swamps. Now the whole peninsula became the Japanese POW camp known as Changi.

Raymond was already savvy in the ways of obtaining, marketing and bartering useful things with the Malays and the like. As one of the 50,000 Allied prisoners who were restrained there, it was vital that business took place in the interest of collaborative innovation. By September 1942 only half this number of men were still at Changi. At times prisoners were sent out in work parties to perform horrendous tasks and often did not return. Others were sent to slave-labour camps all over Asia. Tropical diseases and wounds did the rest.

Because of the unique, isolated position of Changi, the POWs enjoyed a certain amount of autonomy and independence, with the Japanese allowing the officers to maintain their authority and a sense of order over their troops. This complex military administration saw many prisoners go months without interacting with the Japanese guards.

Even though the camp also housed British and Dutch captives, the Australians were renowned

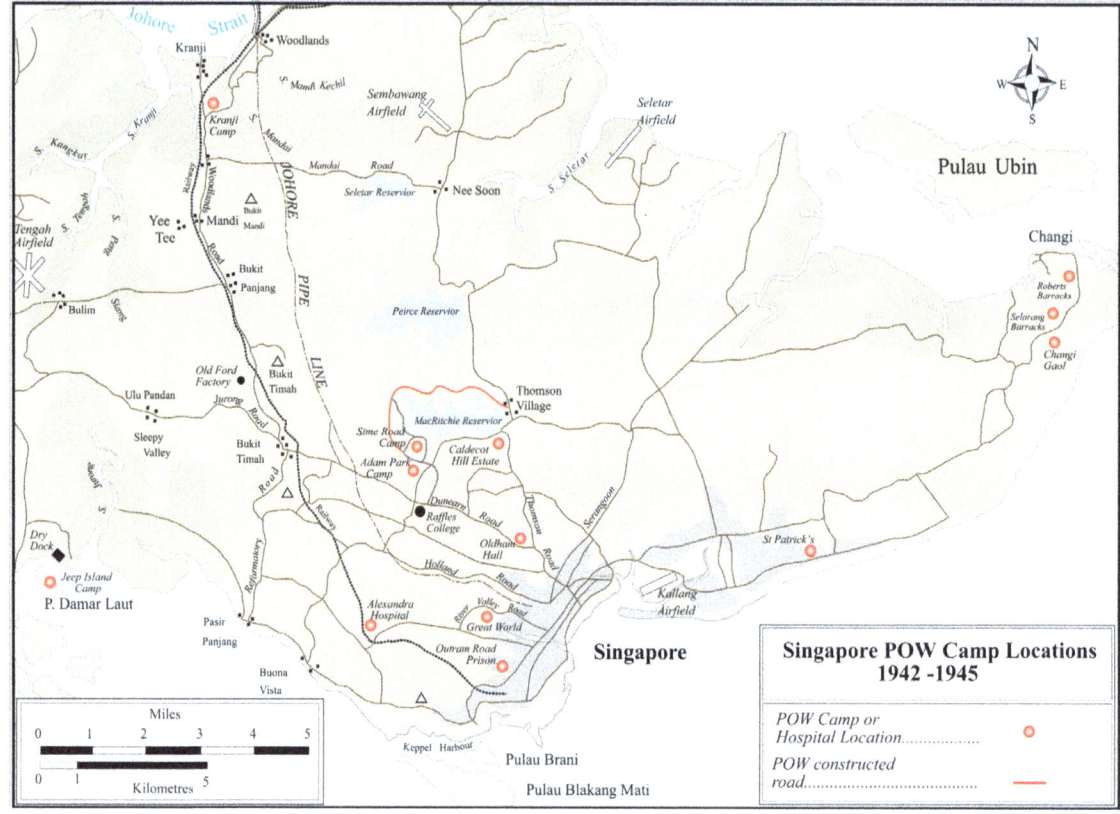

for their organisational skills. Their men were disciplined and attended to things as the need arose, especially with their well-run medical facilities. Each man brought with him unique skills and each man set about either developing these or utilising and contributing them, mostly for the greater good, although not always. As mentioned, underground trade and markets opened up as required. It turned out that these were vital to continue the running of a massive facility such as this.

Underestimating what was possible would be a mistake. The ingenuity and inventiveness of some men even saw them construct the machinery required to manufacture simple things. With the outbreak of beriberi, there was hope of using such constructions to extract vital vitamin sustenance from cut grass.

The main issue all the way through was the food supply. At first the Japanese supplied vegetables, flour, oil, milk, sugar, salt, tea, meat and rice. Back then rice was not part of the Australian diet so the Australian army cooks didn't know how to cook it. Initially they served the daily rice quota as a lumpy, watery, grey porridge.

The method of management of the prison camps by keeping the lines of command in place for each army meant that instruction came through the Australian commanders, not the Japanese. Most Australians followed the egalitarian sensibility path, which saw officers often congregating with their men. This comradeship, or mateship, seemed to make Australians better at working as a team, especially when scrounging things. It is said that Australians seemed to be better at this because they, in fact, did work together, covering each other. But if one was caught, he alone was prepared to take the punishment for all. Stealing was rare and not much of a concern among the Aussie boys, compared with the class-conscious Brits.

For the sake of order and management and control of the interaction between the several camps, in March the commanders decided it a wise move to fence around the individual camps. They sourced their own wire and built their own fences.

Within three months, to ensure self-sufficiency, the Japanese ceased vegetable supplies and reduced everything except rice. They allocated ground for the men to grow their own food. Within the vast grounds of Changi many acres were dug up and put aside for growing food. Pig and chicken pens were created to feed the vast population of POWs.

Life was as good as it could be in a prison camp. To stimulate minds, education and entertainment were also organised by the industrious Australians. The Australian prisoners held their thought-provoking communities in high esteem and proceeded to educate one another through a school that even extended to university level and lasted to the end of the war.

Raymond possessed exceptional energy, which he put to good use. His skills in farming saw him instigate the growing and getting of food in his own way. An imaginative inventor, he was able to make do with things others discarded.

He was impulsive and very bold on occasion, taking on risky enterprises with all the energy he possessed, often believing it was for the good of the community. He was never afraid to assume ownership of something needed, even if it was right under the noses of the Japanese guards. According to fellow captive and author Geoff Bingham, "Crazy Moult-Spiers", as he was called, would walk right up to that needed something and heave it over his shoulder like he had been instructed to go get it by another guard, and walk off with his catch.

His great need of independence saw him doing many things to achieve a level of freedom of action. His altruistic nature knew no boundaries when called on to help the sick or anyone in difficulty. He had his mates and exercised great care for them.

Despite his love of independent action, Raymond responded well to the order, method and balance of army life in Changi. He consistently applied himself to learning French, all the while attending to his love of art and literature. Raymond's diaries were never a consistent daily record of events. They often housed discussions, observations of humanity, reflections of significant situations and, believe it or not, mouthwatering recipes. He frequently listed books and rewrote great lengths of prose from his beloved authors' publications in order to later savour the words again and again.

During the early days, when good health was still apparent, the Australian officers, in their wisdom, determined to curb some of the men's boredom and any sexual preoccupation by asking the Japanese to put them to work trench-digging. This served to tire the men, but then the order to fill them in and dig them again proved transparent, and resentments emerged. However, this was not to last. The Japanese soon began organising work parties, sending them out to clean up Singapore, unload ships and stack food and supplies, eventually even to build an airstrip on the most unsuitable of land. Most men went willingly to break the boredom of prison-camp life.

In August, a failed attempt to escape was made by three men and their corporal. The new Japanese commandant came down hard. He wanted to make an exmple of these men and he wanted the prisoners to sign an agreement stating they would not attempt to escape. This goes against the Geneva Convention. All refused, so on 2 September the Japanese crammed 15,400 men into a space built for just 1200. The Japanese turned the water off to the latrines and threatened to put the hospital cases in there too.

The four caught escapees were executed on Changi beach. They were cruelly wounded with bullets from the Indian Army's men, who were made to shoot them but not shoot them dead. Finally, the corporal who led the escape pleaded with the soldiers to finish the job.

The agreement was signed on 5 September, although often with bogus signatures, like "Ned Kelly".

Because the first half of Raymond's diary is missing, we will never really understand the reason or events that contributed to the following army record, which states that two days later, on 4 September 1942, Raymond was registered as missing.

In his applications for repatriation assistance, he states he had "attempted escape, been put in solitude, been tortured on an ant bed, with water torture and hung by thumbs for two days".

Nothing appears in his war record indicating anything other than Raymond was missing. Perhaps, if he had been caught, he was sent to Outram Street (a prison in another part of Singapore for court-martialled condemned prisoners). In the story of fellow POW Billy Young, author Anthony Hill wrote that the situation at this prison was too brutal to behold. For an insubordinate, or escapee, Changi prisoner to be transferred to Outram Street to be straightened out was to learn what human cruelty could deliver. Once here, it was common for prisoners to be subjected to the torture of solitary confinement. The square prison cells where POWs were confined were very small, scarcely wider than a man is tall. Bed boards were placed directly on the floor. These miraculously floated above the overflow from the excrement bucket.

The constant glare day and night, from a caged globe, made sleep uneasy. There was no water or paper with which the prisoners could clean themselves. Scabies mites, mosquitoes and other insects gnawed at battered, bleeding, scabby and bruised thin skin. The constant itching brought another grotesque level of suffering. Sustenance was merely two spoonsful of grey rice twice a day, eaten with the same unclean hands that dealt with the excrement, followed by a small two inches of dirty liquid char. Even movements were constrained as tormented prisoners were made to assume and hold certain postures throughout the day, such as kneeling or sitting crosslegged in the slimy stench on the floor. No exercise was permitted. Guards often snuck about in slippers, spying, looking for a reason to beat the prisoners.

The threat of being sent there offered some sense of restraint to those in Changi. Raymond may or may not have been there but the brutality gives some insight into the level of punishment handed out by the Japanese.

Sept 22nd 1942:

Everyone getting on each other's nerves – ring fights – no good. A.I.F. soldier bashed and taken to Jap headquarters for stealing a tomahawk which is part of service arms. Twoey was caught for selling petrol and bashed with chunkel handles, one sent to Changi hospital – fractured skull. The other thrown into Nippon jail. Sold issue cigarettes "London" 20c, buy Javanese tobacco. slept nearly all day today.
As regards selling petrol the American Jap is doing the same, taking 44 gal drum on to the mainland selling it to anyone who can pay for it and giving the Aussie driver a good $50 for his trouble – but it still goes on.
One of the cooks of this Bukit Timah camp has been selling the boys rations of meat, sugar and vegetables and we are getting very little so one can imagine when they found out. He was just under guard and is awaiting trial by his own officers. But before he was jailed he destroyed a lot of food and kitchen equipment by throwing it into the latrine pit.
News exceptionally good. Mass bombing by Yanks of Barina – we have upper hand in Timor.
Jap guards here catching all Chinese who are getting rice from our boys over the fence.
I am now called an agitator because so many times I have tried to get better conditions for the boys.

Sat November 23rd 1942:

Marched to River Valley Road camp from Bukhit Tamah after being there in tents for about 2 months but instead of only one army following things up – we had 2 and it was nearly dark before we got our gear and began to settle down. We had breakfast at 7, cup of tea at 4, hot water and rice at 6 – Rations are worst here than any previous camp but the coy broke up and we were issued with a tin of bully and M&V after a lot of agitation – but we got terribly robbed especially with the milk, 2 ½ tins. Commenced work on Mon at Tanglin, shifting cosmetics – smuggled a bit home and shared with boys – we tricked the Japs upon their search. But having got rid of the Baines and Remington we will not sell that godamed lot and a few other things. it's just a case of getting what you can without the Japs catching you. What a life. Done fairly well the first day 5 tubes of tooth paste, coconut shaving creams – but should have done much better as search was not very extensive.

Tuesday November 26th:

Moved to Havelock Rd adjoining A.V. Today camphor balls, shaving cream – and sold package $3, spent $2 on food. Wish had the day at home. Now there is no more money left and I am hungry. But –- we might get paid soon I'll have to put my foot down – but good times will come again. We get a different job here every day only wish we could get back into the money again – money means food. Still in Havelock Rd but now got a way better position ...

Dec 11: farewell

BASHINGS ... at Changi

Coy, abbreviation for company; M&V, possibly meat and veg stew.

Other diary entries might trace some of his movements during capitulation but these ones conclude with large handwritten words sliding down what was left of the page, indicating some kind of unspeakable incident in Changi.

The following diary entry demonstrates Raymond's artistic bent, which combines the need to both write and draw.

> *Christmas Day Dec 1942*
> *Working as usual so chopping wood all day.*
> *There were also wood parties and gardening*
> *parties went to work as usual – Made an*
> *attempt at drawing I have had in mind*
> *for a long time – but with slight attention*
> *"Rhapsody in War". Not at all displeased with*
> *my attempt. I might enter it in a competition.*

Another of Raymond's accounts in his war diary describes being sent out in a work party into Singapore, describing its punishing level of heat and humidity.

> *The sweaty bodies bent forward with the*
> *effort of pulling the sameness of form.*
> *Limb and broadness of back, glistening*
> *with sweat – and so we pull the trailer,*
> *trailers of wood for the camps.*
> *As we top each strenuous hill to lick*
> *our parched lips and throat, and with*
> *one hand dash the stinging*
> *sweat from our eyes.*
> *With heads bent towards the heat*
> *– waves that rush up at us from the*
> *road, a road literally damp with the*
> *sweat of the men before us.*
> *Burning blisters on the soles of bare*
> *feet of those who have no footwear.*
> *Everything a forgoing effect of*
> *The Great Second World War…*

Raymond Moult-Spiers, 1942

FRAGMENTS OF THE SKY

CHANGI

LEFT *Image of war*, date unknown, ink washes on paper, colour source unknown (possibly cochineal or similar beetle) 320x205mm.
Painting from Ray's war diary.

> We left Changi Wed 21st of April 1943 for an unknown destination somewhere north overland to French Indo China. Of course, as usual when embarking on a long journey one thinks of what one's parents etc has told one about being hungry on the train so after selling a few articles of clothing Bill and myself managed to dig up $10.60 for ration purposes mostly for biscuits.
>
> Raymond Moult-Spiers
> 21 April 1943, War Diary

20
The march of the slaves

Before the war the British were leading the world in railway technology and expertise. As the colonial masters in Burma, they had investigated the idea of building a rail system through the dense jungle but, when faced with the extremely steep slopes and the need to cross rivers and ravines, they had concluded that it was not possible.

On the other hand, in 1942, the Japanese believed a 258-mile (415-kilometre) line between Burma and Thailand would help supply their troops in Burma. With masses of POWs in Singapore who had surrendered (rather than being captured), the Japanese believed they had their workforce. On another level, the Japanese believed that surrender dishonoured family and country, and that those who surrendered deserved harsh treatment.

Towards the end of 1942, the Japanese had begun to send big groups of POWs to work on various parts of the construction of a railway line from Thailand to Burma. In mid-April 1943, when the humid monsoon season was just beginning, Raymond Moult-Spiers became one of the last 3662 Australians to leave Changi in what was called F Force. Along with the Australians were some 3400 British POWs. As all were promised better conditions, they went willingly (however, nearly half of the 7000 men would die).

Although F Force was the last labour force to leave Changi, it endured by far the worst and most terrible losses and experiences of the railway's construction. The men, many of whom were already unwell with diphtheria, dysentery and the like, began the gruelling trip with up to thirty men crammed into stifling, enclosed, unventilated metal railway trucks with scarce food and water.

The suffocating conditions were exacerbated as the metal trucks, heated by the sun, were scorching hot during the day and bitterly cold ice boxes at night.

This horrendous train journey took five torturous days, with very few stops for toilet breaks, making the dysentery sufferers terrifyingly desperate. The trip also moved the level of suffering of any unwell men towards life threatening. With thirteen trains transporting over 7000 men, the realisation that they were not going to better conditions slowly dawned on them.

Raymond's personal account of this in his diary, dated 21 April, starts off like an enthusiastic youth getting ready for an adventure. He and his mate Bill remembered always being told as kids to take money on train trips, so between them they pulled together the equivalent of $10 (and a good thing too). With heavy loads on their backs, the 600 men in his battalion were divided into groups of twenty-seven and loaded into steel railway trucks eighteen feet long by seven feet wide (548 cm by 214 cm) – Raymond was six-feet tall (183 cm). The officers were thrown in with the men. Raymond stood next to a captain who fortunately brought some order to the fights that began to break out. It was impossible for them all to sit down, so they worked out a roster system allowing each man time to sleep on the floor.

We left Changi with rather big loads on our backs but at that time no one knew that at some later date we might be marching and carrying gear. We paraded at the Barrack Square at 2 am and with the usual fooling around we got away, 600 of us, 27 in each truck including officers. I was with Capt. ? of the 26th Battalion and with Jim Moreau and Bert in our party.

…

After shuffling around we boarded the train. Our conveyance consisted of an 18 ft by 7 ft truck made of steel so you can imagine the discomfort of the men and then many of the officers in charge, but we were soon to learn that discomfort means little when the Japs decide to do something. Anyhow in this grey light of dawn we moved off on our first stage of our unknown destination.

As they pulled out of Singapore early in the morning, Raymond experienced a swell of gratitude to the Malay people. Still believing in the adventure, he hoped the train would stop in Seremban, his first post on his arrival in Malaya. He dearly wanted the opportunity to visit his much-loved friends there. But the train chugged through under the cover of darkness without a stop.

It was twelve midnight before we reached Seremban and I had no chance to see any old acquaintances but it was rather nice passing through the old places again. The main trouble with these 18 by 7 trucks was that it is rather uncomfortable trying to get ones limbs down but most of the O.C in our trucks have now marked it on the roster system, so every man gets a fair portion of sleep but even so fights are cropping up amongst the men during the night because these fellows want to keep their legs outstretched all the time. We pull up at most of the railway stations to allow the men to exercise themselves and it is just one time when natives and everyone else has to forget about pride and let nature take it's course. In fact, it is almost humorous to see half a train load of men with their posteriors in the air and the Nips afraid of being late shouting at them in 16 dialects to get back on the train. The first two days out from Singapore we had rather good food and three meals a day but as the journey goes on, we are getting one meal each afternoon and told it is cho and only once were we allowed to buy things from the natives on the railway platforms. Passed the Malay Thai boarder on April 25th Easter Sunday then another two days in the hot box before we got out at Banpong. It appears now that we are the first force that has had to march, other mobs got the train further up the line then into Jap trucks.

By 27 April they finally disembarked the "hotbox" at Ban Pong in Thailand. While in Ban Pong for a few days they stayed in labour huts with some dreadful sanitation issues. Then the realisation set in that they were going to have to march. They were told to get rid of unnecessary items in readiness to leave on the second night.

Anyway, we stay at Banpong two days and a night and move out the next. It is here that we first learnt that we could sell clothes and no doubt about it, this was done in style but I am still unable to understand … Sometimes the Nips would buy from us but at the same time being afraid of being caught by our superiors.

Here the Japanese and Thai police forbade the men's interaction with the local people, so the locals would wait until the coast was clear of those two parties before doing business. Raymond states that more often than not they were robbed with a grab-and-run technique. However, he soon realised the Thai police were buying stuff from the POWs and passing it on to the local people … "to look after(!)" … and that the locals were also buying from the Japanese who had bought from the men. Confused, but not defeated, Raymond saw it as a big muddle but he was quick to get in among it all. He was helping out mates by selling gear for those who thought the risk too great and who were not game to enter into negotiations. This was because several of the men had been caught selling to the local people and, in Raymond's words, the "Japs bashed them terrifically". Ray took a small commission for his risk. In a calculated move, he didn't sell much of his own stuff.

At Ban Pong, Ray managed to buy a hat full of tomatoes and a can of Red Cross bully beef, which when coupled with eggs, stew, rice and bananas made it Ray's best ever feed.

The truth of the matter was that, unlike the other men, Ray did not have family or a place he could call home. All his worldly possessions were indeed on his back and in a hand-held pack, along with a pillowcase filled with precious necessities. Loaded like a pack horse was how Ray set off on the march and he wasn't giving it up.

We were in bamboo huts at Banpong but the sanitation was terrible but there were eggs in abundance, even in the winter which we had every meal … Bananas. Some of the boys of other mobs had three meals of bananas. Burlow stayed behind here, malaria, but he wanted a job as truck driver.
So started our march out, for we did not know and still do not know (we have now been on the road 10 days and only had three night's sleep, covered 110 miles, another 80 to do to Rin Tin which is just inside the Burma border.) The first night we marched about 20 miles and reached a camp on the river early next morning. It was then we first found out about

ABOVE *Thailand*, date unknown, ink, crayon, water-soluble stain on paper, 150x200mm, from Ray's war diary. Image held at www.austlit.edu.au, copyright Moult-Spiers family.

blisters. I had started well, I had 5. But as soon as we had landed, we had a good feed with the money we had. I had mamanee [a tiny amount of a Thai fatty cured pork used as a flavouring], condensed milk coffee etc. There were plenty of natives especially girls who were selling on the banks of the river. There was an abundance of eggs and bananas and coffee but one soon got tired of these. Great life for P.O.W.

Ray also mentioned that along the way he was learning a few Thai words and which jungle plants could be eaten. He later describes Bill and himself, with a chap called Monroe, all heading into the jungle at night and in the early morning to find nuts, ending in a feed of eighteen nuts.

Yes a young Siamese girl crashed into me when she was running along the jungle path back to camp and was luscious. I am thinking of

*coming back after the war to complete
my studies in Siamese art ...
A shame to leave so lovely a spot but the
Jap is ... to go on again that night.
... and I forgot to write that it was the
... marching that I had a black-out on
the side of ... And lost my pay book ...*

I was astounded to read that Raymond disclosed having a blackout and losing his pay book. This is the first mention of his lifelong problem with blacking out. It occurred on the march when, in the darkness of night, villagers came out of the jungle and were trying to barter. Even more surprising was that a Japanese guard and another POW actually carried Raymond's gear until he had recovered enough to do it himself. The prisoners were still paid a small wage, which meant they could supplement their meagre diet, if they were able to access food sources available for purchase.

The heat dictated that they walk during the night and rest during the day. Many times the resting periods were on open thorny ground with no shelter from the hot sweltering sun. But, with the monsoonal rains setting in, the conditions soon switched to them sitting in mud. The walk was debilitating, with many men discarding valuable items, like blankets. Along the way, some Thai people were prepared to barter with the POWs, exchanging or selling things for dirty water.

After his blackout Raymond simply had to discard his excess baggage, including two heavy souvenirs he gave to a "coolie".

The monsoon season ensured all things fungal spread unseen into any crevices in the men's bodies. Despite the unpleasant repercussions of this, they clung to the notion they were going to a better place, something they had all wanted to believe.

The trail they were following was easy enough to begin with, taking the rhythm of their march with good intent. But, undertaken at night, the march across these rugged dry plateaus would sometimes pit them against terrible winds that swirled unbearable dry matter into their eyes; they were trudging through terrain they could barely see. The few possessions gleaned and carefully packed on their person were now monstrous burdens. As they marched on towards tropical regions, heavy rain often fell, leaving the warm air dense with moisture. Sticky sweat made everything fix to their skin, including insects, some of which burrowed in.

The march ended each morning with them laid out to rest in a clearing, the enemy pacing, watching, ever vigilant. With each man laying prostrate to rest, pegged out to dry on the open ground, it was apparent each faced the sun's heat as best he could. Each, too, battled the daytime insects and their taunting bites.

Raymond's diary goes on to document the unpredictable and varied interactions with the people who lived in the areas they passed through.

We were partnered all the way by natives who had a usage for fountain pens and clothing. The reason for this clothing is obvious but I fail to see the urge for writing. This camp was exceptionally dry and all water had to be carried, the river being one and half miles away but it was too far for me so I got some out of the natives' well, 5 cents per bucket. The night before we arrived the Thais had attacked the camp with bamboo spears and wounded several of our fellows, the sole reason being for clothing (but the women didn't appear to be too short). Anyhow, the same night they waylaid nine men and demanded all money and clothes at the point of the parang [machete]. The next night they severely wounded a Jap with a parang so the whole Jap guard turned out to stop them making another raid on us.

It was here as POW's that we nearly got stung on Saki, natives' whisky mixed with coffee. It was very good and we sat up half the night singing. It was here I sold the last of my clothes, (all that I wanted to) which realised me 11 Thai dollars and I had already bought 5 lb of tobacco so I was right for a few more days.

It was on the first two marches out of Ban Pong that was the hardest, first because we had just finished a five-day train journey across Malaya and for the most part without sleep and I was carrying an exceptionally big load but I would soon be the biggest part of it. Then the feet started worrying us and everyone was complaining of blisters.

Fourteen days into the march from Changi and at another camp, Ray wrote:

There was about six inches of very dry dirt on the track. The next morning, we arrived at the camp on the bank of the river we had been following. Then there was the unreal Buddhist temple and our camp being down the steps on the flat. The natives arrived in hordes selling sago, coffee, mani [roasted snacks], etc but the river was our salvation in fact it has been right up to the present day … 14 days from Changi.

Following this, Ray had dysentery and had to stay behind in the camp. This tragically separated him from his unit (the diary paper has rotted in places so words are missing).

Then on the 14th of May, after seven marches I am told I have to stay behind. I have dysentery and a temp of 101° this is much to my sorrow as we have never found out that if you get behind your unit you cannot hope to rejoin them again … Anyhow, just after the mob has pulled out it begins to rain. There are 21 men left in camp but … Nips do not worry. Dick Hengoed has dysentery and M____ damn near dead. Everything and everybody gets wet through then they come out and try and make you … the boys but I have made a shelter out of … leaves and lit a tiger fire so I am pretty right … I go next day with 2/30 at the … At the 30

LEFT *Golden Temple*, 1943, 240x160mm, ink washes and yellow crayon on paper, image showing a golden temple at sunrise on the long march through Thailand, from Ray's war diary.

km mark we find that the way …. full of cholera and there is not enough … round. The Nips have brought Coolies and … From North Malaya and they have our [cholera] … and dying at the rate …

The roughly cleared trail bore the unpredictable horrors of sharply cut bamboo, stumps standing upright like blades against the marching feet. But it was the mud that sucked at the boots, wanting them. This monsoonal mud slowly unpicked the stitches one by one, separating the top from the sole, the leather stretching with each wetting, the swelling inside the boot and the propulsion of the next step doing the rest. Fat leeches pooled around ankles.

As the days turned into weeks, precious possessions, carefully toted, were discarded as useless encumbrances. Boots began to shed parts, sometimes retrieved by another coming up behind and used to fix his own. Naked, damaged feet slowly appeared, picking their way across the terrain as it morphed into a thick jungle floor. Some men, once farm boys with feet as tough as elephant hide, had, in one way or another, dispensed with their inconvenient boots, sharing them with those less fortunate, the previous owner more sure-footed without them.

With the Japanese soldiers prone to beat anyone who fell from exhaustion, a preserving perseverance accompanied Raymond Moult-Spiers. Wounds to feet were the worst, ensuring infection would soon follow. To take your boots off meant the chances of getting them back on were limited. Mates often tried to get a fallen man up, but sometimes it could not be done.

MIND THE STUMP

At first the trail was hard and blue
Saki, hard boiled eggs and few
Waiting for the man in front
Watch it mate, JUST MIND THE STUMP
Then dust and Blisters in the night
Gleaming temples. Broad daylight
Whispering with all your might
STONE THE MUNT
Black and stinking filthy mud
Lurching men. Clinging Flood
Then with a curse we hear a thud
MIND THE STUMP
Over a Mountain. Rocks galore
Feet too big and awful sore
That man again yells with a roar

MIND THE STUMP
While dreaming moving. Then a crash
We're walking waking in a flash
The Bloody leg. My what a gash
PLEASE ... MIND THE STUMP

Raymond Moult-Spiers, October 1943.

Original poem kept at Aust-lit, University of Queensland.

MUNT, male arsehole

Once in the Burma Railway camps, dreadful illnesses, like beriberi and cholera, began to spread through all six camps near the Burmese border.

6 MONDAY — 24th day of Panguni — Easter Monday—Bank Holiday
21st day of the 2nd Moon — 19 hari bulan Rabi Alawal — 1942

Maybe it's rather late in the exodus now, seeing that we are on the last leg of the journey, but I feel that I have not given the trip sufficient detail, considering it involved every type of hardship and an enormous amount of will-power.

We left our so-called home Changi on Wed 21st of April 1943, for a trip north that was all we knew. Although several mild guesses were made, the most outstanding of these was Chung Mi in central Thailand, which is the head of the Malay-Thai railway, has a population of over half a million. But we set off with the idea in mind that it would be fairly easy, not anticipating a 200 mile march across Thailand. As I have mentioned before about the train journey, I do not think it is necessary to bring it up again, but there are incidents in that hot box

7 TUESDAY — 25th day of Panguni
22nd day of the 2nd Moon — 20 hari bulan Rabi Alawal

that one will never forget. After four days and three nights we arrived at the terminus of our rail journey, Bangpong, 560 miles over the border, and 1160 miles from Singapore. Our first thoughts on arriving were that we were going to stay here, but the Japs had other ideas, but we did have one nights sleep, and all the next day in which to do a bit of trading with the natives to get some money to feed ourselves, for every camp we went in to, the menu was different, and very little of it. At Bangpong the meals consisted of the usual rice, and vegetable stew, with eggs thrown into it. Eggs and bananas were in abundance here for 50¢ one could get five hands, which numbered about 50 bananas, but the best feed I had was a tin of bully beef which was received ration from Red Cross days. I had

8 WEDNESDAY — 26th day of Panguni
23rd day of the 2nd Moon — 21 hari bulan Rabi Alawal — Passover, 7th day (Jewish Holiday). Last Quarter 12h 13

tomatoes, which I had saved from the camp, but five eggs, stew and rice and bananas for desert. Although at Bangpong I did not sell much of my own gear I sold a lot for people that thought the risk too great, but I made sure I got a good commission. Everything was sold, watches, combs, whites whites, hats, boots, everything. But several of the boys who were caught got terrible hidings from the Japs, probably for selling to the natives because they would come round after dark and try and buy from the boys. It was really amusing, the Japs would have a lighted candle, (as there was no other illumination) so they could see what they were buying, and one of the boys would give the nanny that other Japs in the vicinity but would go the candle and then confusion would follow until the scene was over and the candle relit.

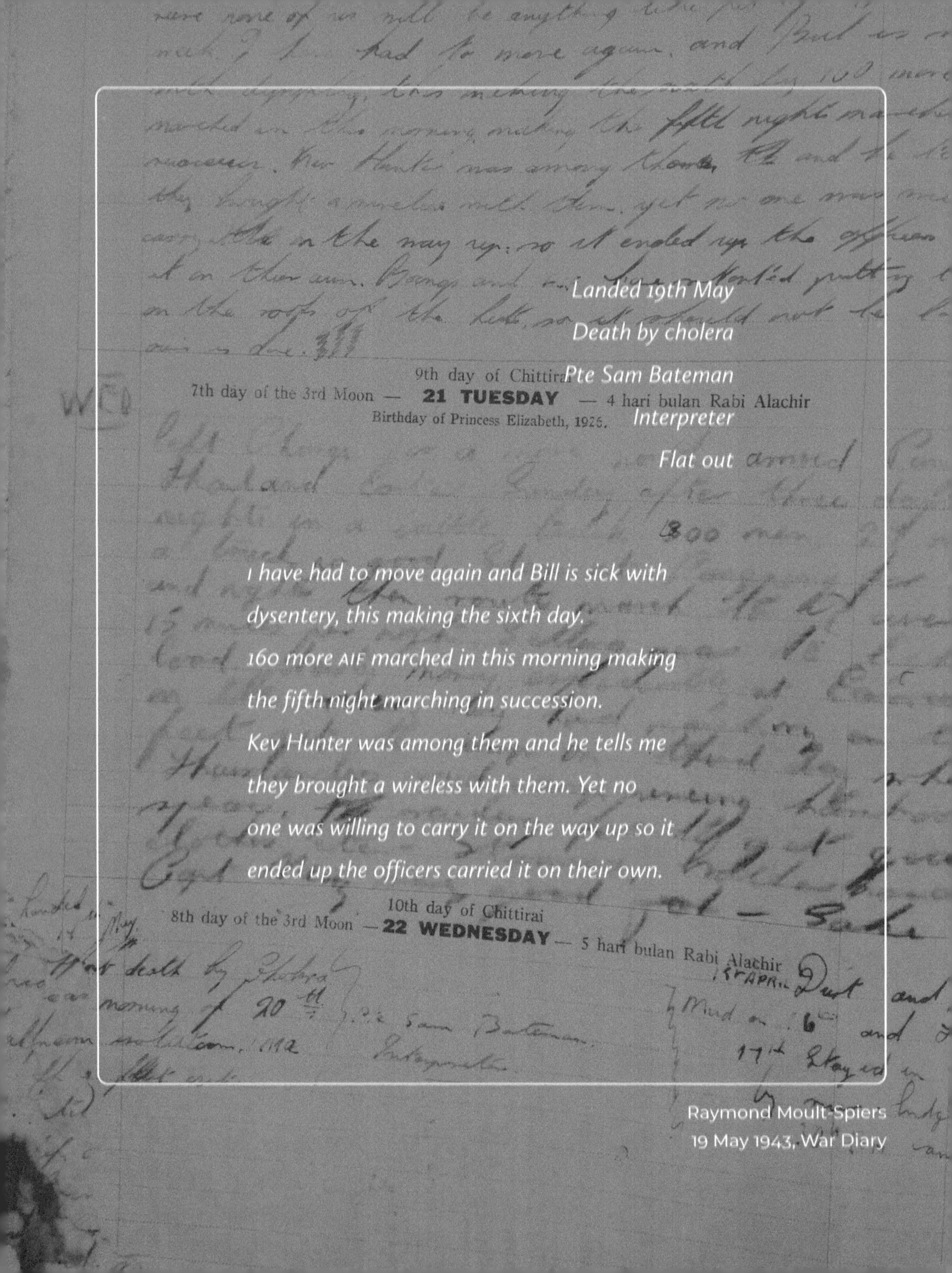

Landed 19th May

Death by cholera
Pte Sam Bateman
Interpreter

Flat out

21 TUESDAY

I have had to move again and Bill is sick with dysentery, this making the sixth day. 160 more AIF marched in this morning making the fifth night marching in succession. Kev Hunter was among them and he tells me they brought a wireless with them. Yet no one was willing to carry it on the way up so it ended up the officers carried it on their own.

22 WEDNESDAY

Raymond Moult-Spiers
19 May 1943, War Diary

21
The Burma railway

At this point Raymond had arrived at the main camp, Shimo Songkurai, where thousands of men were to live and work. This alone presented logistics scarcely imaginable. It was the most remote camp of them all, being well beyond any villages. The only road to it became a quagmire during the monsoon season. This curbed the arrival of supplies. Due to the wet and lack of food, there was an outbreak of cholera, coinciding with Ray's arrival. If it were not for the strong leadership of Major Bruce Hunt, the senior medical officer, who exercised a tight control over food and preventative health measures, things would have been much worse.

When not assigned to work parties, the provosts were required to take and burn the bodies on "Cholera Hill". In his diary, Ray began to diligently keep a daily count of the deaths and of the number of men who had "gone through", a term used to describe an escape by disappearing into the jungle. Some POWs preferred to risk survival in the jungle rather than take their chances with cholera. The problem for the escapees was that the Japanese would pay the Thais to return them to camp, where the guards immediately shot them.

Monday, 24th May 1943. This morning the fifth casualty was burnt by the Provost RSM and nine more fresh cases were admitted into isolation now making it a total of 22 inmates, 12 in the recuperation tent. It has rained continuously day and night for 3 days and the huts still without a roof (which includes ours). Everything we possess is saturated. Several cases of beri beri have broken out owing to the fact that we have very little to eat except rice.
I have been home today with a rash on both legs on the inside which makes it fairly hard walking but the doctor put me on duty, so I have been drying the clothes of the boys who are away ...

Ray also vigilantly recorded the outside news of the war's progress from the valued radio.

At Shimo Songkurai camp, Ray's first POW task was to mix a kind of cement to create the embankment that was supposedly to run from Moulmein in Thailand to Ban Pong in Burma. He was then required to clear the ground to make way for the track.

The monsoon had well and truly started, but many of the huts were still without roofs. Methods of sanitation were unresolved and, with work parties heading out for twelve hours at a time, basic issues were leading to bigger problems. Bad sanitation and being wet through day and night presented all kinds of problems, the most concerning being cholera.

Over the days that followed, Raymond, like most, struggled with numerous illnesses and spent many a long day ill in one of the hospital tents. But, as time went on, he was made to work despite being unwell. Beriberi, dysentery, malaria, skin rashes, tropical ulcers, wounds and infections were commonplace. With the cholera outbreak, though, there were soon more men in the hospital tents than were fit to work.

During recuperation periods, POWs were put on light duties. Raymond, possibly because he was a provost, often worked as an orderly in the isolation hospital tents, where he saw many cholera deaths.

Finally, after some vigilant negotiation with the Japanese by Major Hunt, Raymond wrote that on 27 May 1943 three hundred fit men were permitted to stay in camp for hygiene purposes. They spent the day roofing huts, digging drains and digging and preparing latrines and refuse pits.

These simple changes eventually proved to slow down the deaths, but not before huge losses were experienced. And too late for Ray's best mate.

Sat. 29th May. The best mate I have had since returning from Singapore to Changi died today of cholera – Corporal Bill Borlase – of the Provost Coy, just married before we left Aust, and a baby boy whom he has never seen. His body was taken "up the hill" and he was boasting as how the cholera would not get him but this afternoon after returning from work, I was told he was gone. I did not even know he was seriously ill.
FORGET AND FORGIVEN
MAY GOD SAVE HIS SOUL

By 2 June Ray had malaria, which terminated his job on Cholera Hill. Out of the 1800 men in Ray's camp only 300 were considered fit for work. For their sustenance, the men at his camp were receiving meagre food rations of rice, hot water and a couple of green beans a day. As problems with rice shipments manifested, the rations dropped. The ration for those in the hospital was even worse, as the Japanese had reduced it to three spoonfuls of rice a day.

If a prisoner was afforded the time and energy, scrounging or theft might be considered. Or, if able, hunting snakes, fish, clams or rodents, to share with an inner group of friends, was carried out. In desperation, medical personnel sometimes experimented with local vegetation as a source of potential vitamins. Throughout his diary Raymond briefly mentioned all manner of creative ways he secured extra nutrients.

Finally, Raymond recovered from his attack of malaria and his spirit was lifted with the company of a like-minded soul. Such elevation proved beneficial by establishing a sense of purpose.

June 13th 1943 Discharged from malaria ward after only 7 days' treatment and 2 days con[valence] but Capt Taylor was considerate and put me on a week of light duties.

To my utmost pleasure I found a fellow P.O.W who sees with the same eyes as I do. Eyes of appreciation and that means a terrible lot these days, appreciation of art which includes books, furniture, plays and numerous other things. The feeling was so mutual that I had to agree with him over two of my sketches.

On 22 June, weak from starvation and no longer in the possession of boots, Ray was placed in a work party of one hundred men. Once they reached the designated work area the party was split in half, with one lot going further up the road and the other being divided into groups assigned to road clearing, tree felling and log carrying for the construction of a bridge. Raymond was delegated to log carrying.

BELOW *POW carrying logs,* date unknown, ink on paper, 200x260mm.
Image held at www.austlit.edu.au, copyright Moult-Spiers family.

Normally it took an average of twelve men to bring bridge timber out of the jungle. But this day, with pressure to get the job done, the Japanese bullying reached a new high. They demanded that half that number of men now carry out a log. With just five or six men assigned a log, there was no consideration for the different heights of the POWs, so it was tough on the taller men who were unable to straighten up. Raymond witnessed men crying in agony, but being beaten if they stopped. The last man on the log may have been beaten to make the others work faster. Raymond saw men kicked in the stomach and generally kicked about, slapped, pushed over in the mud and beaten with bamboo sticks.

22 June 1943

A party of five men carrying a high load, the middleman was a six-footer and could not straighten his back. He too was crying. A Jap came up and laid into him with a stick then swung himself to the end of log and jerked it about so much that it was injuring the shoulders of the men. (Men just out from the malaria wards and living on three mugs of rice a day). A Jap then got a bamboo stick and started beating the last man of the carrying party. It was absolutely inhuman treatment. Later a series of beatings were in place by the bridge. It got so intense that the Sergeant in Charge (Graham McKnight) rushed in and took the stick from the Jap and threw it away. The Jap immediately went for an axe to chop the Sergeant's fingers off, but when it arrived, he lost courage and resorted to the old method of punishment

Then, in a hideous turn of events, the Japanese guard appointed just two men to carry a bridge log out. Raymond was one and a small man the other. Raymond immediately took the bulky end. However, by that time of day the task was beyond him and, try as he might, he simply could not work on. The event is described in his diary:

As far as I was concerned in all this. The first log I helped carry was about 15-foot-long, about one foot through. Everyone was straining his utmost, with the threat of a stick behind us. We only just got it there but were immediately sent back for another. This time only two of us were detailed to carry a log of almost the same dimensions as the previous one. I, being the biggest of the two, took the big end. About half way back, tears were being forced out of my eyes, the pain in my whole body was unbearable but we went on until within shouting distance of the bridge when ... cried for help as soon as the weight on my body decreased ... I broke. My whole body and soul were broken and down I went into the mud, and was carried home when the Ration Party went back.

On his collapse, which resulted in him having to be carried back to camp, from this day on, Raymond's health declined noticeably, becoming a constant struggle for him.

By late June Raymond had begun to notice that some men took their own survival very seriously, even at the cost of others. He singled out a few of the officers whose consideration saw them sharing their abundant rations with their starving men. However, more importantly he had noticed the undercurrent of ration theft by some.

26 June

Why waste paper and time criticising the Japs when our own men are making themselves bigger mongrels than ever the Japs were. Firstly, I have been in hospital for four days with exhaustion, along with 1,500 other men. We are existing on three spoonsful of rice 3 times per day and some watery fishy mess just like hot dirty water. The road workers are getting a cup full but they are putting the rest of their ration into the hospital. The officers are getting their full ration and it is now we are finding out who are the men among them and out of 80 odd there are very few. I am in Number 5 Ward and out of the four large huts in this camp three are being used as wards. We know for a definite fact we are not getting our full quota of rice. The issue for the camp was 8 bags of rice yesterday and they can only give 1,500 men 9 spoonsful? For the last three evenings I have been down to the Jap kitchen waiting for the scraps but only got a little one night. But while waiting there it was interesting to see the number of so called Aust walking away from the 2/26 kitchen with rice while hundreds of men are starving. The harder conditions get the worser the men get. Yesterday it was surprising to hear that Major Johnson of the 2/30th Btn. had discharged Capt. Dyer, another mongrel from the 2/26th kitchen and also two cooks for eating meat when they shouldn't have been.

In addition to the above observation is his notation concerning the ever-present search for an element of hope:

Yesterday a man was carried up from work having collapsed on the job, a passing boong [native of Malaysia] wished him good day and gave him coffee and one dollar and said keep your chin up, British here soon. A Force have camp rumbled inspiring a number of men including Col Blackwell. Also see planes have been following road down. Force has seen USA and British planes overhead, in fact there is one is going over now, hope it does not unload here. From the different sources comes the rumour that all POW are returning to Bungong – from Majors Hunt and Johnson – Japs, – and British truck drivers from A Force. Have to see Doc this morning. Hope to stay here until rations improve. We'll see.

In July, he was part of a working party that built a jetty at Neeki to enable supplies to be brought and unloaded closer to the camp, which was still a three-hour march away. After this, things went from bad to much worse at Shimo Songkurai camp.

On 29 July, Major Johnson delivered the news that they would be returning to Changi at the end of August. At this point Raymond was now assigned to the ration party, which was going out to No. 2 camp daily.

He was struggling between bouts of dysentery and collapses but he wrote of the intent to experience "purpose" in his diary:

I am still writing with the same pen in the same book but smoking a different pipe. I am still very tired but have so much to do – mend my boots and clothes. But perhaps I'd better say why – perhaps it is a sense of purpose – perhaps I am losing my grip – but I think not.

But it is his description of the British section of No. 2 camp that was horrific. Here Raymond saw how bad a camp could get without good leadership.

He described the camp as divided in two with 40 yards (36.5 metres) between the AIF and the British.

2 August 1943
… No 2, the ration camp on the river
where there are 1,400 English men …
The camp … filthy men with mud
and flies everywhere and garbage
lying all over the place …
5 August 1934 [sic]
"40 Yards in Front"
After taking a walk around No. 2 today I
reckon H. G. Wells and Quenton Reynolds
[American World War Two correspondent]
would go into holts as to who should write the
story. This would make them forget "London
can take it" and H. G.'s, "Life of man."
About 40 yards in front of the A.I.F. hospital
is the English hospital, where dysentery is rife
and men are dying at the rate of 6 per day.
Yesterday 7 were dead before midday out of
1,400 men. They have lost 360 up to date.
About 40 yards in front is a little red cross on
a bamboo pole. Not enough wind to make it
flutter. it's dead like the men in the atop hut.
They're dead too, cleared to flutter no more. –
They won't eat. They want to get it over quicker.
The place – 40 yards in front, stinks more
than any back street in Singapore Chinatown,
water front, human dung everywhere inside
and outside the huts, in boots, in plates, in
blankets, everywhere – stench – but why
write words – perhaps it's just my donation
of sympathy. Nobody worries about them,
least of all the Japs. Their own orderlies and
mates just ignore them. I went over after
dinner to look for a pair of old boots – mine
were gone. I was lucky, I got about ½ a boot.
it's amazing just how long God, Mother
Nature, Fate, allow things to get on with
and English Bank Holiday has to end
sometime – even if it has a romantic finish.
Yes, 40 yards between the two hospitals
is going the railway track but at present
they are concentrating on the bridge – a
big bridge it's got to be finished.
There are so many in the A.I.F. hospital they
are sleeping 15 men in an area 12 ft by 12 ft
and those who can't get in sleep underneath.
I'm not feeling so tired now, had 5 days in
hospital with dysentery but feeling better.
Reveille [morning bugle call] is at 5.45 and
they come home any time between 10–12
at night. Plenty of rations but not enough
containers to cook them, they sent them
down the river so we are changing the sites
and almost amalgamating under A.I.F.

On 8 August Raymond reported the arrival of huge numbers of starving workers consisting of eight thousand Tamils and Chinese in all. They were coming up from Singapore and, according to Raymond, dying like flies. These people were supposedly replacing the POWs.

The POWs were indeed slowly being moved out but, with so many unfit to march and still hospitalised, hopes were dashed.

Friday September 10th 1943
There are now 1,900 troops here but they
are dying off at about 8 or 9 per day in
the clear ward gangrene has set in …
I hope to start work on staff in a couple
of days although I am still passing
blood, orderlies are urgently needed

Raymond's attacks of dysentery were accompanied by repugnant ongoing skin issues. A month later he wrote of his attempts to supplement his and a sick mate's diet.

Wed 13th Oct 1943
Me and Snow Burbage are battling along but he is sick so I spend a lot of spare time trying to supplement our meagre rations with local fungi which are very much like European mushrooms

Eleven days passed and Raymond now had dysentery – yet again – but unfortunately his mate lacked Ray's foraging and negotiating skills so nourishment was scarce.

Today is Monday 24th October 1943 and we are still in Burma. I have another attack of dysentery and am now a bed patient, but eggs are in and I have no money so it does not worry me greatly and Snow has none and no idea of getting any so we got a $1 worth of weed from the sale of issue cigarettes. Anyhow it's all unfair, a sick man with no money, no eggs etc, and the others, well they get the lot. ... I was thinking this morning of some of the discomforts we have to put up with, lice, skin itch caused by vitamin deficiency, scabies. I have ring worm, tinea all over the body. No sleep day or night for the dysentery and nothing else to eat for six months but rice and stew.

The railway was completed on 16 October 1943, with one in five POWs dying there. Raymond and the remaining men were slowly hospitalised in Thailand for a few months.

The Allies blew up a vital bridge, which once again set in motion the impossibility of supplies getting through.

By 16 November Raymond, who had been battling constant dysentery for months, wrote that the added skin afflictions continued to deny sleep and that the patient death count was 650.

Nov 17th, 1943. I now have scabies all over the hands and prickly heat over my body and legs which make sleep almost impossible but I must consider myself a fit man when compared to some of the poor unfortunates in the hut. Some have scabies on the head or on every inch of the body, hands with no flesh on, abscesses, dysentery, it's just a case of hanging on. We are getting three days scabies treatment and it appears to be doing a bit of good. Nothing definite about move yet but we will be going very shortly if only as far as Cangbune
Nov 19th, 1943 The first batch leave here tomorrow for Cangbune at midday it is rumoured that 200 will be leaving on ... day for the next five days but it is not yet certain so we go to Saigon or Singapore but what matters most is out of this country back to civilisation as soon as ... of course everyone is on tip toe, we have been made every day for the last few months during ... we have learnt what patience means also starvation and a few other lessons.

Of all the groups of prisoners on the railway, F Force had one of the highest death rates. Of the 7000 Australian and British POWs who left Changi, some 1060 Australians and 2037 British died (44 per cent) in the camps dotted along the railway's construction route.

Nevertheless, Raymond was very lucky to have been with Major Bruce Hunt, an outstanding surgeon and efficient camp administrator, whose discipline and fairness kept camp morale high.

Once upon a time in BURMA. A doctor had called the PADRE and said "I don't think this heap of bones will live till morning". So the PADRE went through the motions. Said some kind words about me. And departed with the remark or question. "DID I BELIEVE IN MIRACLES?" I was too far gone to respond. But lifted a hand in thanks convinced I had seen my last bowl of RICE. HOWEVER. About 2 a.m. someone returning from the latrine was yelling about a "BLUE MOON". Madness. Hallucinations. Troppo. but the guards came rushing out so I must have REVIVED sufficiently to beg to be taken out on a stretcher to see this "BLUE MOON" indeed they were right. At a certain time of a century the GREEN HAZE from the jungle covers the moon. And it is indeed "BLUE" 600 witnesses. That was a sign or miracle. And as I relive it. I am unable to stop the tears.

Raymond Moult-Spiers
December 1981

22
Once in a blue moon

According to his December diary entries, after being hospitalised in Thailand, the incapacitated Raymond and others in a similar state were brought back to Changi in easy stages. They travelled to Neeki, from there they went by barge and finally train to Changi.

The size of the actual area inhabited by POWs at Changi was reduced to the immediate environs around Changi Gaol. This meant 11,700 POWs, 5000 of whom were Australian, were crammed into less than a tenth of a square mile (a quarter of a square kilometre).

With the original area of Changi no longer used, Changi was much smaller now and, with land reduced, food production was also down. The pig and chicken pens were gone. There were fewer POWs to feed and manage but most were in poor health.

When Raymond arrived, he was laid up for over three weeks, with a relapse of the stomach and back problems he experienced in Burma. His level of unwellness eventually authorised him to be put in the "art ward". This appears to be his descriptor for the Changi innovation of using art as a healing tool. In the art ward he received a blank drawing booklet and the opportunity to use a few basic materials, enabling him to return to painting and writing diary entries. He immediately wrote that it had been a long time since he had been able to write anything. He questioned the validity of ever keeping his diaries, certainly a risky and daunting task while on the Burma Railway. That foolscap-sized diary having to be hidden, protected and carried was a miracle in itself. But Raymond's ever-present positive self-talk soon reshaped his view, when he noted down that he may be weaker physically but that he was now much stronger mentally.

Raymond's prized Chinese ink was once again put to work, actioned with a pen, enabling him to write once more. He explained in his new booklet diary that, since his log-carrying accident in the remote Thai jungle, he had suffered numerous bouts of dysentery and beriberi. From August 1943, his stomach had not performed like it should. The medical staff said it was just a case of his stomach being unable to continue to handle the poor food. But Raymond implies he knew something more was wrong. He also informed that he had started to give his food away.

Reading on, I soon learned that the act of giving food away was not as simple as might be thought. It was managed like a kind of bartering system. In Raymond's case he could not eat the daily rice or the stew but could tolerate the "doovers" (small items of cooked food improvised with whatever was available like a morsel in ground rice and cooked like a patty). In true Australian fashion Raymond had a mate who organised the exchanges.

This mate was Con, who Raymond had befriended in their early Changi days, the nickname derived from his surname, Connelly. Con was a country boy from Young, New South Wales, whose POW experiences were different from Ray's. Con had been sent out in a different workforce but was back in Selarang (the area Changi had once occupied), or so Ray thought, and Con was well enough to travel through the Changi camp to visit Ray in the recuperation area.

Ray saw Con as a decent kind of bloke who actually cared and who helped him through some difficult times. According to Ray, they treated each other like brothers. He even made a comparison with his own brother, John Luke, which saw Con come in hands down. But with this description in his diary, I am reminded that Raymond was raised in Britain in several foster homes, so the comparison with his brother is a revelation, indicating there was perhaps some contact with his siblings during childhood.

Being British also meant Raymond would not have grown up with quite the same concept of "mateship" as did the Australians. The British, with their class system, certainly did not have the same philosophy of caring, so it is entirely possible Raymond may have misunderstood exactly what mateship meant.

With this background, it is the friendship with Con that takes some understanding. For Raymond it seems the urge to be close to another human being is fraught with difficulty, from the perceived point of view of the fellow soldiers, as well as the challenge presented to Raymond from within. He was concerned that he would be the biggest loser. The struggle with sharing, the very essence of what it meant to be genuinely close to another human, was constant. But Ray wrote that he thought (or liked to imagine) that Con on occasion saw deep inside Ray.

Con sometimes sees the impulse that drives the brush and turns the pages.

In past diary entries, after Ray had experienced a rare, deep and significant communication with another POW, he usually wrote about it as a connection and understanding of minds. His love of the arts, books, beauty and nature shared with another like-minded POW was a unique occurrence he genuinely valued. In these new entries there was no hint of this type of connection with Con; instead it hints at something deeper. Neither is it to be confused with any kind of carnal urge. It is a known fact at this stage of the game that the likelihood of any kind of expression of sexuality or encounter was well and truly replaced with the sheer battle to stay alive.

With his return to Changi, Ray's new diary entries slowly extended to observations that give an overview of the whole camp. He watched the ebb and flow of rumours and their effect on the men. He wrote about the rhythm of hope and despair, saying how rumours came in about once a week, elating everyone, but then the resignation set in following the realisation that nothing was changing. This was summed up with:

> *Fate holds out the apple then pulls it away.*

Raymond termed it as a kind of "blighted hope" that kept everyone going. He equated the unrelenting urge to return home as the same feeling as that of

> *... a small child that is dilly dallying home, stopping now and then to gaze and stare but gradually getting home because it knows it has to.*

Indeed, the urge to go home never left these grown men.

The civilian jail at Changi is described in his diary with despair. Raymond was aware of the wretchedness of many civilians who had been in the gaol at Changi for two and a half years and that babies had even been born behind bars. In comparison, the POWs had much more freedom. He told of a certain Japanese officer who made it known that he wanted his way with a beautiful Eurasian girl and, when their baby was born, he removed the newborn and shot the poor little thing. Raymond states that no one will ever know how many died at the hand of these captors. No records were kept.

He was also disturbed by the cross-cultural tensions in Singapore. How the back-biting and animosity between all the different races had progressed to unprecedented levels. Raymond expressed in words that being on the Burma Railway

> *... builds a hard crust over one's soul that even the Japanese could not knock off, not even with their axe handles.*

He remembered that, when things were at their blackest in the railway camp, a bloke called Phil Bailey gave him a lecture on the introvert and the extrovert. But Raymond didn't think he could access his extrovert at that stage. Now that he had been "dry docked" for a period of time, he was beginning to understand the lecture and was starting to find his extroverted self again. Although he could barely eat and was just skin and bone, this revelation seemed to bring him strength.

That may have been but, in the next few pages of this diary, he turned inward to explore the meaning of all "this business". His intuition, his sense of knowing, certainly played a big part in his ability to reach an understanding and to realise his resilience, especially in dealing with the multitude of highs and lows concerning the many rumours of peace agreements or defeat of the Japanese and the resulting much-dreamed-about rescue of the POWs.

June 1944

If I read enough of H. G. Wells I will soon be able to write like him he is like a certain food one likes but if taken too much of at once tends to spoil the taste for ever; but in small doses and not too often; well, he's acceptable. I am not copying from H. G. himself but what has happened is that I have had a lot of time to think of late being sick for two weeks. I have read a few books and done a little painting but very little eating. But the so-called army doctor says Mist Alkaline B1 four days and work, so what is one to do, but having a good sergeant in charge of us he says work when I feel like it, and <u>so</u> I do. And so it is. But I have been filled with a lot of conflicting emotions and impressions recently, in fact they have got jumbled to such an extent I find I have to take time off to sort them out.

July 12th 1944

I am still loafing or not exactly loafing but taking things easy. In fact, I have done no actual work in the last month, but it's not my fault. I have suddenly lost my appetite. That thing that has caused me so many hours of anxious, painful agony, hungry enough to eat anything even to picking wild green berries and boiling them up in fact anything at all that is edible, but now I cannot look at rice or stew. I was paraded before the doctor recently and he tells me that the muscles of the stomach have collapsed and the only help he can give me is to put me on a pap diet. Pap for breakfast, lunch and the usual stew, rice and doovers for tea, but being unable to eat the stew and rice I can usually swap it for a doover.

As time went on it became obvious Raymond was not recovering.

About August 1944 Raymond wrote: "Eighty-two bags of mail have turned up at Changi."

He appeared to have expected "the same bundle of letters from Rosemary", to which he added "turns me cold". Earlier in the diary he wrote about how much he craved the "companionship of a girl again, not physically, but just to be able to talk of what doesn't matter". And yet he is not happy about the prospect of getting letters from Rosemary. Raymond apparently had called off their engagement some time ago (but perhaps she didn't get that letter). The struggle with this dilemma was ongoing for Ray.

In this diary Ray reported the death of an Indian commander called Chandra Bose, who was actually wanted for several political murders back in India. But, according to Ray, when this unsavoury high-profile chap turned up in Singapore, the Japs put him in charge of the Indian independence army. Raymond wrote that Chandra was:

> ... recently put in charge of the whole works, in case any Japanese decided to make a break for it. But it appears someone had it in for old Chandra. He was assassinated in Johore Bahru. A Chinaman never forgets.

However, this information of Raymond's does not match the suspicions of the historians who have still not agreed on his place or style of death. (Current records say he died on 18 August 1945 in a Taiwan hospital.)

In a moment of reflection, Raymond remembered having arrived at the precipice of death in the railway camps and Padre Duckworth coming to him with prayers and hymns. He recalled the flood of memories from his childhood, "every little thing, every little gesture". He remembered his tears when Padre Duckworth came as a sign of Ray's impending death and his later tears at the miracle that was to be "once in a blue moon".

As a consequence of his own reaction to the Padre's religious input, Ray now questioned all men's response to religion, to the unknown in death. He appears to see it as a rush to seek refuge in God at the end. Although, he states, prior to this need to commune with religion when one is in dire straits, "How many of us do not have time for such things in life?"

5 August 1944
Have done 3 days on the Changi Aerodrome and in the AGH with dysentery. Now have a sore mouth. Con is working on the drome and all POW are to go to Changi Jail ... the near future also it is believed steak and eggs are just around the corner.

But then he and all the POWs were swallowed up again with the tempo and high pitch of the rumour machine. It was so high they all believed the war would end within the hour.

Into the trough wallowing about until another tidal wave sweeps them out.

He says there is no choice in this POW existence, that they are like

... draughts pushed and shoved around depending on who is playing with them?

But liberation does draw near. To suffer or not to suffer became another topic he wanted to explore. He questioned the belief that through suffering a person comes to find the fullness of life. Although

Yea I am expecting a letter from Rosemary, but what does she talk about? First, I suppose the reason that while she writes in that school girlish style is because red tape says you be careful how and what you write and then again, I can tell by her pen just what her mind is thinking, but like most people she does not write what she thinks. Why cannot she stop being so foolish, what does she think I am, that such piffle should interest me.

But she does not know, she cannot possibly know that I am not the same soldier that left her almost four years ago, and I should be grateful for the girl's letters regardless of what she writes.

You see she has not lived yet, in fact she had not even got ¼ of the way, but she tells me she knows how. But she is no exception. The majority of the girls are more or less the same make up. But I have often wondered what prompted her to write to me after that first meeting. And why after I told her the engagement was broken off, does she still continue to write me of her love and how she is preparing for that day when we will be joined together in holy matrimony.

You see I have tried to forget the girl.

To ignore her existence even – I just glance through her letters once and put them away – she's unfortunately only living on the surface of things, but perhaps she feels that in time she will realise the fulness of life ...

he now knew that nothing could ever be as bad as working on the Burma Railway, Raymond argued that it is through beauty that we find the fullness of life. Despite the inhumane hardship, Raymond continued to express an immense gratitude for all that he had, for his health (such as it was) and for the situation in which he found himself. He often wrote about how grateful he was for the goodness in nature, citing various aromas and sounds, magnificent visual glimpses into the beautiful natural world around him. He wrote:

The way to God is through the aesthetic sense pertaining to all things beautiful. Beauty belongs to all men in common and it was through beauty, that they came to God.

Raymond committed to paper that he "hoped to enjoy the sweets of the world again". His advice:

Living life to the full and enjoying life to the full or else we miss such a lot.

Aside from philosophising and spending time observing humanity, Raymond would often write out long lists of books, appreciating writers like Oscar Wilde, H. G. Wells and Aldous Huxley, to name a few.

It is evident he was inspired and passionate about the books he read, as he liked to savour their words by rewriting sections of prose. But equally he would seek out recipes, recording them to stave off a different sort of hunger, not that these foods were ever available.

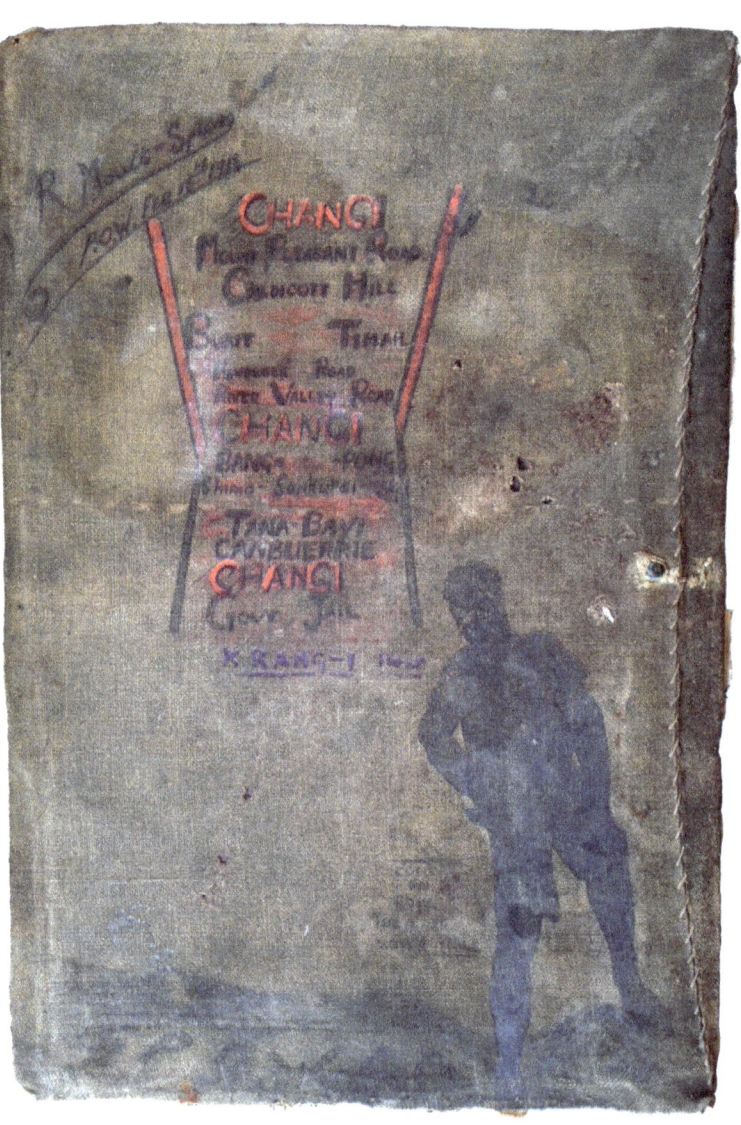

ABOVE The cover of Raymond's war diary. Stitched in old army uniform, listing the POW camps he found himself in from 1942 to 1945. 350 X 250mm

Fried rice, fried tomato, bubble and squeak

Macaroni, pork, chicken and grated cheese topped off with 2 fried eggs

Toast SPREADS instead of butter or jam

Cottage cheese olive spread

1 cup cottage cheese

2 tablespoons of cream,

¼ cup chopped olives,

1 teaspoon onion juice:

Blend cheese with cream, until right consistency for spreading – add salt, onion juice and olives (chopped nuts or chopped pimento may be used instead of the olives).

Prune and nut filling

To layer of chopped prunes add;

1 tablespoon of lemon juice

1 tablespoon orange marmalade,

1½ cup of chopped nuts

blend together and use on all bread.

Peanut Butter and 1 Banana Spread

½ cup peanut butter: ¼ cup cream ½ cup banana pulp

Mix peanut butter with cream until smooth

And light in colour; then combine with

Banana pulp and lemon juice:

Chocolate syrup

3 oz chocolate or 2/3 cup cocoa; 2/3 sugar

1 ¼ water ¼ spoon salt:

Melt chocolate over hot water, boil 3 minutes: Add salt: turn into a jar when cold seal and store in fridge.

And so it seems a finer race,
Must universally take its place,
Amidst a tranquil, awaken world,
And flag of truce, it is unfurled.

I am in fairly good health, clean living, an hour or two each morning in the POW garden. Clean – but patched clothes – plenty of water – a good bed – am giving up smoking – to get more food – in good health eventually. But it's tragic – it's absurd – good health but my soul is sorely wounded

Raymond Moult-Spiers
28 July 1944

23
Kranji

Towards the end of the war and still suffering with the terrible back injury and stomach affliction, Raymond was moved to a POW hospital at Kranji. Here he was described by fellow inmates in Geoffrey Bingham's book, Love Is the Spur, as "a tall bony Canadian man who was in the Australian Imperial Forces and whom had been on the Burma–Thailand Railway". In fact, he was soon to meet Bingham at the camp and the two were to become close friends.

Kranji was near the Kranji river mouth and was where the Japanese had crossed the Johor Strait in strength to take Singapore. They chose to do this because it provided the least amount of water to cross after the Allies had blown up the causeway previously joining Singapore to mainland Malaya. Here the Japanese only had to face a few Australians, Raymond among them.

Once Singapore was occupied, the Japanese reserved Kranji village as a POW camp and, with its cemetery still on the hill, they allowed the Allies to perform burials there throughout the war. These all took take place to the haunting sound of the bugler's last call. It is this hill that has come to be known as the Kranji War Memorial.

Being returned to Changi did not help Raymond's stomach issues, and he now had no desire to even forage for extra food to add to the rice or stew.

Raymond was into his fourth month at Kranji Hospital Camp when, on 14 December 1944, he wrote in this his diary that he wanted to volunteer to return to Changi, primarily to be with his mate Con, but his ward master advised it would be a mistake. Even though the food might be considered better, Raymond would not get the care he now received at Kranji.

Since returning to Singapore, Raymond's diary entries changed completely. Although he struggled with separation from his mates at Changi, he was seeking depth of thought, the meaning of life. He expressed his need to connect with deep thinkers,

ABOVE *Swamp*, date unknown, water-soluble stain and ink on paper, showing the swampy landscape around Kranji, Singapore, 160x210mm, from Ray's war diary. Image held at www.austlit.edu.au, copyright, Moult-Spiers family.

writing that he had no time for shallow folk. His interest in books led him to the library at Kranji where he met and was befriended by fellow POW Geoffrey Bingham, a lay preacher. Here, discussions on philosophy were not unusual. Bingham was partly trained in theology and was very keen to introduce love and gratitude back into the lives of POWs. Sharing a love of life was an undercover operation, with meetings with like-minded POWs held in the blacked-out X-ray room. After years of cruelty and without the certainty a family provides, Raymond found solace with this group. The force of love ignited the urge to connect with some of his fellow POWs on surprisingly deep levels, the intensity of which was almost too much. At those times, he hid in the sanctuary of his hospital bed.

Ray claimed in his diary that the optimists said, "It will be a race between an invasion and the coming of the Red Cross ship. If the ship comes it will be the third in three years." Raymond considered this a good effort by the Red Cross. He reported that the men in the work parties who went into Singapore said they saw Indians unloading Red Cross stuff – a mystery perhaps.

On 1 April 1945, pamphlets were dropped warning people who lived near the Japanese military concerns that bombing would start soon and they were advised to move away.

In his diary entry on 5 April 1945 Raymond explained that, unlike his Burma Railway entries, he was "no longer interested in the fastidious recording of dated events". Instead, he now preferred to write in a journalling style. He stated, "The Burma Railway seems like it was years ago but it was only eighteen months."

Still in April 1945 he tells of a big clean-up at Kranji by a working party, where four hundred patients were returned to Changi. Ray called himself "one of the lucky ones", as he was left behind. He stated this, even though he was unwell and had to dig in the grounds for tree stumps to supply fuel for the cookhouse, thereby receiving a meal. An interesting system.

He described his life as a series of flashes or phases, "so many phases to a period, so many to this POW".

His diary reveals the finding of another kindred spirit. Ray described how important it was to him to find someone with whom he could act foolishly, without judgement, and with whom he could speak. This helped him to sort out some kind of anchorage for his jumble of distorted thoughts.

At one of the meetings in the X-ray room Raymond wrote that he asked the group leader (not Bingham) a question concerning the part kindred spirits play in life. The chap replied that his kindred spirit was in a bottle of Scotch! This answer made Raymond realise why actual kindred spirits were so few and far between. But, with all the incitement to love and care for one another, I can't help but wonder if the ignition of love in a bruised and battered soul didn't arouse the cells of his body to repair.

The entries in this later diary became intermittent from April to July 1945 and processed some intense feelings Ray had been developing for a POW called Rye. However, another POW named Fick was also involved, a three-way friendship, which inspired some intense feelings in Ray. Ray wrote that he tended to head for cover and said he preferred self-imprisonment under the mosquito net over his bed to getting tangled in others' emotions.

ABOVE. *Desolation, the Wilderness of Our Souls, Self-portrait as POW*, 1945, ink washes on paper, approx. 160x210mm. Image held at www.austlit.edu.au, copyright Moult-Spiers family.

ABOVE *Huts* (possible view of huts around Kranji Hospital Camp, Singapore), date unknown, ink on paper, 250x210mm, in Ray's war diary.

Books soon replaced the strain of the triangulated friendship once his camaraderie with Rye was intercepted by the third party. Life certainly was safer back in the confines of the hospital bed. Here, netted in retreat, his mind was able to dream up recipes and travel to faraway places, embracing customs, structures and exotic foods, or it could tangle itself in philosophies and arrive at its own wisdom. He busied himself with illustration, embracing the beauty of nature, which could be either painted or penned as a poem from the heart.

Raymond's war diaries reveal he learned French and gained dexterity in painting and drawing. This later diary is littered with scenes of daily life around the camp, as against in the camp. He was not concerned with the horrors of the camp but rather sought the bigger picture; the beauty and power of nature seemed to fascinate him.

Geoffrey Bingham also wrote a number of short stories that often referred to, or were about, Ray Moult-Spiers. He described Raymond's antics in his short story called "The Cat and the Clown".

The original story was somewhat distorted when told to Bingham third-hand and, like Chinese whispers, had altered a little along the way. Raymond wrote to me in the 1980s, when Bingham's book came out. Ray was very displeased with the final rendition of the tale that ended up in print.

It was here that Bingham described Ray as a tall, extroverted Canadian with an artistic nature. Tall he was but Canadian he was not. Possibly this affectation was to avoid any association with the folly of the British army's ridiculous mistakes in the loss of Singapore. We will never truly know why.

Bingham's story describes Ray as coming across a little cat belonging to one of the Japanese guards. As quick as a flash Ray had swooped the little cat up and thrust it under his shirt, continuing on his way and sauntering across the campgrounds bowing to guards and saluting where required. His charade and outlandish actions were not missed by the hungry POWs, and by the time he had arrived at his destination bets had been laid as to whether or not he would even make it across the compound.

Ray had no intention of eating the soft, trusting little cat, an idea his conscience would not allow. He did not want the guard's cat to be in his belly, but neither was he going to let it free. A cat was a huge bargaining chip. A group of men were waiting in his hut and had begun to barter for possession. The exchange was a windfall for Ray and a heck of a story for the fellas to dine out on … in more ways than one.

As far back as March 1945, the Japanese were facing the very real possibility of defeat. Rations were hard to come by, but it wasn't until 15 August, when the bombs were dropped in Japan, that defeat was realised.

As the end of the war approached, food and medical supplies continued to decrease.

A strange illusion occurred when the rescuers arrived. With the end of the construction of the Burma Railway came the return to Changi of the surviving but very unwell men, bringing with them their starvation and diseases. To the untrained eye of the liberators, this influx of malnourished men made it appear as if life in Changi was hell on earth, but this misconception was not the case at all. Changi was always a well-managed haven.

ABOVE Untitled, date unknown, coloured crayon and ink, 155x250mm, from Ray's war diary. On the reverse is a recipe for potted beef.

When, on 2 September 1945, Japan formally surrendered, the jubilation was intense. It was equally matched by a sense of dread among the POWs, as it had been rumoured that the Japanese did not intend to leave any POWs alive. Indeed, in Singapore, General Saito refused to surrender, despite the emperor doing so. It was not until 12 September that Singapore was surrendered to the Allies.

The gates of Kranji prison were opened, but according to Bingham scarcely anyone moved towards them. Eventually some of the men who were in Bingham's secret group made a move. Bingham wrote that "Crazy Moult-Spiers was with me, and we all laughed and walked and talked and then returned to camp".

At the end of the war in Singapore, but still at Kranji, some of the POWs were able to get their hands on fresh clothes. Moult-Spiers found a couple of formal-wear all-white uniforms and matching white leather shoes. There were no epaulettes or insignia to signify rank but everyone knew white was worn by officers. He and his mate Bingham were soon wandering about Singapore in these stunning outfits, eventually arriving at the wharf. Here they noticed a decommissioned submarine that had been gutted by the Japs and made into dormitory-like accommodation. It was during the early days of the surrender and the Japanese sailors were still on board awaiting their transfer to POW camps.

As brazen as you like, Moult-Spiers and his mate Bingham stepped on board and, on seeing it was a disemboweled vessel, they entered the hull. The hull was now full of two lines of bunks with Japanese sailors scrambling to attention at the end of their bunks. Each bunk had a samurai sword at its head. Moult-Spiers was in, followed by his more dubious mate, Bingham. Together they made an inspection, strolling right through the middle of their former enemies, who were bowing in respect all the way. With not a weapon between them and Moult-Spiers struggling to stifle his laughter, his mate constantly urging him under his breath "to keep sober", they made it to the end. But Moult-Spiers wanted a samurai sword for a souvenir and, with all the bravado needed to take one, he turned to make his choice. Amazingly when they turned there was not a single sword to be seen. It was time to swiftly disembark ... no doubt with the same flair of affected arrogance.

Paperwork states that on 20 September Raymond Moult-Spiers was found alive at Kranji.

Finally, when Bingham and Moult-Spiers were shipped out, they boarded the hospital ship *Oranja* for home. Because Bingham was suffering with kidney stones at the time, he needed a stretcher. Being stretchered onboard and escorted by his extremely thin mate ensured the two attracted the eye of a very beautiful matron, who assigned them to a freshly painted, highly polished luxury cabin with fresh towels and linen. An unbelievable moment. Ray had survived and was on his way to a new life.

In addition to the Victoria Cross awarded to Lieutenant Colonel Charles Anderson, other military decorations were awarded to the members of 2/19th Battalion including two Military Crosses, two Military Medals and seven mentions in dispatches. Raymond Moult-Spiers could stand proud indeed, having served with such fine men.

ABOVE *View*, date unknown, water-soluble stain and ink painting, 160x210mm, from Ray's war diary. Image held at www.austlit.edu.au, copyright Moult-Spiers family.

However, of all the Australian battalions in Malaya and Singapore, the 2/19th had around 1500 men, but had sustained the highest casualties of any Australian Army unit during the war. Only 271 men survived Yong Peng and were withdrawn to Johor Bahru, where they were joined by 650 reinforcements. By the time the war ended, 620 men from 2/19th had died and 197 were wounded. The 2/19th battalion was disbanded later in 1945.

Scrutinising Raymond's survival, it seems that, to keep his soul alive, he practised painting scenes from countries he had never seen. To keep his heart, he wrote of love, appreciation and gratitude. To keep his mind, he practised French, read widely and contemplated philosophy.

To keep his body, he scribbled recipes to feed his hunger. In this way Raymond Moult-Spiers kept up his hope.

BELOW Replacement medals after the theft of Ray's original medals in the late 1980s.
1. Prisoner of War Medal (unofficial). c. 1992.
2. Star 1939–45;   3. Pacific Star;
4. Defence Medal;   5. War Medal 1939–45;
6. Australian Service Medal 1939–45

Prisoner of War Commemorative Medal

Tasmedals of Hobart, Tasmania is pleased to announce the issue of a very special medal to honour the sacrifice of freedom suffered by Australian Prisoners of War.

The specifically designed medal is only available to those members of the services who were prisoners of war or to the families of those veterans now deceased.

The medal is in the shape of a cross bearing the badges of the four services. For the first time, the nursing service's badge is depicted in honour of the sacrifices made by so many nurses.

The medal is suspended by a single haunting thread of barbed wire indicative of the deprivation and affliction the POW's had to endure. Above are the words PRISONER OF WAR. In the centre of the medal is a raised map of AUSTRALIA in enamel to signify national identity.

Issued on 15 February 1992 by
Tasmedals, 8 Orana Place, Taroona, Tasmania 7053
To Commemorate the 50th Anniversary of the Fall of Singapore
1942–1992

RIGHT Raymond Moult-Spiers with his medals at Anzac Day service on Stradbroke Island.

MEDALS WORN BY RAY (L-R):
1. Star 1939–45;
2. Pacific Star;
3. Defence Medal;
4. War Medal 1939–45;
5. Australian Service Medal 1939–45;
6. Prisoner of War Medal (unofficial). c. 1992.
7. Burma Star (unofficial);
8. Australian Ex-Prisoner of War Medal (unofficial).

"A certain blue enters your soul."

--Henri Matisse, artist, 1869-1954

part four

THE ARTIST

I have to hide what I hold inside
Like a mother not me to decide
The colour the bloom
That fills up the room

Raymond Moult-Spiers
date unknown

24

The artist and his army of paintings

I gazed in wonder at the discovery of an old photograph and painting at Raymond's daughter's home in 2019, both depicting the interior of Raymond's Horsley Park studio. With this pictorial evidence, along with Lili's first-hand description, I was able to imaginatively explore Raymond's creative haven.

I could see hanging from a hook on the railway sleeper mantel that he kept a dusty well-worn digger's slouch hat. A silent rifle leaned up against the stonework and collided with a shirt caught on the top corner of a set of dark wood bookshelves. A pair of gumboots stood stiffly to attention in the centre of the space.

Further exploring Uncle Raymond's creativity led me to something quite unexpected. Reflecting on his work, as a resettled Englishman and POW in relation to Australian art, brought some revelations.

Dadaism started in Europe during the horrors of World War One, but it didn't show itself in Australia until the 1950s. Instead, in reverse order, Surrealism had come first. Dadaism centred on deliberate irrationality and negation of all that had gone before, particularly in art and literature. Surrealism, on the other hand, attempted to focus on the dream-like, unconscious qualities of the mind.

The reason Surrealism had reared its head before Dadaism was because Australia, as a relatively new nation, was vastly different from well-established Europe. But Raymond was from the UK and already stained with notions of the rebellious Dadaist concepts and the will to reapply broken or torn pieces, rebuilding anew from the old.

In the relatively untouched sunburnt Australia, the dream-like notions of Surrealism had stepped forward. This was possibly because Australia was not as affected by an outdated class system or the destruction of war, as in Europe.

In response to the lack of a class system, even in the POW camps, Ray's wartime work had begun to appear Surrealistic although it could be argued

ABOVE Ray Moult-Spiers' Horsley Park studio in the 1950s, photographer unknown. Private collection.

it was built on a Dadaist foundation. By the time he arrived back in Sydney at the end of World War Two, Surrealism was old hat and Dadaism was yet to be understood. Ray quickly enjoyed the vast equalised society now available to him.

Following his betrothal to Australia, and having been locked away in Changi with "scarcity" keeping guard, Ray satisfied his need for self-expression through innovation. He was drawn to capture moments in the environment. A capture was instant, done on any found material at hand. For Ray the realism of the moment was caught in the gesture of the stroke on a telling support. Was this Dadaism through necessity, through the loss of rationality and another war?

Like any Dadaist, Ray found refuge in his sense of the absurd, his sense of humour and irony. All of these were on a collision course with authority. This was survival for Ray; he knew only too well how to live under the veil of oppressors. Raymond's life was already cut up; he already knew how to let the pieces fall and how fate would pull things together. He knew how to be an anarchist, just slightly under the oppressor's radar. He knew how to capture the spirit of the time and turn it on its head.

Despite the disconnect from his family, Raymond's unfathomable appreciation of the arts surged through his veins. He came from creative stock. His people had flair and were well versed in creative decision making. Although cut out of his family's life through no fault of his own, like a true Dadaist he collaged himself into various life situations to survive. He was no stranger to play-acting and mimicking the ridiculous.

This was done by engaging pure chance and unorthodox methods to produce relief from tedious or tenuous situations, but it also involved the use of materials not normally employed to make art. Whatever else, it was often provocatively spontaneous work.

Anything could be used and nothing was taboo. Dada art challenged the notion that an artist had to be trained or skilled to create relevant artworks. Scarcely out of his teens, and a POW in a war, Ray certainly was not trained in the true sense of art school indoctrination, but he was visually very vocal in what he had to say, with whatever it took to say it.

It could be said Raymond's artistic side was awoken as a young soldier, chosen because his skills in camouflage surpassed many, making him sought after to do this job out in the Malay jungle where he hid the Australian army's presence so well.

Ray Moult-Spiers, the English immigrant, mysteriously and mistakenly thought to be Canadian, returned to Sydney a hospitalised ex-POW, with a few tricks up his sleeve. In the Thai and Singapore POW camps, he had been a practising Dadaist out of sheer necessity. He had challenged the status quo most of his life and, when it came to producing art, he was ready with whatever it took. While in Changi, his approach to creating art was imbued with self-expression. He was not concerned with how it looked. His concern was the moment and what his work evoked. He sometimes explored the imagined landscapes of distant lands, as seen in his diaries.

Perhaps for Ray Dadaism had actually begun in the 1920s, with the deconstruction of his English family. It was then incubated in the POW experience until the mid-1940s, when Ray absurdly began to rebuild a life for himself as a make-believe Canadian in Fairfield on the outskirts of Sydney.

But, for the rest of Australia, it wasn't recognised until Barry Humphries' absurdist acts began to challenge exactly where and how art occurred. It was then that the concept began to be understood. Humphries, a Melburnian, was apt to perform these absurdist acts or statements anywhere, ensnaring the viewer with humour. It is safe to say Ray himself, described as an extrovert by fellow army mates, was not afraid of absurdity. With author Geoffrey Bingham expanding on Ray's clowning acts in his short stories, this aspect of his nature is not in dispute.

Somehow Raymond returned from the war with a huge folio of work. As the only possessions he had, he wasted no time in utilising them. Even though he was laid up in the army hospital, he was busy with the Red Cross organising an exhibtion of his works.

In a review of his first Australian solo exhibition (with the Australian Red Cross) in 1946, his wartime pictures were surprisingly described as being futuristic. The reviewer stated they tell of searchlight advertising (could this be the imagery from laser projectors we see today?) and of Ray's prediction of the partial surrender of the human personality to a socialistic process. He also seems to have been aware of a change in the status of women, ultimately liberating them. (Did he really know of the future success of Women's liberation way back in 1946?)

The reviewer stated how "Moult-Spiers has the ability to touch the vague memories of others with his communicative powers". The reviewer revealed this appears to happen most when viewing the artist's landscapes. He declared there was a kind of universality that Moult-Spiers had collected from his many travels and observations of the beauty in landscape. His tropical landscapes were described as rich adventures. The reviewer concluded, "Many of the works are not so much a technically skilled capture, but a capture nevertheless. It is a capture of the mind of the artist as prisoner in the midst of suffering and suspense."

The world wars challenged belief systems (in the midst of collapse), while the arts expressed both what had and was happening, along with what was to come. Ray, like other freedom-loving Sydney Abstract Expressionists, imposed a redefinition of the boundaries of what art could be. Sometimes it was irreverent and perhaps even irrelevant, but his work must have startled in its day as it was often referred to in Sydney newspapers with awkward reviews that cited both intellect and reason juxtaposed against dream-like qualities such as:

'R. Moult-Spiers' "Post Atom" is vital with thought, Surrealism in conception and yet worthy of reason.'

Prior to Raymond's arrival in Australia, in the late 1930s, Sydney artists had begun to explore Abstract Expressionism. It was this approach that set Sydney artists apart from their Melbourne counterparts. Broadly, Melbourne's arm focused on Surrealism while Sydney went the way of Abstract Expressionism. Back in the mid-1940s with war wounds unseen, Abstract Expressionism is what lay in wait for Ray. Surrealism, too, was tentatively making its way in both Sydney and Melbourne. This was apparent with a series of exhibitions in both cities. The old guard was still involved with defining Australia through landscape, and national identity through portraiture. They imposed their views and rules on the nation's notion of how art should look.

The Contemporary Art Society of Australia stood up against the old guard with vehemence but it wasn't long before the various new creative expressions within the Contemporary Art Society itself were separating and weakening its hold on the ground it had gained. Without the availability of the rich history of Europe, Australia certainly appeared to lack the understanding of the context for modern art. Australian museums and art institutions did not yet have large collections to draw on and certainly no budgets to bring out touring shows. With only the Impressionism of the Heidelberg School amid traditional landscapes and portraiture to look at, it is no wonder Australia was slow to embrace what Ray and his contemporaries had to offer.

Although both the Victorian and New South Wales modernist groups had come together to form the Contemporary Art Society, which was set to face down the traditionalists, the Sydney artists, among them Ray Moult-Spiers, were affiliated more with Abstract Expressionism and disliked the dominance of Surrealism in the Melbourne group. Not so the rebellious Ray; his work embraced both styles.

Ray was a maverick and had no wish to follow any conventions. This was spotted during his time at East Sydney Technical College under the Commonwealth Reconstruction Training Scheme 1947–49. At this art school Ray appeared to be adept at expressing himself and challenged belief systems behind some of the school's expectations. He wrote in a letter that an art teacher once described his work as "flotsam and jetsam", but added "you find unusual and beautiful things where you least expect". Ray was an individualist and nothing was going to change how he expressed himself. His sharp mind and curiosity seemed to prevent him remaining too long in one arena.

It is reasonable conjecture that Ray knew or came into contact with many prominent artists in Sydney. Prior to the late 1940s, Grace Crowley and her pupil Ralph Balson were among the artists who were inspiring the avant-garde in Sydney. Crowley, who had studied art in Europe, was considered the most experienced modernist painter in Sydney. An outstanding force of nature and an inspiration to aspiring female artists, she had co-run an art school and later an art studio in George Street, where the City of Parramatta Art Society opened its doors in 1950, with Ray as a foundation member.

During Ray's time in Sydney, Balson was teaching part time at the East Sydney Technical College (1949–59), so it is likely a keen Ray would have rubbed shoulders, if not with Balson, at the very least with Balson's ideas via his students. Being a student at East Sydney Technical College meant Ray encountered Jon Molvig, Robert Klippel, Tom Bass, Tony Tuckson and John Coburn, all of whom were returned soldiers enrolled under the same scheme and destined to become some of Australia's great artists. All were training under artist-teachers such as Godfrey Miller, Wallace Thornton, Dorothy Thornhill and Douglas Dundas. The ex-servicepeople followed in the path of artists like Margaret Olley, who had also trained at the college, graduating as a top student in 1945. But this group of ex-servicepeople were especially renowned for their dynamism in making up for lost time.

Ray, now with proper art materials, began to produce works even his beloved Parramatta art group found hard to define. This did not worry Ray; with every painting he was releasing surreal abstract versions of his unreal former life.

THE VISION

His days may be numbered
But lay he encumbered
All winter and summer unseen
But a date he must keep
after such a long sleep

Raymond Moult-Spiers
date unknown

25
Paintbox or letterbox

Rosemary Riley, Raymond's wartime love interest on paper, wrote to him for four long years, penning words of marriage, perhaps to keep him alive.

The Japanese sometimes withheld her letters, sometimes destroyed his. Gaps in correspondence confused things but she remained faithful. She lived on her parents' dairy farm in Bega, writing to the rhythm of the clanging in her father's blacksmithing shop.

Life on the dairy farm was no match for life in a prison camp. And with the ever-present redaction of anything that gave meaning to his experience she was never going to know the full extent of the difference. She wrote by choice about the weather, the cows, the pasture, what she and her mother baked, of knitting socks and other duties for the war effort.

He was unimpressed by this. His imagination did not allow wandering into the mere daily activities of the free. He grappled to rein in his imagination as he pondered the words of philosophers and swam in the deep waters of a soul struggling to keep its body alive.

He instead contemplated the very real emotions of deep friendships with men who understood the slow loss of a vital life force through the starvation of the body and soul. Interaction with real people was more compelling than the hollow feeling of unrelated words filling space on paper.

Although Rosemary was added to his army papers as his fiancée in 1942, Raymond appears to have become involved with an older woman, a Miss Elma McKay Gibson (1909–1977). We are not privy to how they met but meet they did. Elma appeared to be the deep thinker he craved; she understood him in ways he did not expect. They married in 1946, not long after his release from the army and hospital. He was twenty-six and Elma, some eleven years older, was thirty-seven.

The star burst that was Elma sparkled her way

ABOVE Elma McKay Gibson.
Date and photographer unknown.
Family collection.

Ray and Elma, 1940s, place and photographer unknown. Family collection.

through all the layers of war trauma and lifted Raymond up and out of the malady that was pinning him to the army recuperation hospital.

The intensity of Elma's presence may have been enough. This woman could reach in and grab your soul. She could cut to the core of a person. No use in waving a distracting facade here. Raymond needed someone who could see the real him, not all the cover-ups he had put in place since childhood. His wartime diary (in journalling) cried out for a person of depth. In seeking and believing he had found a caring person of depth, Raymond flew towards Elma like a homing pigeon.

Not only did he marry at speed but, within months of arriving back in Australia, Ray had exhibited some of his war paintings. In the same year he exhibited his new semi-abstracts with the Contemporary Art Society and began to be "mentioned in dispatches", sharing reviews in the Sydney papers with contemporaries such as Arthur Boyd.

This may have been so, but Mr and Mrs Ray Moult-Spiers received their mail at the Railway Hotel at Fairfield from July to December while he explored various potential futures.

The civilian job department invited Raymond to make a start in "stationery", which was bound to have been too still for a man like Ray. From there he went on the road as a travelling salesman. He resigned a few months later, receiving a "Golden Pencil". Word had it that Elma worked as a stenographer. Together they pencilled up enough money to buy a little farm at Horsley Park, where Ray attempted to raise pigs that were far too smart.

Meanwhile the lure of stationery presented yet again, this time put to good use being sent or received in the mail. Ray posted an application to run the small post office at Horsley Park.

ABOVE Postage Stamp Ray. Date and photographer unknown. Family collection.

Horsley Park is west of Sydney, near Fairfield, where the smart pigs were stationed. Here, "Arty Farty Moult-Spiers" created his version of "Animal Farm", spirited, of course, by his small battalion of savvy pigs. However, Ray and his pigs appeared to have had a falling out and all focus soon moved to the post office. Stamped with approval, he took on the position as postmaster and the pigs were relieved of their duties. The small acreage was then handed over to earth-bound birds, who ruled the roost. Much like the postmaster, the geese began to scream warnings of a possible postal activity while the ducks, with their uncanny knack for survival, waddled about, their exuberant behaviour never ceasing to entertain.

But what of "The Gibsons", Ray's new flock, featuring one heck of a bird called Elma?

Elma came from a prominent, hard-working, well-liked Fairfield family. She was one of seven siblings all born above the family's grocery store. Her parents, Walter and Ethel Gibson, were highly respected for their extensive involvement in the community. Walter was an alderman on the local council who often topped the polls on election day. He later served for many years on the Parramatta School of Arts committee (a favourable sign for Ray). Ethel, his wife, brought up their seven children while maintaining involvement with the Red Cross, church work and the wartime effort. The family was a strong and supportive unit.

Ray taking up duties as the Horsley Park postmaster was something the Gibsons might well have influenced. After all, living and working in a small rural community was what they did best, and supporting Ray and Elma to take charge of Horsley's so very important correspondence depot had the effect of elevating the status of the two newlyweds in that community. It was an opportunity too good to miss.

Raymond had busied himself learning the Postmaster-General's rules and regulations, which governed the way it all proceeded. He assisted the district's largely resettled international community, selling postage stamps (especially for overseas destinations), managing banking and money orders (a way of transferring funds), processing the mail and telegraphs going in and going out, and weighing letters and parcels. He generally felt the encumbrance of responsibility that ensured everyone local was able to run and communicate their business, as well as keep in touch with distant loved ones. But Ray's real passion for painting was running alongside his new position, and Walter Gibson's active role in the arts made doing it all seem possible.

With their hearts in the right place, the Gibsons undoubtedly welcomed the war-weary Raymond into the family. Walter's backing of the arts must have struck a home run for Ray, because after the war Ray's full commitment to painting began to reveal itself when he enrolled at East Sydney Technical College.

This all lined up very well with the 1950 emergence of the Parramatta Art Society. Whether with the support of the Gibsons or his own life direction, Ray was guided to be part of the society from its outset. His presence as a foundation member gave Ray the charge he needed.

Raymond also surely felt his purpose forming through the supportive reassurance of the art group. It was a kind of re-emergence and a revival of the International Arts Union and School of Arts, which was set up in Parramatta in the mid-1800s. However, due to a late-1800s banking crisis in the colony, the union and school folded before 1900. But nothing could take the arts out of a forward-thinking artistic community like Parramatta. In 1950 the mayor of Parramatta formed the Parramatta Art Society and the reinstated School of Arts was resurrected in 1951. Ray was part of, folded into and nurtured by a group whose primary aim was to encourage, promote and foster appreciation of the arts.

Ray Moult-Spiers was reborn a self-made artist. His height, added to by a mop of thick carefully groomed hair, enabled him to effect a striking figure, which, with the addition of a pipe, made him appear very knowledgeable and considered. His creativity and tendency to seek progressive ideas

FRAGMENTS OF THE SKY

LEFT Ray in early 1949, place and photographer unknown. Family collection.

RIGHT Kyle (surname unknown), Art School Portrait of Ray, c. 1947, ink on paper. Brokensha collection.

saw his ego and mental energy very much aligned. His sharp rise to Parramatta fame was quickly proved with his exhibited works and his aspirations were held high and documented in print for all the world to see.

The unusual Horsley Park Post Office was established in 1933, just after small plots of land were released in that area, perhaps Australia's inspiration for the future hobby farm. The unofficial building called the post office was casually set and casually run in its rural surrounds. The only thing marking its purpose was a roadside noticeboard that indicated the house was used for official post office business.

Once Ray and Elma were installed on their dual-purpose property, changes began immediately. As indicated, Ray's farming techniques may have been a little unusual, but then so were the Moult-Spiers. They further divided their home into more sections. The first division was already in place, with a small room at the side of their living quarters being the local post office. The second division was Ray's creation of a studio around the back.

As tough as she was, Elma yielded to Raymond over and over. She loved the arts and supported his every endeavour in his pursuit of artistic expression. It is said she could work a room for the

ABOVE Ray Moult-Spiers, *Storm*, c. 1949, oil on board, 54x66cm. Auction houses.

good of the artistic community. Taking her sense of humour out and about, spreading optimism, she was popular, and her company was sought after and appreciated.

It wasn't long before the third division emerged, when Elma, daughter of storekeepers, and a clerk before the war, had hatched the idea of being a sub-agent for selling newspapers. This single act was a lifeline to her community in the middle of nowhere. In the early days she managed the sale of newspapers, an important commodity, but then she slowly added useful stores.

In order to supply the basic needs of the rural community, and with prior family knowledge of the business, Elma's newspapers became a small shop and agency. The store was not permitted to be part of the post office. In the early 1950s the Postmaster-General (now Australia Post), did not permit the two overlapping businesses to be in the same location, so Elma had to set up her shop in a completely separate room in their house to sell papers, jams, lollies, butter, sugar, flour and all other items of necessity.

Elma was indeed a community-minded woman, a caring person, and running a general store offered her all kinds of opportunities. A commonsense sort of person, she could be considered one of the early "little Aussie battlers".

Her living conditions could be described as challenging. In one way or another she was forever having to define boundaries. With books and magazines everywhere, and Raymond's interests always butting and pushing her interests around, she, like Raymond, enjoyed learning about things, pursuing intellectual pleasures and the ensuing discussions. Elma had a sharp mind and was quick to debate issues. Her eclectic interests always made for quick-witted responses. These were the things Raymond enjoyed most about Elma.

In turn, he seemed to intrigue Elma. He was different and so was she, and they both liked different. Raymond liked Elma's "go get it" attitude. He appeared to like her tenacity and original outlook on life. In truth she could handle him like no other. But that didn't mean she succeeded – it simply meant she was able to see things through with him.

She wanted to know his history (and later the history of the objects they collected). They certainly both shared a love of antiques and their intriguing stories. This woman needed a creative outlet, a way to expel the ebb and flow, with the highs and lows of feelings and energy she experienced. Her history reveals she baked. It is said she loved to cook, and indeed cooked her way into the hearts of the community.

Raymond, who in the 1950s still had an ongoing struggle with the war injury to his stomach, had to stand to eat. So receiving her nurture through food was fraught with unknowns for them both.

Raymond's tendency to go through periods of intense highs, when he was excessively optimistic, seemed unnatural at times and, as with all highs, a fall was inevitable.

Over time he and Elma developed a kind of dance medley in the way their relationship worked. A mix of the passionate tango with the energetic, partnered jitterbug, followed by the stand-alone twist. And then would come the call – "change your partners please". Fiercely focused on her one minute, then aloof the next, his attention simply elsewhere.

OPPOSITE Ray at the pub. Date, place & photographer unknown. Family collection.

Ray behind the microphone. Date, place & photographer unknown. Family collection.

The "on again, off again" nature of their relationship soon made itself apparent. Raymond wanted to be friends more than anything but she could be moody and difficult to understand. This was a man who wore his heart on his sleeve, frequently jumping in, reserving his harsher judgements until after he was entrenched in a relationship.

Raymond's intelligence gave him the kind of mind that was able to inspire confidence in those around him and he was not afraid to take on risky enterprises with all the energy he possessed for the good of the community. This trait was evident during his war years and he was able to transfer this energy into his new life.

An expressive, animated speaker, Raymond often gave rise to some very witty and playful banter. His mischievous sense of humour was never far away, with his absurdist nature available in sudden flashes. Knowing him was transformative.

As he was considered a "good sort", people often responded to his calls for help. However, he sometimes abused this help by repeating the same mistakes, relying on others to again rescue him. He felt secure with Elma but his social popularity brought a flirtatiousness that regularly led him into trouble with a capital T.

His proud, loner-like behaviour could be and was indeed very attractive to some women. The twinkle in his eye could draw some a little too close. But this twinkle was developed from his sheer willpower to pull himself into a new out-of-the-ordinary life. He relished new experiences and, by surrounding himself with original people like artists and writers, they were plentiful. His love of literature brought out his perspicacious side and added to his ingenuity, intelligence and originality, all of which gave him the capacity to raise eyebrows.

Raymond had talents that he seemed to take for granted. He, with Elma, not only invented their own dance medley of life but embraced the local dances, art and theatrical groups, which they appeared to enjoy tremendously. Ray was often asked to be the master of ceremonies at social functions. Neither was he a stranger to playing character roles, which his popularity in portraying Fats Waller or Johnny Ray at community events proves. It was fun for him to be other than who he was for a time.

At the time, Horsley Park was mainly inhabited by Italian and Maltese immigrants who kept small plots of varied produce. Elma and Ray's small plot of three acres may have stretched from their back door, though exactly what Ray intended for it is another thing. But more about that later.

Ray and Elma lived next to Frank Borg, who in 1955 bought out Elma's newsagency, though they kept running the post office, and set it up right next door, opening the first real general store in Horsley Park. Frank was a short, outspoken Maltese man who ultimately gained position in the community by taking over the selling of Elma's newspapers and other necessities. He and the tall, outspoken Ray frequently encountered differences of opinion, with Ray often leaving Frank bewildered.

Running errands in Horsley Park meant encountering one or other of these characters.

Frank was also subjected to overhearing Elma and Ray's many feisty arguments. Elma was a tough nut to crack, but Ray wasn't one to give up. He could pursue her relentlessly, arguing his or even any point until at last he was satisfied he had won that round.

I thought my turn would never come
That I was just another bum
Of canvas paint
And in-between were pictures
I had never seen
Of dreams come true and oh so true
You needn't travel very far
To step onto another star

Raymond Moult-Spiers
date unknown

26
Fantasy-land

For Raymond, living in Horsley Park and still working as a deputy postmaster may have seemed off the beaten track. However, from 1952, the sculptor Gerald Lewers and his wife, modernist designer and painter Margo, lived not far away on the Nepean River. They were innovators in the understanding and promotion of non-representational artwork in Sydney, and in 1951 had moved to Emu Plains, a twenty-minute drive from the Moult-Spiers' place in Horsley Park. Gerald Lewers was a founding member of the Contemporary Art Society in Sydney, and was one of eight artists who participated in the 1939 ground-breaking EXHIBITION 1, held at the David Jones Art Gallery.

The avant-garde David Jones Art Gallery was a place of great importance in Sydney at the time. By presenting the contemporary modernists' Abstract Expressionist show, which demonstrated the principles of Constructivism and Cubism, it was set to challenge the predominantly Surrealist modern art group in Melbourne.

Ray was engaged with this group of contemporary artists between 1946 and 1955, during which the Contemporary Art Society (sometimes with Ray) held three major shows at the David Jones Gallery. The Lewers were on a mission to promote the arts as a powerful device that could be used to overcome contentious nationalism and the devastation of the world wars. They were accepting of every form of creativity and artistic freedom, all of which would have been very appealing to Raymond.

During the 1950s the Sydney arts community was small, with everyone among the visual artists, architects, writers, poets, journalists and musicians aware of each other. Despite the distance, many travelled to Emu Plains to visit Margo and Gerald Lewers. It is possible that some, on the way to and from Emu Plains, may have stopped over at Ray's studio and that the Moult-Spiers travelled there also.

Meanwhile, the government of the day made a magnificent and rare gesture of support towards the Australian public, with an authentic exhibition called French Painting Today. The exhibition was arranged between the French and Australian governments to tour Australia. The show arrived in Sydney in January 1953 and laid the ground for aspiring Abstractionists to dig in and stand firm against the figurative Surrealist artists of Melbourne. It appeared to engender a split in Australia's Contemporary Art Society. But survivalist Ray, ever the chameleon, was able to stretch himself over both schools of thought and even on occasion pleased the more traditional old guard.

Raymond's work and potential career as an artist was thrust into the public eye when, in February 1953, he achieved a full-colour two-page spread in the popular *Australian Magazine (A.M.)*. He had sent this enlightening article to me in his first 1980 letter.

It was written by Herbert Hull and described Raymond's POW struggles to procure materials. Hull said Raymond professed to developing the knack of cutting bamboo sticks so they could be used for brushes. He tied a tuft of hair at one end – "real sable", he called it. For pigments he used red and yellow clays. But his greatest painting possession was some Chinese vegetable black, two sticks of which he managed to hang onto throughout the whole deadly war story. Hull went on to imply that Raymond attracted other former-POW artists to join the City of Parramatta Art Society.

ABOVE Original article, by Herbert Hull, sent to the author in 1980. Family collection.

ABOVE. Ray Moult-Spiers, *Hurricane*, 1950, oil on board, 48x40cm. Location unknown. A fantasia painting from his 1953 Sydney solo exhibition at David Jones Gallery, which eventually linked Moult-Spiers to Walt Disney (although The Wonderful World of Disney did not introduce its "Fantasyland" until the following year, 1954–55).

In July 1953, Raymond's enthusiasm for the arts, his wartime resilience and his painting talent were proved with a startling one-man show at the David Jones Gallery.

The show was reported on in *The Sydney Morning Herald* on 15 July 1953:

Raymond Moult Spiers is showing some of his fantasias. Indeed, there is a certain proximity to Walt Disney's creations of a more fanciful type. "Musical Phantasy", "Ballet Musical", "Dreaming of Olwyn", "Hurricane", and "Rebirth" are pretty and ephemeral in a manner which may make them acceptable to film audiences; as paintings they lack that element of the concrete which even the strangest forms must attain here. The exhibition will be opened by Brigadier F. G. Galleghan at 3p.m. to-day.

Raymond's solo show of fifty-two paintings in July 1953, opened by Brigadier Galleghan, his commanding officer during World War Two, was reviewed by highly respected art critic and painter

James Gleeson. Gleeson described Raymond's work as "watercolour fantasies", saying, "Unfortunately his technical resources are not strong enough to sustain his flights of imagination and the result is confusing to say the least. Greater discipline is needed if these images are ever to become decipherable." Gleeson had said much the same thing about the founder of the New South Wales Contemporary Art Society, Gerald Lewers, and his two person-show with wife Margo Lewers, the year before.

Using the word "fantasies" to describe Raymond's work appears to have stuck. Fantasy lends itself to Surrealism, not Abstract Expressionism, and, as Ray was more often than not dabbling in both, confusion followed about exactly what he was doing.

But Sydney was not without its purist Surrealists. Sydney-born James Cant, who was in London prior to the war, at the time of the explosion of international Surrealism, touched down in Sydney in 1955. Although he later went to live in Adelaide, it was during his brief time in Sydney that he no doubt brushed shoulders with the tentatively declared Surrealist, Raymond Moult-Spiers.

There are some distinctive similarities in their approaches, although it is safe to say James Cant was a beacon for Raymond, not the other way around. This is because Cant painted with the conviction of someone who knew a thing or two that other "would-be" artists had not accessed. While in London prior to the war, James Cant had been introduced to the Mayor Gallery, where he first showed in the 1935 group exhibition beside the great Surrealists of Europe, Ernst, Klee and De Chirico, and where he was subsequently invited to become a member of the London Surrealist Group.

ABOVE Newspaper review written by the acclaimed art critic James Gleeson. Brokensha collection.

But Raymond's elasticity enabled him to extend to all three schools of thought. A traditionalist one minute, Surrealist the next and now Abstract Expressionist, all three with his natural Dadaist foundation.

Despite Gleeson's judgemental review addressing Raymond's lack of technical resources, his first major solo exhibition in the David Jones Gallery made a big splash. It achieved an enviable turnout to the opening, followed by reviews and mentions in many Sydney newspapers.

Interestingly, reviewing the same exhibition, The *Sydney Morning Herald* took a different perspective and retold the story Raymond shared with Chinese artist Madame Yee-ping Shen Hsu. It is reported

ABOVE Ray Moult-Spiers, *Mystery Bay*, c. 1953, black and white photograph of painting. Location unknown.

that Raymond said, "I like the Chinese", going on to explain that, while he was a POW in Changi, the Chinese pushed a large parcel through the barbed-wire fence to the prisoners. It contained five hundred Bibles. The padre of the camp was purported to have said: "I am sure the Good Lord wouldn't mind if you made cigarette papers out of the pages, provided you read them first."

In 1954, Raymond participated in the fourth Annual Exhibition of the City of Parramatta Art Society. One reviewer observed that, while the show was full of predominantly conventional styles, this was not the case with the works by Raymond Moult-Spiers. The reviewer noted that "his pictures must hold some attraction", adding, "Despite his Surrealistic treatment of his subjects, Moult-Spiers' use of brilliant blues on both canvasses creates a bright interesting impression." Another review of the following 1955 Annual Parramatta Art Show, written by art critic Muriel Staunton, further singles out Raymond. "Moult-Spiers once again draws attention and causes the conservative to realise that this painter is unique. His 'Summertime', primitive in conception, is powerfully mystic."

FRAGMENTS OF THE SKY

ABOVE Ray Moult-Spiers, *Hut on the Hill*, c. 1954, paint on card, 25.5x21cm. Private collection.

ABOVE. Ray Moult-Spiers, *In the Beginning*, 1954, oil on board, 49.5x60cm. Auction houses.

FRAGMENTS OF THE SKY

Ray Moult-Spiers, *Agony of Being Lost*, c. 1956, oil on water using bleed technique on paper, 18x20cm. Private collection.

Raymond's dexterity was evident with his paintings of realistic landscapes, along with more contemporary Abstract and Surrealistic works. His commitment and fervour to his practice earned him respect and support, but it appears the conservatives in the City of Parramatta Art Society were often perplexed by his unusual approach. "Fantasy" was the term used and one thing led to another, with the idea of working for Walt Disney arriving in Ray Moult-Spiers' pigeonhole.

The wonderful world of Walt Disney animation would have been splashed across the movie theatre screen at the Roxy in mid-1950s Parramatta. It would have been all framed by a proscenium arch fringed by Mesopotamian bull sphinxes. And so it was that the notion of "Fantasyland" was transferred to the public consciousness. Everyone knew Walt Disney was the leader of the pack when it came to the magic of animation, and there was something about the whimsical way Disney portrayed his Fantasyland animations that provoked viewers of Ray Moult-Spiers' paintings to suggest the two belonged together.

Ray certainly would have been there to assess this as he sat in the dark picture theatre. His experience was no doubt enriched by the illuminated colour palettes activated by the light shining through the film strips that had captured the animator's paintings. Ray's landscapes soon moved towards magical, and he was convinced he had what it took.

The spirited Ray's decision began when he sent Walt Disney a letter with the newspaper cuttings citing the reviews of his work in reference to Walt Disney's fantasy world. This fervent, outrageous act of blatant self-confidence actually got him an offer of a paid job trial.

On the strength of this, he left his position as deputy postmaster at Horsley Park and, with streamers trailing to the sound of "Auld Lang Syne", set sail for Hollywood. The long departure blast of the foghorn belonged to the cruise ship, the *Orsova*, which left Sydney Harbour in the summer of 1956, with Ray and Elma on board.

Raymond had begun to follow his dream. He was resolved to take his skills to America. They arrived in San Francisco one month later, and Raymond met with the Walt Disney studios and negotiated his trial.

Although Raymond was ready to begin his adventure with Disney, the Disney studios were, in reality, not hiring that year. The Disney machine had its sights set on creating the real live three-dimensional world of Disney on an acreage to be called Disneyland. This was not the only hindrance. In a letter to his brother, Raymond explained that he and the Disney studios did not always see eye to eye. Disney's reputation for being difficult appeared to come into play and was juxtaposed against Raymond's own free-spiritedness. Disney was notorious for being challenging to work for and given Raymond's artistically expressive temperament this was never going to be a close marriage.

Disillusioned, Raymond found alternative, casual work as an extra in films and then more permanent work on a horse ranch in California, which set him on another path. Working with animals was a great way to console himself after the loss of his dream. He, like his father, possessed a great affinity with horses. His knowledge of breaking in and training horses on the ranch, called North Ridge, was valued by its owner, a Mr Lomax.

Ray had worked with horses in his youth and

identified them as friends. This is attested in letters and by the titles and subject matter of many of his paintings. It is also possible that his father may have been a wanted man who changed his name in order to continue horse rustling from the UK into the US and Canada.

In Hollywood, Ray's likeness to film star Lee Marvin attracted a slight glimmer of attention. At that time Marvin had been playing hardboiled characters in supporting roles in westerns, war and detective suspense movies. Marvin was not yet in the big league and it wasn't until the 1960s that his fame really set in, with his star role in the western comedy Cat Ballou. Although urged and encouraged to try for a role as a Marvin stand-in, Raymond was back in Australia before filming started. It is, however, very probable that Raymond had trained some of the horses used in the film. While the idea of working as a double was floated, it was not going to be a reality, at least not exactly as envisioned. Raymond played on his "skirting with Lee Marvin" fame for the rest of his life, even pursuing further Marvin stand-in parts, such as one for an intended production of Patrick White's novel Voss by the South Australian Film Corporation, which unfortunately was never realised.

In a letter that his brother John Luke wrote to Raymond, while he was working with the horses and not with the pencils, there is some acknowledgement of the Disney debacle. John Luke certainly invited him to stay with his family in the UK during the festive season and offered the use of a chalet on his property for a studio.

Prior to this Elma and Ray had managed to visit Austria, England and Paris; however, problems with Elma's visa prevented her staying in America with her husband and sent her home mid-year while Raymond stayed on.

Sadly for Elma, her father passed away while she was on board ship and she missed the funeral.

John Luke wrote to Ray in the US at the time, enquiring as to whether Ray had found a nice girl yet. This question certainly indicated there was trouble in Elma and Ray's marriage.

OPPOSITE Ray and Elma dancing on board ship in fancy dress, 1956, photographer unknown.

For all this love is new to me I

might as well be up a tree

But she is kind considerate too

And never makes a fool of you

Her lovely voice I can't forget

And music is her laugh and yet

When sad comes down upon her eyes I

join with her and wish otherwise

Raymond Moult-Spiers wrote everything as though paper was scarce. He wrote from one side of the paper to the other regardless of paper size. Any attempts at considered conventional line breaks rarely exist in his poetry. This one has been slightly structured for ease of reading.

Raymond Moult-Spiers
date unknown

27
Horsing around in Horsley

By Christmas 1956, Ray was back with Elma and back in the Horsley Park Post Office. Whatever was occurring in their relationship had been preparing the ground for things to be different. It wasn't long before Raymond's studio took on a new meaning.

The Moult-Spiers' home began to reflect Horsley Park with its divisions into small allotments. The attraction to the area for new Australians was spectacular. A small acreage was all you needed to make a go in the "Lucky Country". The gathering of the predominantly Maltese and Italian international community was being added to by a smattering of South Africans.

Two miles (3.2 kilometres) from the post office lived a young mother with Zulu in her English blood, Frances Brokensha. This woman was to play an extraordinary role in Raymond's life.

She and her white South African husband, Colin, and their three-year-old daughter, Priscilla, were drawn to Horsley by her sister, who had already discovered the bounty of cheap land and opportunity. They had escaped the tricky business of apartheid back in Durban. Most of Horsley Park appeared to be established by escapees from hideous situations in other parts of the world and the South Africans were part of the next wave.

The new girl in town and her family had slipped away from the trouble in South Africa in 1954, on the *Ixion*, arriving on 15 September at Albany, Western Australia. All three were born around Durban, KwaZulu-Natal. But, as apartheid was gaining a stronger foothold and with Frances circulating her Zulu and English heritage in her mixed blood, the decision to move on was wise.

Colin wanted five acres and a dairy cow so they had made their way to a very affordable small acreage in Horsley Park. Frances's appearance in rural Fairfield made an impact. She stood for things most women had never dared think about.

FRAGMENTS OF THE SKY

ABOVE Ray Moult-Spiers, *Twisted Trees*, c. 1952, paint on card, 13x10cm. Private collection.

ABOVE Ray Moult-Spiers, *River Park France*, c. 1957, oil and wax on board, 192x85cm. Private collection. This painting explores the difference in light in France captured on his trip back from the US.

HORSING AROUND IN HORSLEY

ABOVE Ray Moult-Spiers, *Totem*, c. 1956, oil on board, 122x183cm. Family collection.

Colin, a dashing, hard-working electrician and former air force mechanic, was unable to use his qualifications to attain employment due to the difficult Australian regulations. Consequently, Frances took work as a nurse at the Lidcombe Hospital. This she did at night while her husband retrained in horticulture during the day.

The young mother enjoyed the new freedom available to her since leaving the fearful situation in South Africa. There was plenty to explore in her new community but whether she did or not is another thing. Groups, clubs, sports and the arts could have all benefitted from her accommodating and gentle charm, personal magnetism and easygoing nature. Instead, she seems to have put everything into her calling as a nurse. The hospital may only be 15 or so miles (25 kilometres) from Horsley Park but even today it takes over two hours, one way, by public transport.

The first part of the journey was to ride her bike to the Horsley Park Post Office, where it was agreed that she could leave her wheels around the back. From there she would catch a bus to the Fairfield train station for the hour-long train journey to Lidcombe. Once at that station she walked to the Lidcombe Hospital.

Frances was a colourful character. The local drama group would have marvelled at her ability to reach in and understand how to play any character she may have cast herself in. According to those who knew her, Frances was a very animated person who could and would spontaneously play-act different types of people.

In reality, other choices were more appealing. The "old-time dances" held at The Rivoli in Parramatta, Western Sydney, a marvellous social venue, were a wonderful outing for the people of

ABOVE Frances Brokensha.
Date, place and photographer unknown.
Family collection.

Horsley Park and surrounding areas. These were spectacularly significant, heart-warming events, with a fourteen-piece band being recorded and broadcast on Sundays to over fifty radio stations throughout Australia. There is no doubt that Ray and Elma attended these.

Ray had warmed to Frances and Colin from the outset but it was Frances with whom he enjoyed philosophising. This came easily to Frances, as did debating an issue. She was fun – there is no doubt of that – and her laughter would warm anyone.

Ray was to find out that she was not like other men's wives and their ideas around extramarital affairs; she would not be tied to the trappings of convention, any convention.

But Ray Moult-Spiers had fallen for her almost immediately. She was no shrinking violet. She was straightforward about what she wanted and, when the time came, she was equally clear about not wanting the complexity and needy behaviours of a lover. Spontaneous excitement was what she was all about … at least that is what it appeared to be. In fact, Frances had an instinct for moderation that kept her afloat. She was cool headed and could detach herself from the emotional turmoil of others.

Frances loved a genuine backstory in people who interested her and for Ray's part he was quick to supply. He, in turn, found in her genuine counsel, something he had rarely experienced before. He felt good, he felt healed when he was with her.

Their bond was to be lifelong but when Frances fell pregnant to Ray things took an unexpected turn.

Contrary to all her bravado and abilities, she went the way of the strongest opinion when it came to anything that personally affected her. This characteristic appeared to play straight into Ray's insecurities around what family meant.

For Frances, life revolved around diplomatically navigating her way through it. With Raymond floundering around with his own inner conflicted notions of his right to a family, Colin's strong and clear love of children and family carried Frances straight back home.

Whichever way Colin looked at it, Frances was an asset, his asset, a gorgeous wondrous asset at that. But it was their love of children that kept them close. It was children, along with their shared fondness for nature and animals, that made life worthwhile. So, when Frances fell pregnant, sometime during the festive season of 1957, Colin, oblivious or not to the misadventure, was soon ecstatic with the prospect of more children.

Just how did Frances come to fall pregnant to Raymond Moult-Spiers, with him not long back from his overseas trip and into the arms of his spritely wife? A wife who could be insecure about their relationship, a wife who at forty-eight was somewhat older and headed into menopause. Elma, with her already-established struggle with moodiness, could have been challenged by many things that would have seen Raymond spending more time in his studio.

The Moult-Spiers' dance-medley relationship was being played. Either way, "change your partners please" was the call of the day when it came to Frances. And the studio held the key, with the pushbike of hers resting against the wall like that … it was just a matter of time.

As for oblivious Colin and his blind eye, he was busy with his own life. Despite his caring and loving nature, he was a man missing in action!

With lots of good and wonderful qualities going for Colin, not surprisingly, or perhaps very surprisingly to some, he and Ray continued a constant friendship all their lives. Colin was a compassionate soul with a strong sense of humanity, humour, insightfulness and feeling for the arts. However, it is safe to say Colin knew more than he let on. His children described him as very intuitive.

With silence the preferred choice, he knew better than to challenge his perception of "his family". Yes indeed, when "his" second daughter, Lili, was born in 1958, he was a very proud dad.

It appears Colin had absolutely no intention of stepping out of his marriage and was resistant to letting go of his notion of what his marriage might be.

Colin, Frances, Elma and Raymond would spend hours happily debating issues, swapping sides, looking at the issue from all angles. Their discussions tied them in knots and held them tight. But Colin's destiny was to raise not only one but two of Ray's children as his own.

The second child, a boy, was conceived in October 1963 at the height of Raymond's involvement in the Sydney art scene. By then Frances was no spring chicken and complications occurred. Things were difficult for this little one, who was born with spina bifida, manifesting as the lifelong accumulation of fluid on the brain. Drains were put in from the infant's brain to his stomach, which allowed Leonard a reasonably normal life.

And so it was that life continued in Horsley Park for another three years, before "change" came a-knocking at the Brokenshas' door once more.

OPPOSITE Frances Brokensha. Date, place & photographer unknown. Family collection.

BELOW Raymond with horse. Date unknown.

Have plenty of paintings.
And will send you one if you like.
Abstract or traditional.
Take your pick.

Raymond Moult-Spiers
date unknown

28
A brush with his studio

By the 1960s the primitive studio tacked onto the back of the Horsley Park Post Office had taken on a different look. By all accounts it was like entering Aladdin's cave. Four-by-twos provided rudimentary shelving on which were placed what appeared to be hundreds of small paintings. The bejewelled effect filled the space, making it sing with colour. A large timber rack stacked with the bigger canvases ran down the centre, dividing the room. The stench of turpentine prevailed, in spite of being mixed with various oils, both studio and artist heady with the intoxicating world of painting. This studio and its occupant attracted many interesting people for intellectual and art-practice discussion.

On the other side of the rack was a tall, steel-framed workbench, and built onto that were shelves resting on bricks, exhibiting books and many beautiful objects. Exquisite keepsakes from faraway places perhaps. Urns and vases everywhere held vast quantities of paint brushes. Tubes of paint and pigments were everywhere.

Inside the dual-purpose abode was Elma with her newsagency and small store. Outside the dual-purpose abode but inside the dual-purpose studio was Ray and his sometime lover. Fantastical and extraordinary perhaps, but then so were the players.

Ray had suffered intolerable human cruelty, but he was not about to give away his new-found freedom for the sake of social principles. He was, after all, trying to make his way in a country not of his birth but where opportunities were abundant, and he appeared to be taking as many as he could.

Sometimes when Frances left her bicycle against the outside wall of the studio while she worked the nightshift she encountered Raymond at work in his studio, and it wasn't long before she was lured into his mystic palace of delights.

Earlier, in 1957, back from his skirmish with America and the world at large, Raymond's

FRAGMENTS OF THE SKY

LEFT Ray Moult-Spiers, *Ray's Casting Couch*, 1960, oil on board, 97x65cm. Private collection.

BELOW Ray Moult-Spiers, *Totem in Surrealistic Landscape*, c. 1957, oil on board, 88x104cm. Auction houses.

ABOVE Ray Moult-Spiers, *Roo Country*, c. 1959, oil and wax on board, 46x90cm. Private collection.

ABOVE Ray Moult-Spiers, *Wild Horses*, 1958, oil and wax on board, 60x90cm, (exhibited again 1962). Location unknown.

paintings were again receiving press, as evidenced in a cutting from a local Fairfield newspaper article dated 5 January 1957, which both discussed his work and announced he had been studying painting overseas.

This is further substantiated with a 1957 exhibition catalogue citing Ray Moult-Spiers in a two-person show with up-and-coming Melbourne artist Ronald Kirk at the Dominion Galleries in Castlereagh Street, Sydney. This gallery was known to support some of the country's top artists.

Raymond was indeed back and had sprung into action when he also exhibited with a group of five young contemporary artists in a show that was very much concerned with the concept of "anti-art school". Their view challenged a belief that art schools could strengthen contemporary art movements and their own place in art history by following a certain "school of thought". These five rebellious artists wanted their freedom from this misconception. The show was taken to the people and, in a Dadaist act, held in the CWA Rest Rooms, Fairfield, an odd location to say the least. One newspaper review (no date, author or newspaper title noted in the clipping) claimed:

There is more humanity – and kinship with humanity – to be seen in this small exhibition than is likely to be seen in a multitude of art galleries and exhibitions arranged by those who profess to know what life is all about and tag it with an "ism" or an "ist".

The Biz art critic, Evelyn Walters, discussed Ray's work (again no date) with reference to his brief 1956 sojourn in Paris, as evidenced in his paintings.

Walters wrote:

Most prolific exhibitor is Ray Moult-Spiers, whose compelling work includes some done locally as well as some he painted while abroad last year. This imaginative artist varies between strongly dramatic contrasting paintings and contrasting misty paintings which never the less emphasise appropriate treatment (note no. 26, "Loch Duich"), while the second is best expressed in "Summertime", with its delightful fantasy.

In 1959, two other ex-POWs, both artists like himself from the City of Parramatta Art Society, joined Raymond in another deliberate Dadaist act. They contrived to take their work out of the gallery environment and display it to the people, roadside. Like renegade artists from the front line, these three attracted a crowd and the press. In an ensuing 1959 newspaper article about the "road show", titled "Blood for Paint", Ray claims that during the war it was out of necessity that he painted with brushes fashioned from bamboo and human hair, using pigments made from clays, metals, dyes and human blood.

In 1961 he won the Parramatta Art Prize with his painting titled *The Mourners*, purchased by the Parramatta City Council, and now in the City of Parramatta Cultural Collections. In 1962 he won the Parramatta Contemporary Art Prize. This recognition and being a foundation member of the Parramatta Art Society led the way to involvement in other art groups.

Before long Raymond was on the executive committee of the prominent and progressive Australia Art Associates, the biggest nationwide organisation for modern painters, architects,

ABOVE Ray Moult-Spiers, *Surreal Figures at the River*, c. 1960s, size, title and medium unknown. Location unknown.

ABOVE Ray Moult-Spiers, *Horse Play*, c. 1960s, size, title and medium unknown. Location unknown.

ABOVE Ray Moult-Spiers, *The Mourners,* 1961, oil on board, 60x90cm (1961 Parramatta Art Society Contemporary Art Award). City of Parramatta Cultural Collections, NSW.

sculptors, designers and creators in plastic arts. The organisation was the first of its kind to address the need to tour original works of art to all major centres throughout Australia. The Cumberland Argus picked up the story on 9 May 1962 and in bold text cited artist Raymond Moult-Spiers, winner of the Parramatta Council's special Contemporary Art Award, as one of the executives of Australia Art Associates, said to be the largest arts organisation in the Commonwealth.

Raymond powered ahead and in 1964 held a two-person show with Collinridge Rivett, who was secretary of Australia Art Associates. The exhibition, at the Penthouse Gallery, Church Street, Parramatta, was opened by David McMillan, the University of Sydney archivist. Perhaps well before its time, proceeds went to the International House Appeal in aid of multicultural understanding and acceptance. An initiative by both the University of New South Wales and the University of Sydney. The review describes Ray Moult-Spiers as being "recognised as one of Australia's most creative and original contemporary painters".

Ray's interest in taking elitism out of the arts and inspiring people to reach for their own creative expression stayed with him all his life. He appears to have travelled extensively, enthusiastically moving about his district and interstate, entering art

BELOW Raymond Moult-Spiers preparing for the 1959 "Road Show", an exhibition he and two other ex-POWs took out of the gallery environs and to the people. His absurdist wit at play: "At first I painted for me – no returns. Next I painted for peanuts – better". Family collection.

prizes for the purpose of promoting and fostering an appreciation of art. He wanted art to be available to everyone and with an open heart encouraged emerging artists of all ages to develop their skills. The essence of this practice was certainly set within his co-founded City of Parramatta Art Society from its inception. Perhaps eclipsing Raymond's bigger view of sharing the arts nationwide was that this concept carried through to Australia Art Associates.

During the process of research and writing I came across a magical find during an internet search. It turns out artist Ambrose Reisch had encountered Raymond during the late 1960s, a meeting that changed the course of Ambrose's life. Then sixteen, Reisch recalled the air of anticipation as he sat in a meeting of the Cabramatta Art Society while Raymond was sliding and pulling his large painting down the passage, finally dragging it into the meeting room. According to Ambrose, before Ray started to speak, "you could hear a pin drop".

For Reisch that first meeting became the inspiration that swung his choice to pursue a career as an artist ... and a successful one at that, crisscrossing between the Australian and international art worlds, and including lecturing at the National Art School in Sydney.

LEFT Ray Moult-Spiers, *Old Inn*, oil on board, 39x49cm, 1969. Private collection, UK. Written on the back; "Back entrance of an old inn in New South Wales where prisoners from England loading boats to go up-river were chained to posts in the yard".

ABOVE Ray Moult-Spiers, *Horsley House,* oil on board, 100x79cm, c.1965. Courtesy of Fairfield City Council, NSW.

Reisch framed Raymond as "debonair" when he stood to speak, cigarette in hand, describing the background to his painting as being set on a south coast beach. Ray professed befriending another artist on that beach who was also working. This artist was Brett Whiteley. Ray had depicted him standing next to a carved lectern on which lay an open book with the word "Baudelaire" written across it. Reisch explained it was Ray's referencing of literature along with the intensity he stirred that captivated him. Reisch said, "That was for me, at sixteen, a seminal experience."

Apparently, Raymond enhanced his story with affect, causing the eruption of gasps throughout the room with his account of how Brett Whiteley had also used blood in his painting, albeit shark's blood. Reisch acknowledged it was "very theatrical but Ray brought a lot of excitement to the meetings".

His painting *Boudin in Tourville* (see page 284, a later rendition representing the principle) connects to Baudelaire's 1859 salon review, citing the lack of urban landscapes. Boudin was soon one of the first artists to paint outdoors with his painting of the popular resort beach at Tourville.

Reisch also sent me a written portrayal of a later visit to Raymond's Horsley Park studio:

For my youthful experience, the studio was filled with mythical magic. The artist, the thinker, the dreamer evident everywhere. Now that I cast my forensic eye over that experience, I feel I am right.

Ray was not a production artist, on the art treadmill, but more a romantic artist, enacting his forays into the surrealism of his experiences. These are of course my impressions from the time.

LEFT Ray Moult-Spiers, *Rainmaker*, oil on board, 50.5x49.5cm, c. 1970s. Private collection, UK. Current owner reports, "my mother asked him why he always seemed to paint in blue (a colour she disliked!) so he said he would paint something red for her".

ABOVE Ray Moult-Spiers, *Moulin Rouge*, oil on board, 60x48cm., c. 1960s. Private collection, NSW

ABOVE Ray Moult-Spiers, *The Race*, oil on composition board, 61x90.5cm. 1967, location unknown.

In conversation he was interested in the surrealists but more importantly in the poetry of art.

With these descriptions of Raymond's Horsley Park studio, the impression is that Raymond's whole life was a Dadaist collage.

Where could all this prize winning and executive positioning in the arts have gone? Why did he slowly slip off the artistic ladder of success?

What was happening to this artist during the late 1960s? It seems he was seduced by the world of antiques and the vague knowledge of his father's antique shop in London. But perhaps it was the desire to understand his father, by being more like him.

Ray's love of beautiful things is undisputed. Whatever else, he was drawn by the wheeling and dealing within the industry and began to buy and sell collectables. At the same time, the proprietors of an antique business in the Sydney beachside suburb of Cronulla, close to an hour's drive from Horsley Park, which Ray had come to frequent, recognised the potential for informal dealings with the artist.

In Raymond's letters to me in the 1980s, he often wrote that in those days he could knock up a traditional landscape in no time. It appears Raymond's ability to do so may have successfully coupled with Cronulla's luscious antiques store. The teaming up of stylish antiques with Ray's traditional paintings must have worked well, possibly inspiring buyers to purchase. Original landscape paintings no doubt looked magnificent against tasteful in-store arrangements. It seems the couple who ran the business could sell them, and sell them they did. Raymond implied he also became a scout for the owners and appeared to buy collectables for them. He continued this association, no doubt informally and under the radar, for a couple of decades.

ABOVE Ray Moult-Spiers, *Lowestoft*, oil on composition board, 38.5x38.5cm. 1967. Private collection, UK. Boats racing off Lowestoft on the east coast of England.

THIS IS JUST A BEACH IN TIME

OF ENDLESS SANDS

THAT CONVERGE THE STRANDS

OF FINE ENDURING TIME

TOGETHER SPENT

EACH MOMENT LIVED NOT LENT

Raymond Moult-Spiers
date unknown

29
Horsley and Away

During the late 1960s, the Brokensha cottage in Horsley Park was a rental – a three-bedroom fibro build, painted blue, complete with outside toilet and laundry. Its copper boiler and double concrete troughs were not so perfect for the modern working woman that Frances was.

Horsley Park was a God-fearing location, where it was purported there were more Christians (mostly Catholics) than in any other area of New South Wales. Worship activities often took place in a hall. Exactly opposite the God-fearing hall was the post office and the not-so-God-fearing deputy postmaster, the bedazzling Mr Moult-Spiers.

The post office was at a ninety-degree angle to the road, facing Frank Borg's General Store. Inside the store, which did face the road, was Frank Borg's massive taxidermied eagle, suspended over the counter. A strange sight indeed for those not in the know.

General store items were not all that Frank Borg sold. What happened around the back was another thing! Built onto the rear of his shop was an extension where he housed his staff, his beloved family. His wife and children were all expected to work in the shop, and they did. But it was what else that went on around the back that raised eyebrows.

Frank Borg might have been a small bloke, but he was the big man in town, exercising a big idea. His big idea attracted a clientele who had no problem frequenting his big-idea establishment, Borg's "sly-grog shop". It operated as an attractive option for the Horsley hunters, a group of mostly Maltese men who liked to hunt ... the taxidermied eagle now explained.

The post office, too, operated another world around the back and sat on what seemed like three acres of geese, such was the piercing sound. But around the back of the house was the artist's studio, spilling its contents all about and attracting some very weird types.

Actually, noticing it was the Horsley Park Post Office required local knowledge. For a long time, the only indication that there may be some kind of public facility somewhere around was the community noticeboard up by the road. Eventually the Postmaster General put a bright red post box and bright red public phone booth out the front. Still with no signage roadside and a dip down to the house, guesswork followed as customers made their way along a kind of brick-paved laneway to the side of the house facing Frank Borg's General Store, some distance away.

The part-time church and community hall standing on the opposite side of the road surveyed the goings-on at the post office. And rightly so, for the deputy postmaster was a man ahead of the times and the times were headed towards the "free love" of the 1960s. Fortunately "God-fearing" only occurred on Sundays.

The deputy postmaster, who had been "countering the culture" of apparent religious fervour, was busy germinating the seed of the 1960s way back in the 1950s.

Mr Moult-Spiers' first Horsley Park love child, Lilian, gave the following description of her early encounters with her yet-to-be-realised birth father:

> *His voice I remember well as a little girl of four years of age, living with my parents in a small but quaint country town located in the western suburbs of Sydney. A place called Horsley Park.*
>
> *One of the most prominent places in Horsley Park and a hive of activity for many of the local folk was the post office. This oddest of places remains vivid in my mind. Just like the rest of the folk in Horsley Park a visit to the post office was a regular occurrence. My Mum would grab her light green, hard plastic with embossed flowers shopping basket from the back door. With back door key and red purse in one hand and shopping basket in the other, it was off to Borg's shops for milk, bread and if we were lucky, "Iced Vovo biscuits" for morning tea. As we approached the shops Mum would call to me, "Lili, could you pop to the post office to see if there is any mail?" Off I would trot past the shops and down a narrow dirt path, past a hedge, turning left towards the post office.*
>
> *As a brash impatient four-year-old, I would make my way along the cobbled mossy brick path, past the geese and chook pen to the front door of the Horsley Park Post Office.*
>
> *I recollect clambering up the mossy, grime encrusted, redbrick stairs. Stretching up on tippy-toes to open the threadbare squeaky screen door I would bellow, in my well-rehearsed rowdiest voice, "Any mail for Brokensha?" I commanded to be heard, as only the very top of my head could just be seen over the post office counter. I waited patiently for someone to appear to serve me.*
>
> *As I waited a haunting feeling fell over me, as a soft flush of blue-green in the shape of an ornamental chimpanzee caught my eye when I fastened my stare on a collection of small creatures behind a glass window. Perched high out of the reach of children, suspended in time, individual ornaments, meticulously placed, with fixed eyes intently leering back at all who visit.*

I was often startled by the tall thin-framed man standing in the doorway of the kitchen leading into the post office. He would look down at me tenderly.

"Yes Lili, what can I do for you this morning?"

"Any mail for Brokensha?" I strained with all my four-year-old might. The weight of his gaze frequently drained me, making my little heart beat faster.

"I will just have a look, yes, look what we have here for your Mum."

He would then lean over the shiny well-worn wide wooden counter. My tiny hands stretched up, reaching into an unwavering grip. I would pluck the thin smooth folded paper from his long tapering fingers. Clutching the blue telegrams and white envelopes with the stamps of the queen's head, I would turn on my heels, never glancing back. Pushing the screen door open with one hand, stepping out into warm sunlight, I could always breathe away my jitters. Slam, goes the screen door, leaving my encounter with the tall thin-framed man behind.

Lilian's brother, Leonard, also remembers as a child going to the Horsley Park Post Office with his Mum. He remembered a lane leading to the post office door then up a couple of stairs to some kind of canopy. He recalled opening the creaking screen door and going in where a huge counter stood bearing a set of equally huge scales and old Commonwealth Bank money boxes. He remembers the pigeonholes for sorting the mail, but most of all the peculiar man behind the counter, who he was told to address as uncle.

The peculiar deputy postmaster in his post office set at its odd angle facing the Borg's, also faced his own yarded gaggle of geese. This rather bizarre placement of Mr Moult-Spiers' goose run was nothing short of astonishing as it appeared to be attached to the wall of Frank Borg's General Store with his massive taxidermied eagle. The neighbourhood was well and truly alarmingly feathered.

Lili says until she walked down the cobbled brick path to the squeaky door of the post office to pick up the mail, she had never heard such a sound as those hissing geese. No doubt both Mr Moult-Spiers and Mr Borg were well wired to all those sounds alerting them to possible custom … or discovery. From Lili's description the layout is further coloured:

The geese were to the left … the front yard to the private house of the post office with a high hedge was to the right … up two steps to the front screen door … which led into an open but small room that smelt of busy-ness. I was always captivated by the neatly positioned animal ornaments … a pale green monkey … a pig … a rooster … and a giraffe … all wanting so desperately to escape so I could play with them.

These ornamental creatures were the foundation members of the Moult-Spiers vast array of "collectables".

Horsley Park lacked some community essentials. The use of the hall for worship, or churches in other districts, was due to the youthfulness of the area – it could not afford an official place of worship.

There was no church for decades. A travelling Catholic priest performed baptisms and confirmations at people's homes and conducted services in the hall once a fortnight for his zealous congregation. In time, a portion of land on Horsley Drive was donated and a Catholic church was built in 1961 ... but not in time to save the free-loving postmaster.

Lili's recollection of the implied Horsley religious fervour stretches to the Anglican version:

For the "other" Christians of Horsley ... well ... we had Sunday School ... Sunday night Church ... Fellowship tea once a month where we brought a plate ... and Rally every Friday night for the young folk of Horsley Park ... Mr Morrison was the priest/pastor of this small congregation of "other" Christians ... and he would ... religiously ... pick up all the young folk from their front door in his white van ... so we could attend such weekly "get togethers" ... in the large hall across the road from the post office.

Behind the hall was the local sports ground where Lilian played soccer. Having the local hall with its practising devotees and all its community activities opposite the post office put the Moult-Spiers in prime position.

By 1968, every morning Frances, with her two younger children, aged around four and ten, would amble along the road towards the school. Frances was nearing fifty and their house ticked over like a finely oiled machine. It had to, there were secrets to be kept hidden in the tidy cupboards. Frances and Colin's seventeen-year-old daughter, Priscilla, looked on, believing it all.

Between their home and commodity outlets and on a slight gradient, stood the little school.

Prior to living in the rental property, Lilian says her parents had owned their own home in Horsley Park:

Mum and Dad owned their house on Horsley Road ... sold it in 1965 and moved all of us to South Africa in 1966 only to return to Australia the following year.

The Brokenshas were still living at Horsley Park when the Moult-Spiers began to grow restless. By the late 1960s, in an unusual move Ray purchased a property at Warwick in Queensland. But perhaps he was planning ahead? A few years later he purchased another at nearby Allora. This could not have been done lightly as both were a good ten-hour drive away. It appears they were purchased for the purpose of storing a collection of massive antique furniture from the Duke of Bedford's estate in England. Some people may have purchased a commercial storage facility for this purpose but not so the Moult-Spiers. By all reports these houses were crammed full of expensive old furniture and other collectors items.

Ray wrote to me in June 1980, listing some of the duke's former possessions:

And the antiques at WARWICK. Came from the DUKE of BEDFORD's estate. Carved oak side board, marble credenza. Queen Anne bed. Admiral sea chest. etc.

In another letter later in the 1980s, Raymond wrote that he had not been allowed to keep the antiques in their Horsley house anymore. This is possibly because there was no room left for the occupants. Troubled by what to do with them, he also sought to sell some of his rapidly growing collection, although which came first is difficult to determine. Between the selling and the buying Raymond began his business relationship with the Cronulla antique dealer. The shopfront seems to have been situated on Cronulla Street, which ran along the bay and the ferry dock. The owners lived across the water in Bundeena, on the edge of Royal National Park, and would catch the ferry to work each day. Mrs Antique Dealer had become an agent for the sale of Ray's more traditional artwork. In exchange Ray appeared to act as a sometime scout and buyer for their shop. Ray's involvement with Mrs Antique Dealer was to play out years later in a drama set against his children.

All in all, life was changing. Elma was now approaching sixty and the Moult-Spiers began considering a move for retirement. Perhaps not so in the case of Ray. Still in his late forties, he was planning his future career prospects in creative ways.

In July 1970, Ray Moult-Spiers, aged fifty, resigned as deputy postmaster of Horsley Park and he and Elma went to live in North Parramatta. Perhaps Elma or even Ray received some kind of inheritance, because Ray began investigating purchasing a property in Fiji before deciding an island closer to Australia might be the better option. With their stuff stashed between Allora and Warwick, they tried a few locations.

Before long they discovered the charm of an island just off Brisbane. With Elma's love of the sea and the discovery of North Stradbroke Island, they soon purchased a holiday shack there, then another and another, and more still.

Big old Buick cars were added to the collectables while passports were stamped over and over with trip after trip to the exotic "Far East".

The Brokensha family, too, began to explore other possibilities. They even went to live in the Moult-Spiers' Allora house for a year, although it was a squeeze with all the oversized furnishings. Leonard was about sixteen then, and had to navigate his way through this strange antique world to get out the door and head to school in Allora.

The 1970s certainly produced a restlessness with both the Brokenshas and the Moult-Spiers shifting feet. But the children still did not know their true heritage as they bobbed around and past the unusual possessions belonging to Mr Moult-Spiers.

Trees in Horsley Park

OPPOSITE
Elma & Ray 1971

YOU MUST HAVE STUDIED MY FAVOURITE ARTIST
ROBERT RAUSCHENBURG. HUGE. BLOODY GREAT
ORCHIDS BUT MOSTLY FOUND THINGS. LIKE
BRUSHED CAR BODIES. FRIDGES. PEOPLE. DEAD
GOATS etc. he is an intimate of Peggy Guggenhiem
of gallery fame, NOO YORK. WHERE BLUE POLES
CAME FROM. SHE RECENTLY OFFERED TO BUY
THEM BACK FOR 45 MILLION. WE SHOULD ACCEPT.
I OFFERED A REPLACEMENT FOR A MERE 2 MILLION
CALLED RED SAILS IN THE MORNING. NO GO. SORRY
MATE. GET TO THE END OF THE QUE? LINE ...

Raymond Moult-Spiers, 1991

30

The artist and the island

Ray's passion for collectables and big old American cars grew. He set up a studio haven on Stradbroke Island and carried on working, entering prizes and selling his work through various art galleries in Sydney. In 1972 he held a solo show at the Penthouse Gallery in Parramatta.

The world of Raymond Moult-Spiers' creativity had arrived on Stradbroke in the early 1970s. It came in bits and pieces, slowly building to the crescendo called his studio. Much like a painting is made, so his island studio was made with layer upon layer. At first, he managed his island life like a getaway, an escape to a haven shack in a fishing village.

With Elma's love of the sea it was decided to make this place their home. They often left their country estate in Warwick, packed to the rafters with antiques, and went to live the life of islanders.

Raymond and I were still unknown to one another in 1970, but it appeared to be a time of change and adjustment for us both. At about the time Raymond moved to the island, I had begun art school in Perth. I was dressed by my mother in a twin set and a pleated navy-blue crimplene skirt, completely the wrong fit. But at seventeen and a shy country girl, there was no way I was able to look like an art student that first day. By the end of the week, I had realised self-expression started with your wardrobe. After that I realised my grandmother's packed lunch was also the wrong look. I opted instead for a can of Tab (the first diet Coke), and then after a time added a cigarette to my lunch. With hunger ever present, that lasted as long as it could, until I discovered the Claremont shopping precinct at the top of the park and across Stirling Highway. With funds an ever-present problem, that too lasted as long as it could.

By 1974, I was dressed in long skirts I had made from old flags found at a rubbish tip. I had a perpetual tobacco stain on my middle finger, oil paint under my nails, in my hair and always on my clothes, and had been through a flotilla of

FRAGMENTS OF THE SKY

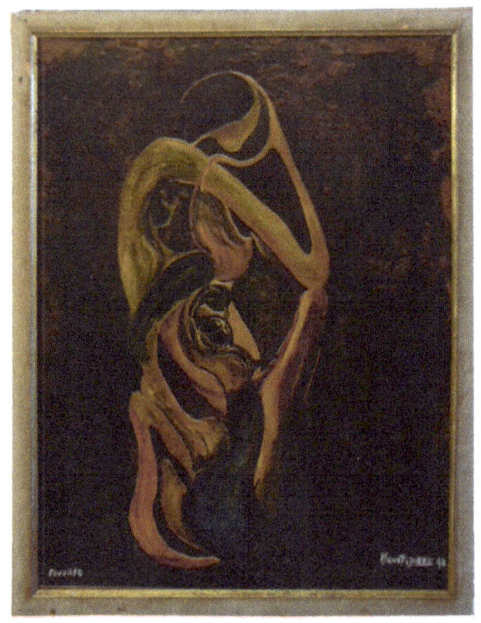

LEFT Ray Moult-Spiers, *Reverie*, 1972, oil and wax on board, 56x45cm. Private collection QLD.

BELOW Ray Moult-Spiers, *Tobacco plantation*, oil on board, 39.5x29.5cm, 1953. Private Collection, UK. The date is a conundrum and may point to numerous other works yet to be discovered done in this style since the 1950s. The current UK owner recalls and verifies the date, "the painting was a (belated) wedding present to my parents who married in 1950."

ABOVE. Ray Moult-Spiers, *Campbell House Amity Point*, c. 1973, oil on board, 65x90cm. North Stradbroke Museum Collection, QLD.

RIGHT Ray Moult-Spiers, *Trees,* oil on board, 69.5x55cm, c. 1970. Private collection, UK.

FRAGMENTS OF THE SKY

ABOVE Ray Moult-Spiers, *The Pool*, c. 1990, size, title & medium unknown. Location unknown.

LEFT Ray Moult-Spiers, *Blue Lagoon*, c. 1973, oil on board, 100x60cm. North Stradbroke Museum Collection, QLD.

boyfriends ... most of whom were dreadful mistakes. But I had graduated from art school and had started a couple of part-time lecturing jobs, one in adult education and one at TAFE lecturing on the history of costume in fashion design.

Raymond, on the other hand, was in a shiny sharkskin suit, being photographed chatting with the then prime minister, Gough Whitlam, who was to open the art exhibition Raymond was showing in. Raymond arrived at the exhibition in his 1950s Buick. Curiously Raymond's association with Whitlam was renewed in the 1980s, when he was invited on board Whitlam's boat on Sydney Harbour (this time sporting his crocodile-skin boots).

Raymond and Elma's purchasing of real estate continued, with a collection now of eight holiday properties on the island (some freehold), along with their country houses in Warwick and Allora. Raymond's purchase of more American cars seemed to be headed towards owning a fleet of them. Their trips to Asia throughout the 1970s were so frequent one cannot help but wonder if they were perhaps buying collectables for the antique business in Cronulla.

Lili related her 1980s experience of arriving at the island studio as always inducing piercing screams from his relocated gaggle of geese. My imagination heard it like car horns tooting at a country football match, announcing a visitor like a precious goal. She said that standing on the cobbled path at the edge of Ray's property frequently led her to gaze down at the crazy paving. This further indicated to me his ongoing tendency to collage, demonstrating his urge to reconnect the broken pieces of his puzzle-board life, but never completing the task. His lifelong attempt to manage chaos.

Lili described the path as splitting a course between the shrieking geese on the left and the silent sheds on the right. It appears the tangled garden fringing the structures attempted to warn of the idiosyncratic occupant. The house, at the path's end, was covered in an applique of found objects. Lili discovered it was not unusual for him to be at the door holding a live rabbit, illegal vermin on the island. However, once inside, the rabbit would be put into a cage under the kitchen sink and covered with a curtain.

She recounted the home as a few small rooms, all littered with strategically layered keepsakes hiding oversized furniture. Ray apparently slept in the second room but its entrance was set like a booby trap, with a huge block of timber teetering from the slightly ajar door. Should anyone have made the mistake of pushing the door open, even slightly, they would have found themselves, or at the very least their toe, crushed by this massive piece of timber!

It all invited the question as to what exactly had happened to this man that he needed his sleeping quarters protected.

From Lili's description I could see the house as a wonderland of half-done projects, but I am fooled by the mention of white goods scattered about the yard. One would be wrong to presume its occupant was only interested in repairing these white goods. Casting my imaginative eye about, his interest in art always rushed forward, only to be pipped at the post by the collectables and antiques. Plants and wildlife would then clamber for position amid antisocial slogans and pictures of UFOs.

Lili commented that kept newspapers attempted to meet the ceiling in places, perhaps guarding his keen interest in not-so-current affairs and politics.

Raymond Moult-Spiers, c. 1973, with then Prime Minister Gough Whitlam. The third person in the photograph is unknown. Family collection.

ABOVE Ray Moult-Spiers, *Bird and Goat*, c. 1973, oil on board, 35x82cm. Family collection.

LEFT Ray Moult-Spiers, *Kapoc Tree*, oil on cardboard with printed text showing through, 21x14cm, c. 1985. Private collection, WA. On the back is the text, "Blessed are the young, for they shall inherit the national debt." Herbert Hoover.

BELOW Ray Moult-Spiers, *Creation*, c. 1985, oil on board, 39x97cm. Private collection, QLD.

FRAGMENTS OF THE SKY

LEFT Ray Moult-Spiers, *Collaged*, c. 1975, mixed materials on board, approx. 75x55cm. Location unknown.

ABOVE Ray Moult-Spiers, *Totem*, polymer on shiny card, 21x15cm, c. 1980. Private Collection, WA.

She told me he buried money in the garden, no doubt hoping for the ever-ellusive money tree to sprout.

Lili described the back yard as spilling out into the bush and down to the swamp, where a massive London double-decker bus stood. My mind mistakenly saw it as a monster from the everglades that, not unlike Dr Who's Tardis, appeared to have landed at a random intergalactic location. But, instead of a police box full of deceptive space, the bus was apparently packed tight with more valued objects.

Among this, but on the outer edge, was his studio. An arbour led the way in. It was constructed from bush poles and scarcely supported the vine growing on it and the entwined resident carpet snake. The slabs under it were, more often than not, covered in a mat of snake skin and leaves. The studio glass door exposed the contents. My artist's imagination did the rest. I saw colour with palettes and brushes lying in wait where they were left, surrounded by every type of tube, tub and tin of paint available. This was where art was made, where his collages were constructed onto misshapen boards and paint took the eye into a deeper dimension. Paintings were done on anything that would support application. Easels gathered and stood firm, holding these images up. Enthusiasm was apparent, the creativity showing in surges. The walls were reinforced by shelves of all kinds. These were filled with a range of objects, apparatus and nature yields, all shelved but ready for their moment, the possibility of being selected and dropped into a pool of wet paint great. Set about him in the tiered auditorium, the clutter was his audience, his witness to his acts of artistry and musings.

In spite of his New South Wales press coverage slowing down, work in his studio did not. Sadly, with Elma's death in 1977, Raymond was left to gradually reinvent himself, slowly but surely becoming a recluse. His island neighbours say his paintings were sometimes given or exchanged for goods. Most recipients were uncertain what to do with them.

At this time Raymond Moult-Spiers' passion for collages had bloomed. As explained, his studio started to fill with all kinds of things he had found. Creating collages was not a "scissors, glue and magazine cuttings" experience for him. He would embed crazy stuff and all manner of things directly into thick house paint applied to miscellaneous surfaces. These works spoke to him in a language he understood. His war experiences of scrounging during his POW days proved invaluable in the manufacture of this new work, produced in his Stradbroke Island studio. The collages began as he made his way along his crazy and sometimes shattered life path. Perhaps he was attempting to piece it all together. His creative acts on random assorted surfaces mapped progress. His letters to me in the 1980s demonstrated his response to touring shows and his personal activities:

RENOIR IS COMING FLOWERS ARE ALL THE GO AFTER VINCENT TWAS SUNFLOWERS NOW IT IS IRIS IN THE SNOW BULLDUST

And:

26 Aug 1988
Dear Julie, hope all is well with you and your ART IS FLOURISHING. I GET Sydney Exhibition in September 30 paintings – BIG 3' x 4' BIG MONEY Ha Ha?

I did not find any evidence of this September exhibition in Sydney. In 1992, Raymond sent me this description of his work:

> UNABLE TO GET BOOKS. ART ON TAPIES TAMAYO, YVES TANGUY ZAO-WOU-KI etc. MIRO BUT DEFINITELY NOT BETTE MIDLER OR ELKE SOMMER. I USE COLOUR TO PAINT ENCHANTED FOREST AND YOU KNOW IT IS A FOREST, BUT NO TREES. ATMOSPHERIC PAINTING I CALLS IT. LET THE COLOUR SPEAK LOUDER THAN TREES. AND NO ONE TO TELL ME IT'S TIME FOR DINNER.

Driving his American cars on Stradbroke set him apart but then the "druggies" came to the island in the 1980s, when he was occasionally robbed and beaten. These events began to reshape his reasons for doing things. Electrical devices, long since deceased, were kept as decoys all around the garden. Perhaps this smorgasbord of items, there for the taking, was set like a distraction, an offering to a would-be robber. A TV, like a useless plastic duck on a pond, decoys both, attracting more of the same. He began to litter the yard with his decoy white goods. But the most stunning of his decisions was when he took to wearing a pair of colt revolvers, stating in his letters that he had converted his wealth to gold, which he now wore in a money belt.

Raymond maintained his expansive, ever-increasing eclectic creative interests all the rest of his days on Stradbroke. His studio a treasury, a potpourri, a compendium of how his mind worked. A place of excitement and wonderment, of ideas yet to be realised, right up until his untimely and mysterious death. Although hidden from the Queensland art world, his mark was made. Ray was part of the artistic foundation constructing an Australian identity through its art. He sustained a freedom of expression by keeping his own individualism alive, spreading it like a contagion wherever he went.

None of his works was ever mistaken for a masterpiece, but he was prepared to be involved in waking up a nation to its own creative potential.

Ray's contribution to the arts was recognised by the National Gallery of Australia when they acknowledged his passing in 1995, with a small obituary indicating Raymond Moult-Spiers played a role in the nation's art world and that his involvement was valued.

THE ARTIST AND THE ISLAND

OPPOSITE Ray Moult-Spiers, *Boudin in Tourville*, c. 1980, paint on particle board, 22x9cm. Private collection, WA

ABOVE Ray Moult-Spiers, *Dreamtime*, c. 1990, oil and polymer paint on card, 26.5x18.5cm. Private collection WA. The painting has been done on the back of cat food packaging.

BELOW Ray Moult-Spiers, *Driftwood*, polymer on card, 26x18.5cm, c. 1980. Private collection WA.

THE ARTIST AND THE ISLAND

OPPOSITE Ray Moult-Spiers, *Avalanche*, c. 1980, paint on paper, approx. 21x14cm. Private collection, WA.

ABOVE Ray Moult-Spiers, *Thirty Knots*, oil on paper, 21x14cm, c. 1968. Private collection, QLD.

BELOW Ray Moult-Spiers, *Kakadu*, polymer paint on board, 97x39cm, c. 1990. Private collection, QLD.

FRAGMENTS OF THE SKY

ABOVE Ray Moult-Spiers, *Blue Moon Three Pagoda Pass*, 1994, polymer on paper, 27.5x23.5cm. Private collection, QLD.

OPPOSITE. Ray Moult-Spiers preparing for an art exhibition, 1994.

PLEASE

I WOULD NOT INTRUDE BE RUDE
OR ENCROACH UPON YOUR SOLITUDE.
JUST SIT AND WAIT BY YONDER GATE
AND IGNORE THE RAUCOUS MULTITUDE.
I WOULD ONLY STAND AND STARE

AT THAT LONE FIGURE ON THE STAIR
THINKING OF A TIME WHEN I
FELT NO BIGGER THAN A FLY
COS I WAS LONELY ALL THE TIME.
SING QUITE SOFTLY AND MAKE UP RHYME.
WITH FAMILY GONE THE CUPBOARD BARE
TWAS AWFUL COLD UP THERE

SO, I MADE MY OWN SMALL CELL
WHICH NO ONE ELSE COULD QUITE DISPEL.
SO, IF I SHOW A DIFFERENT FACE
IT'S NO REPLACEMENT OR DISGRACE.
TIS JUST A WAY OF HIDING ME
FROM THAT CRUEL WORLD
THAT TORTURES THEE
YOU KNOW I CANNOT HIDE FROM YOU
WHO KNOWS THE DIFFERENT
BLENDS OF DEW
FOR ONLY YOU WILL SEE MY FACE
THE ONE THE OTHERS HAVE NO TRACE
SO, THINK ME NOT OF DUBIOUS SELF.
THERE IS NO ROOM LEFT ON THE SHELF.
YOU ARE ALL I HAVE TO SHARE
SO GRATEFUL THAT YOU ARE THERE
YOUR VOICE YOUR SOUND
BE MINE TO KEEP
FOR THERE'S MILES TO GO BEFORE I SLEEP
THE PRODIGAL [FATHER]

Raymond Moult-Spiers, 1989

31
The prodigal father

The story of the man on the island still holds many veiled secrets, but when I finally made contact with Lili for the first time in 2019, the lights came on about his life around her in the late 1980s and early 1990s.

Lili told me it all began with Frances's sudden insistence that she wanted to holiday on Stradbroke Island with her daughter and grandchildren. Initially no one other than Frances and Ray knew why. All that Lili knew was that Ray and his deceased wife Elma were long-time family friends of her parents.

These visits to Ray by the family – his family – in the late 1980s were very mysterious to Lili. Her mother and Ray were still maintaining their secret. It seems Frances initially took it on herself to re-acquaint Ray with their offspring and then their grandchildren. She did this without acknowledging to Lili or Lili's children this was the reason for the visits to Stradbroke Island.

Lili described meeting up with Ray on Stradbroke after having very little to do with him for some twenty-six years. She still believed he was her parents' friend and it never occurred to her he was her biological father, although she had noticed her brother looked more like Ray than the man they called Dad.

Lili's description of the first of many trips to Stradbroke Island captured the experience. Like all island visitors they had to first drive their car onto the vehicle barge to be ferried across and unloaded at the island dock, where Ray waited.

Lili recalled her first sighting of him from the ferry, saying he was "a slim tall man with unmistakably hastily combed white hair who rested against his Cadillac with a smile beaming larger than life". She recounted Ray's smile "as always widening as we pulled up alongside his huge vehicle. 'Follow me,' he would urge, before he entered his Cadillac head first through the driver's side window!" Lili implied he was very flexible, describing him as "swiveling his lanky body until he would position himself finally, sitting erect facing the steering wheel".

Their experience of following him always filled them all with a "mishmash of excitable giggles and tummy butterflies", she said. "I can only describe our visits as days of a circus carnival. Each moment filled with outrageous disbelief."

Ray's driving style was reckless to say the least. Lili reported his hell-raising technique of suddenly taking a sharp left: "Turning off at the intersection was a technique Ray seemed skilled at. No indicators, no slowing down, just a sudden swerve of his oversized car."

When they first arrived at his studio home Lili's account brings to mind a kind of compound that, according to her, was "cloaked in bamboo on the southern side of the property hiding the geese and chook pen". But her description of the dilapidated structure that served as a carport says a great deal more about Ray and his lifestyle.

> This ramshackle construct of rusting corrugated iron featured a central large telegraph pole cut in half, balancing on a seriously distorted lean and propping up the uninhabitable piece of architecture. An old fridge was perched on the passenger's side and appeared to be supporting one portion of the carport. The fit was so snug for the Cadillac that all three doors could only slightly open (the driver's door never opened), while a Humber took pride of place on the other side. Shiny and black in colour with white wall tyres, it slid meticulously under the iron sheeting. Head room only. I always looked on with disbelief.

On this first visit Ray apparently called out, "Don't move a muscle," as a red-bellied black snake removed itself from under the fridge. Lili says Ray was chuckling when he said, "We must have startled it." Lili reported the snake then slid "intuitively across the dry dusty road into the wetlands of paperbark trees adjacent". Her description of his instructions continued with, "Coast is clear, make a move for it, I'll put the kettle on. Just make your way up the path, oh, by the way watch your step as you come up the back stairs as one of them is broken."

Lili further characterised Ray: "A Canadian man, with a slither of swagger attached to his stride, who often wore straight-legged blue jeans, held up with a well-worn leather belt attached to a silver buckle with an American eagle coin secured in the centre, topped with an open-necked shirt. His crocodile boots completed the tall thin frame."

She said that on their first visit she saw him looking on tenderly, admiring his visitors walking up the path made of cobbled mossy bricks. Lili's account tells of her daughters' reactions having gotten over the broken step:

> Larisa (aged ten) and Lee (aged thirteen) suddenly came to a grinding halt in front of me, their gaze focused on an odd screen door consisting of a large unframed painting of two kangaroos. This painting seemed to be strapped to the doorframe with what looked like shredded decaying pieces of cloth. This substitute for a screen was seemingly to keep the flies out.

They found Frances already seated at the kitchen table, with her red handbag placed neatly beside her. Lili explained:

> We tentatively stepped inside where the smell of small rodents and old wares permeated the

air until the three of us were overwhelmed. We precariously filed into the kitchen where we simultaneously launched backwards with a full whiff of the odour, the girls exclaiming "What's that smell?" In scanning the kitchen, we found ourselves shrouded with an eclectic ornamentation of stuff. An accumulation of antiquated, old wares enmeshed with inexpensive clutter. The kitchen seemed to be the place where the exclusive distinction of eloquence met with worthless adaptations. Where the extraordinary uniqueness, which cost a pretty penny, brushed up against the dirt-cheap watered-down versions. Where dried rare frogs, caught in the paperbark swamp across the road, were spray-painted with gold paint and their withered remains fossilized onto exorbitant priceless bone china vases.

Lili's story further evoked the image of Ray frantically pushing a clumsy pile of art books to one side of the table, while dusting a chair with the back of his hand and offering "Tea, all round, China Black or Russian Caravan?" Lili said Lee's focus zeroed in on a classic, rare piece of Royal Doulton crockery when she asked if she might have her tea in that cup, pointing to the shelf above the stove, where the Royal Doulton cup and saucer sat suspended in a space, dejected and undusted until that moment! Ray's demeanor changed almost immediately appearing opposed to the idea and scoffing offhandedly, "That's a bit bold of you."

But, according to Lili, he stretched up and carefully took down the cup and saucer from the rickety wooden shelf, and placed both, ever so delicately on the table for safekeeping. At that very moment his cat jumped up on the table and Ray hastily lunged at it, intent on scooping it up and discarding it out the door. The cat, however, with claws outstretched, clipped the Royal Doulton cup. And smash! The room turned coldly silent. "Bloody cat" was heard from Ray, who took no responsibility for his part. Frances then apparently jumped to her feet and offered to clean it up, asking where his dustpan and brush were. "No such thing here," chirped Ray with a smile. Frances then found a piece of cardboard, bent it and, using an old hairbrush, swept the broken pieces off the kitchen floor. Lili noted that all the while Ray appeared to enjoy the fussing.

But Lili's next description holds a glimpse into their secret. "I remember Ray reached to help my mother up and their eyes fastened. Ray held her while exchanging a fleeting loving glance. In that instant I saw a sensitivity towards each other."

That moment gone, Lee and Ray apparently continued their search for the perfect cup and saucer in another room, finally deciding on a retro set, but instead of making tea Ray changed direction and Lili's version of the story goes on with Ray's next announcement:

"What if we skip tea here and go for a drive to Point Lookout for coffee?"

Lili reported that "his way of influencing our decision further was by grabbing his car keys off the cluttered surface of the table, calling out, 'Any takers? We can all fit in the Cadillac.'"

Lili noted that her mother, clasping her handbag, was exhilarated by this and had sprung into action.

Lili says they were all mesmerised in their fascination of Ray's potency to influence. Lee immediately saw the joy ride as a "lookout Hollywood" opportunity and they were off.

The story continued. The motor of the Cadillac was humming on their arrival at the carport. Ray

Ray in the kitchen, his rabbits hidden behind the curtain, c. 1990, photographer unknown.

then reversed abruptly and with no time to spare had hopped out and opened his arms to usher them into the back seat.

Lili described him as "seamlessly manoeuvering rapidly around to the other back passenger door, slipping and stepping, as if in a silent dance".

Then he called "All in" while bumping shut the car door with his hip. With agility, he dived headfirst into the driver's seat and swivelled effortlessly to face the front ... when Larisa piped up from the back, "What, no seatbelts?"

Lili says Ray glanced around the car, even looking under the front seat while still driving and saying they were here somewhere, then laughed at his own joke before taking a sharp left in his usual unconventional style.

It was an uncomfortable drive full of dust, swerves, jerks and sudden breakneck speed, all to the sound of old Fats Waller songs as they whizzed past glimpses of Amity Point. They finally arrived at the lookout, where he announced, while staring at Lili in the rear-vision mirror, "This is where I want you to throw my ashes when I die."

She was dumbfounded at this request but even more bewildered by it being directed at her.

Evidently, the Cadillac came to a sudden halt in the carpark and they were directed to get out. From here they wandered down to the point, along the way taking a moment on Norm's bench. This is where Lili's love of watching the dolphins skimming through the waves as fish hurtled high in the air, avoiding being eaten, first occurred. That and the stunning views, including the effortless misty movements of the whales and their enchanting songs, which became more frequent and closer to the point.

With everyone back in the car, Ray then headed to the Beach Hotel for lunch on the terrace overlooking the ocean. The Beach Hotel sat high on a piece of land that suddenly dropped away down to the sea. A fish-and-chip lunch was consumed and Lili's tale continued when they headed back to the carpark. Apparently, Ray hopped into the Cadillac in his usual unconventional fashion and started the engine – rrr, rrr, rrr – it backfired. Lil says the Cadillac initially rolled across the carpark, backwards, in the very direction of the drop-off to the beach. Ray turned the key again – rrr, rrr – the Cadillac continued to inch closer and closer to the drop-off each time he attempted to start the motor. Lili observed that the people enjoying their lunch had begun to look up, as others stood up, staring in disbelief. Perhaps all were aghast at the possibility of this huge car toppling rear end first, down the embankment.

Lili professes Lee and Larisa began to die inside with embarrassment at the spectacle, hiding their blushing faces from the gathering crowd on the deck. Then Ray shouted, "Hop in as soon as she starts. I don't want to stop her just on the slim chance she doesn't fire again."

Lili's immediate thought was "No way am I getting in the car."

With all of them ready to crawl under a rock, Ray cranked the old girl over again and it finally belched and bellowed white smoke from the tail pipe as it roared to life. The breeze from the ocean gently pushed the blanket of fumes towards the pub, leaving the lunchtime crowd drenched in a cloud of fog. But, added to that, Ray planted it. The Cadillac lurched forward with back wheels screeching. The smoking tyres adding a thick blue to the canopy of white exhaust, all of which was headed towards the guests.

Ray called out, "Jump in. I'll keep the revs up." Lili affirmed they all piled in like lost puppies, clambering for a space on the long back bench seat. Then, to the sound of screeching tyres and the clapping and whistling crowd, they were off like the start of a drag race. Lee gave voice to the moment while punching the air: "Nailed it."

The rest of the holiday was summed up by Lili in this nonsense statement: "Ray's 'horsing around' antics enticed and enchanted us all. Each day the topsy-turvy fun tumbled involuntarily into the next, meshing with moments overflowing with convulsive humour, hunches of spontaneity and dashes of tame idiocy."

That was Lili's introduction to the man on the island.

As she explained, the frequency of their trips to the island increased and so her stories began to eclipse my own abstract experience of Ray through his letters, photographs and small paintings slipped inside envelopes. His news had begun to tentatively mention his children, something from which he had previously excluded me.

With the story of his new crocodile boots and his visit to Sydney, where Lili was living in late 1989, Raymond's true role as her biological father was uncovered. Lili had "joined all the dots" and boldly signalled her suspicions, allowing him the opportunity to address the issue directly with her in his way.

Once the situation was acknowledged, Lili's newly formed father–daughter relationship was immediately more complex and demanding. For Lili, his outpouring of poetry slipped into his constant letters was more than she could respond to. With an already busy family and work life she had no time to write letters. At times it was almost too much. She instead made a weekly phone call, time permitting.

Further to this, Lili added that as the increase in trips to the island followed so did Ray's hypnotising charm. Some of their memories around Ray's back yard alone took some comprehension and entailed exploring his British double-decker bus.

A 1966 Routemaster, the double-decker was apparently adapted into a den of iniquity, with adornments of lace, silk and satin drapery and bed accessories, which allured unsuspecting guests of the female kind into its seduction.

Ray's back yard begged explanation as it included a TV set along with other odd items. He explained his fear of things being stolen so he considered this the most obvious deterrent.

With every arrival came the inevitable departure says Lili. "The daily grind would always call us back. Crunching, ear piercing, reverberating metal scrapes and scratches of the Straddie Ferry which widened the gap as the tug pulled away distorting Ray's broad smile. Ray, the 'islander', would begin to evaporate into the sunset. I could see a place inside him that only we could fill. He always lingered by the edge, watching, waving, stalling his invading feelings of loneliness, before surrendering to his place of solace."

With this need understood, Ray and his newfound family always honoured his war days by marching in the Anzac Day parades down the street from the Little Ships Club on Stradbroke. Above all else, Ray's resilience consistently showed in his creative spirit. However, in April 1995, Anzac Day was more intense than most, with the echoes of World War Two swirling around more persistently than before, as fifty years since its conclusion was commemorated. That same year, war biographer

Ron Mumford noted in his research that he was concerned for Raymond's mental health, while my research revealed some of Stradbroke's inhabitants had begun to see Raymond as a menace (their words). According to them he had been randomly firing his Colts, so the police sensibly confiscated his guns, perhaps leaving him vulnerable.

His body was found some time in July of 1995. According to locals, the island's big flesh-eating monitor lizards had found him first. Reported too was that he had been robbed. Officially it was declared he had passed away from a heart attack. The robbery was left unsolved as it seems no further investigation took place. To the distant onlooker, none of these indications bring a satisfactory conclusion as to his end.

Meanwhile, days (or perhaps weeks) after his death a phone call was made to his much-loved daughter. Lili relayed the story of the late-evening call to her home on the Sunshine Coast. Lee and her three children were staying with her at the time. Lee had just put her children to bed when the phone rang. She rushed to answer it before it woke her babies.

"Hello," she whispered in a dubious tone.

"Hello," a male voice replied. "Is this Lili?"

"No, I am her daughter, Lee. May I ask who is calling?"

Lee reported that a cold spontaneous shiver had already stirred up the back of her neck.

"Is she there?" requested the person on the line.

Lee apparently watched the goosepimples rising on her skin before turning to her mother, who was sitting at the kitchen table, within hearing distance of the phone. She could hear the other person's voice and their request to talk to her. But, not wanting to talk to anyone at that time of night, Lili had held her hand up and shaken her head.

"No, she's not here. Can I take a message or have her call you back?"

"Yes, if you could, please let her know I have some sad news. Ray has passed away."

"I will tell Mum," she replied slowly, her voice quivering with the sound of sorrow and shock. "I missed your name."

"Oh, it's Allen. I'm a friend of Ray's. Your mum may remember me – we have met – and so so sorry to bring this news to you this late at night."

Lili says Lee replaced the receiver without saying goodbye.

And with numbness consuming each word spoken repeated, "Ray has passed."

Lili experienced a deafening sound echo through her as her thoughts twirled about with "Never again will I see Ray, never again will I hear Ray, never again will I laugh with Ray", until the night shrouded his death in its cloak of darkness.

The very next morning they made their way to Stradbroke in a silent trance. Glimpses of Ray's mad-hatter days collided with the stabbing sorrow of dormant memories, all the while wrestling with thoughts of Ray being alone in his last moments, before surrendering his life forever.

After much ado and his long-ago bidding adhered to, he was cremated and, in a mark of respect, his friends from the First Nations Quandamooka people stood across the Point Lookout rocks, which they had covered with flowers. They stood high above Lili, who was at the interface where vegetation met the water's edge. Everyone faced the ocean while Lili fulfilled his rear-vision mirror request. At the very moment she released his ashes, a curl of wind took the soft powder, unfurling it back over her and the island.

Raymond's Sky

... We will stand alone against the final sky
Staring at the vista with a piercing eye ...

Raymond Moult-Spiers
date unknown

EPILOGUE
The Spirit

In 1995, when Raymond's body was discovered on the island long after his death, an estimate as to the time and date of his passing was made, with mention of a robbery, but no mention of how much investigation was carried out.

Beginning my own investigation in 2015, from my circular island, the papasan in the middle of my living area, I embraced Raymond's story and began to research and write. The dimensions opened up around me as the alchemy began.

Fortunately for me, and mixed into all this alchemy, was my cousin Anne. We two, the eldest of our Western Australian clans, joined forces to seek understanding of how Raymond fitted. Anne had names and dates in files begging to be understood and I had Raymond's letters, not to mention Raymond on my shoulder. In 2019, Lili, too, was on board. We three in cahoots began to piece the story together.

That year his larger-than-life personality invigorated me while the rest of my life force was mending my broken bones. I found energy where there was none. Was this synchronicity, defined by Carl Jung as "a meaningful coincidence of outer and inner events that are not causally related"?

As we went, the foundation of collected facts began to firm up and I was able to write the family's early history. Once we had the "bones" sorted, the urge to share the information with all of Raymond's bloodline was great. I found a Moult descendant in the UK who had been working on the Moult family tree for many years. I wrote to him and was intrigued to find he, too, was involved in the arts, working as an art historian and librarian in London. Antony, our newly discovered relative, was pleased with our contact as he had been unable to trace the families of Ann Moult and her brother John Thomas Moult. There was no doubt Antony was a descendant from the Moult lineage, and even more astounding (alongside both Raymond and myself referencing Native American culture) was that he was married to a Native American.

Timing is everything, so they say, and timing flipped into action as my initial reluctance to contact Lili began to inexplicably shift.

Back in early 2019, I did not know Lili at all, but she was my linchpin and I knew much rested on knowing her. Her brother was not forthcoming about her, although he communicated freely about his own experience with his birth father. Over the years I had thought of Lili many times and I had believed the feeling I got back. It felt like or signified a kind of armouring around her energy; consequently I had kept my distance. I had no idea how or if she would respond. Was she similar to Ray? Would she understand my modus operandi?

I wanted to give Lili time to prepare but there appeared to be a kind of "divine timing" – things were falling into place at speed. It turned out Lili had retired from a stressful position in child protection the week before I contacted her and, if I had tried any sooner, she said she would not have responded to me.

When I pressed send on my introductory text to her, on 5 April, unbeknown to me the very thing that caught her attention was the time it arrived – 5.55 pm. Ray's number-watching had spilled over into her consciousness. The number five was one of Ray's constants and fifty-five was the street number of three of Ray's houses. A convincing and potent sign indeed. She responded to my text straight away.

Later I realised the divine synchronicity aspect. Prior to calling Lili on 5 April, I had been frantically searching the internet for any information about her grandmother, Elizabeth Keogh. In doing so I had "inadvertently" stumbled across an image of Elizabeth with her baby, John Luke, in a group photograph at her cousin's wedding in 1914. I felt enormous empathy for this woman. After my initial communication with Lili, which incomprehensibly began on Elizabeth's birthdate and concluded on her death date on 14 April, I was convinced Elizabeth was able to somehow influence us. I imagined synchronicity had spiritous portals through which things like anniversaries could generate enough energy to implant earthly opportunities.

Our connection was made and so Lili and I began to spill and share the information we had gathered and held dear for so long.

On 26 May I emailed Penelope (Raymond's niece) in the UK, letting her know I had made contact with both of Raymond's Australian children. I was also able to tell her that his will was mysteriously changed three months after he had consolidated it to leave everything to these two offspring. In the end, however, his children did not inherit any of his estate. The antique dealer and gallery operator from Sydney did.

I sent Penelope the draft of the researched Moult-Spiers family history and later also sent through some photographs Lili had sent to me to identify. Penelope responded, helping us learn who they were. She said she found the history very interesting and corrected a couple of Raymond's misleading descriptions of her and her father. Curiously, Penelope, like her father, and indeed Lili, had worked in the care of children.

As I had sent both Lili and Penelope what Anne and I had stitched together about their lineage, and both had responded with interest, I was surprised when Penelope's last email implied that she had no more family information to offer saying she "had been in the dark all these years". She effectively stated she was unable to answer any more of my questions and stopped communicating. All my quizzing about the whereabouts of her father in the 1990s went unanswered. I wanted to know if he had an antique shop in North Arm, Canada (as Raymond claimed to have had shares in this business with his brother). Did she know anything about Raymond's Canadian accent? Other questions about her grandfather, John Thomas Moult-Spiers, and Minnesota simply could not be answered. Penelope had cut herself free and drifted away from us again.

In a curious link to Minnesota found among Raymond's paperwork was a document describing shares in Minnesota Mining and Manufacturing, a company that started with making sandpaper in the 1900s and advanced to abrasives, adhesive tapes and so on in the 1950s. Why did Raymond have this document? Could it be linked back to the man called John T. Spiers and his wife, Elizabeth, who were living in Minnesota until the 1950s? Was this anything to do with Raymond's father, or was it sheer coincidence?

Lili, on the other hand, was struck by the similarity of the families' life paths. Having now learned about her ancestors, Lili noted her two granddaughters had taken on similar careers to those of her great-aunts back in the early 1900s. The aunts were in the bespoke fashion industry as Court tailoresses in London. Lili's granddaughters also worked in the bespoke fashion industry but in Melbourne, where they were charged with dressing female ministers of parliament and the like. Lili even noticed that another of her young granddaughters had uncannily been given the same names as two of Lili's great-aunts, Eva and Grace, and that Eva Grace's birthday was the same as another of her great-aunts, my grandmother, Annie.

Lili enthusiastically suggested coming to Queensland but I was still far too broken and in too much pain to consider travel for a few more months yet.

On 25 July (unbeknown to me at the time, the date Raymond was thought to have died), I worked out the best travel dates using divining, or so I thought. I contacted cousins Anne and Lili with my suggestions. All agreed on the dates so we booked our flights the next day, unwittingly to arrive on Lili's birthday, one month later.

When my text of travel dates appeared, Lili says that at that precise moment she was talking about what she might like to do on her birthday, and so it was decided she would meet her kin for the first time.

Curiously, a century before, in 1919, Ann Moult left for Australia, thus separating from her Moult family of origin in the UK. In 1920, the year Raymond was born, she was followed by her grown children and their spouses, so that all her immediate family were now living in Western Australia.

Now, we three having reached out and touched each other with curiosity, our kinship was reestablished across the wide expanse of a foreign land called Australia.

Anne and I flew to the Sunshine Coast, arriving on Lili's birthday. Neither party knew what the other looked like, but Lili quickly picked us out from a disembarking crowd of around three hundred. Having been gathered up in an absolutely affirming way, we then met Lili's extraordinary husband, who drove us to their rural property, where he is regenerating rainforest.

On day three, scarcely knowing one another, we comfortably set off for Stradbroke Island, crossing the bay to the island on a vehicle ferry. Once there I was swept up with the most overwhelming urge to cry. The emotion was so great I could barely function. Lili assured me it was normal.

Lili, however, had the island's magic well in hand. What she asked for she got. Perfect weather, whales, dolphins, koalas. The whales appeared around the section of coast where Lili had released Ray's ashes on the day of his funeral. Unbelievably, the whales were swimming belly up and waving their flippers in the air, a magnificent sight. While Lili and Anne were getting to know one another, they had walked around the coastal track and were watching the whales.

Meanwhile, I had walked back to the little bridge that crossed the tidal ocean, entering a pretty little rocky cove. Closer to the shore was where Lili had released Raymond's ashes, or tried to. The view from the little bridge enabled me to imagine the scene and the ashes blowing all over Lili and back onto the island, and her laughing at his final shenanigans. Lili had described members of the local Indigenous people standing on the rocks above, that they had covered in flowers. Suddenly my reverie was broken by a flock of screeching, colourful green and yellow lorikeets jostling in the pandanus trees above me, as if cheering.

The next day we spoke with a number of people who remembered Raymond. It became apparent he did not integrate with the mainstream community but rather kept them entertained from afar. As always, he was described as often wearing a big cowboy hat, belt with an impressive buckle and cowboy boots with spurs (a little overimagined perhaps)! And that he never walked anywhere but always drove one of his big American cars, and he lived in a shack. They said his yard was a mess of bamboo, ducks and chickens everywhere, complete with a feral attacking rooster.

Most appeared to think he was a Yank. Many spoke of his wickedly sharp wit, delivered with all the finesse of a skilled comedian. "A very funny man, absolutely hilarious." Remembering his wit and implying he didn't mix with island mainstays made him into something of a fringedweller.

We found the same neighbours still lived next door to his now-annihilated house and cleared-away garden. A new beach house stands in its place. Apparently, the person who had inherited Ray's property and all it held bulldozed the lot.

The former neighbours further told of his sarong-wearing days, confirming he was often seen with ducklings following him about. But they emphasised he was a quiet man and a recluse hidden in his overgrown garden of bamboo, like he was still in Changi.

They told of his acquisition of the bus, which sat at the back of the block with its upper deck filled with costume apparel for entertaining his lady friends. The neighbours said he gave them a painting as a wedding present, ten years after their wedding! Some twenty years later they donated it to the Dunwich Museum. This was done at the very same time I had first contacted the museum for information about him in 2015. It seemed possible that Raymond, now an ethereal being, was leading us all towards some kind of goal.

Visiting the location, I learned I had visualised Ray's abode and surrounds completely in reverse. Like I was looking at it in a mirror. This was not the first time my all-seeing, all-knowing eye had shown me a mirror image.

When we returned to Lili's home on the Sunshine Coast, we began to go through Ray's personal papers, which Lili had responsibly retrieved from Ray's house after the funeral.

ABOVE Bulldozing Ray's studio home, 1996. The red double-decker bus is still on the left. Photograph gifted by Ray's neighbours.

Anne and I itemised it all as we searched for the clues now folded into this story.

Amazingly among it all we found a list of places he had lived, all containing the word "North":

North End, England
North Arm, Canada
North Bend, Indiana
North Rocks, Sydney
North Ridge, California
North Stradbroke, Queensland

At the end of August, we met Larisa, one of Lili's daughters, and her family for the first time. Her daughter boldly declared, "Mum never has people to stay."

But even more surprising was that Larisa had married a man whose surname was Northover.

Both her little daughters were filled with excited curiosity about us. "I love you so much" cards suddenly appeared, made by Ruby, the youngest. Larisa and Lili announced that they suspected Ray communicates through Ruby.

The following day we three distant cousins travelled to Leonard's home in a nearby town, where we enjoyed lunch with him and his new wife. When love was not available to him in Australia, Leonard, like Raymond, had also sought to find it in the women of Asia. And, like Raymond, had begun to woo his new love with the written word (albeit his postings were electronic). Getting to know Leonard was fraught with little surprise memories of Raymond. Leonard, himself an artist, was exploring some very interesting atmospheric imagery. His interest in what the skies might hold uncannily reflected his father's visions.

A little strange, perhaps, is the fact that Leonard, Lili and I had kept everything Raymond had ever bestowed on us. We three had kept these things carefully for between twenty-five and forty years.

The plan to return to Leonard's a few days later was mysteriously interfered with when Lili's electric car would not start. This effectively took Lili out of the visit and brought in her daughter Larisa, who picked us up and drove us to the markets in a nearby town, where Leonard would collect us. On the way Anne and I saw a sign to "North Arm" of all places. This coincidence focused our attention as we had not long learned that was where Raymond claimed to have had shares in his brother's antique shop, at North Arm, Ontario, Canada. Yet another mystery.

On the way to Leonard's home, we followed a big red bus eerily reminiscent of the double-decker in Ray's garden. On Raymond's death, Leonard and his then wife had the job of cleaning out that bus. Coincidently, we were headed to Leonard's to see the memorabilia retrieved from it. We were soon photographing Ray's scrapbook with all his newspaper cuttings about his art exhibitions, and the one and only picture of Ray's dad, John Thomas Moult-Spiers.

Travelling back to Lili's that night, Leonard was unsure he would find the rural property, so rarely did he see his sister. Anne and I tried to help but he randomly announced Lili would be standing out the front. It was dark and Anne and I thought it improbable. But she was!

Later that week, after an intense day sorting his papers, Anne and I went for an afternoon walk down the country road on which Lili lived. When we turned to walk back, to our surprise we were face to face with a sign that said "Ray's Place". We burst out laughing as we looked at it perched on a letterbox.

The next day I was silently typing up one of Ray's poems, which happened to be about his childhood at North End. In it he wrote about the two little girls who were there with him. They were called Maizie and Dot. At the very same time, Anne had been sorting through piles of Ray's letters and was randomly reading one out loud. It was a briefly worded Christmas card sent in 1994 from someone called Dot, which simply said "memories of North End". Both Anne and I shrieked!

A few days before this, Lili and I had decided to have thirty minutes together with a psychic. She had asked if we knew a Martin, but we both looked blank! She said it was a healing perspective and moved to it to being Martine, a sister of mercy, a nurse. On Sunday evening, among the data collected I came across St Martin's Church at North End, which revealed the church group who had fostered Raymond out. At the same time Anne noticed Raymond's birth was registered at St Martin (St Martin is the registration district for the Carnaby Street area, London). We also found papers that indicated Raymond signed up to go to war at Martin Place in Sydney. None of these Martins seemed to be healing indicators, more like signs for the worst yet to come in Raymond's case.

Back home in November 2019, and after reading and summarising one of his war diaries I had begun to write about his observation of the bugle playing "The Last Post" whenever they buried anyone on the hill at Kranji, when I suddenly heard it being played. All of which seemed spooky until I realised it was exactly 11 o'clock and Remembrance Day! Too many dimensions operating perhaps.

Home still with Ray, my invisible tenant, a funny thing had been happening to my keyboard spacer, which had been driving me around the twist for a number of days. When I pressed the spacer, it did nothing, so all the words joined together and I had to keep going back over things separating words by hitting the space bar extra hard. During the slow process of fiddling around trying to re-space the words, I lost a huge cut and paste. Furious, I went out for a walk. At the time I was trying to write about his entry into my life in the 1980s, which of course was leading me to write more about my life and less about Ray's. I think I got "told". I went back to his "difficult to read" letters and came across his story of a near-death experience and the miracle he underwent when the "blue moon" had appeared in the railway prison camp. In this 1980s letter, he wrote that he was crying while reliving it to write it down. Then, without prompt, a text arrived. Unbelievably Lili had sent me an image of a painting Raymond had done called The Blue Moon. A miracle in itself. All this led me away from the 1980s and back to the 1940s and the Burma Railway, where his seeing the beautiful blue moon worked like magic to save his precious life. Compelled to type the story about the moon, I found the spacer on the keyboard had started working properly again.

Synchronicity is strange indeed.

As to the mystery of his death, there is no resolve.

Lili was told it was a heart attack, but where is the proof? She does not have the death certificate. His body was cremated.

Could someone have really robbed him as he lay there? Was he still alive when they did this? Who was this robber? Was it investigated?

As Lili's and Leonard's birth certificates do not show Raymond to be their father, they lost their court case to the gallery operator, because their birth father's paternity could not be proven at that time.

Penelope's retreat means she can no longer be reached in the hope of organising a DNA test. I am too far away in the family lineage to affect any investigation or suitable DNA. Without proof of paternity no one can access his death certificate until the prescribed period of time has passed. An application can be made but you need vast ID proof of your relationship to the deceased and/or good reasons why you need the death certificate, and the fees are excessive.

Proving he was robbed has long since been lost in time.

A fifteen-minute visit to yet another psychic, this time in Western Australia, and again without prompt, revealed Raymond's spirit arriving to her (in the reading) in a big old vintage car (that convinced me he was there) and then she said he asked her to tell us that he had a massive stroke. She held the left side of her head and said he experienced severe pain here before passing.

He has been with us all in unexpected ways all this time. Even as I pause at the crunch time, the disappointment of not knowing the exact truth is strong but the way here has been extraordinary.

The experiences I have been through have taught me there is more to intelligence than measured IQ; there is a multi-intelligence at play, comprised of intuition and body and spiritual quotients.

With effort I had begun to understand the person I called Uncle Raymond, not only through historical documentation, his diaries and letters, Lili's stories and the psychological consequence of his early life, but also through the characteristics cited by others who had encountered him. Putting it all together created an underlying alchemy for my creative imagination. I was equipped to proceed with cautionary interest.

Raymond's POW experiences exposed some serious consequences of a cruel captivity during the war, which cannot be taken lightly. That and his varied experiences of having been raised from a very young age in several foster homes, would have all contributed to the creation of some very strong emotional complexities.

As with many who experience unreasonable, punishing captivity or the like, a sleeping dragon is awoken every now and then. With it comes the desire to play the captor, which overtakes all logic and reason. Violence used or even displayed abuses trust and violates the "other". Rescuing Raymond from himself during such times would have been a tall order and may have seen Elma fall victim to his dark side, as it emerged just enough to keep her in check.

"Hurt people hurt people" is a potent saying.

Raymond's terrible war experiences, both as a fighter and a prisoner, leave us with the knowledge that "wars are never won". The consequences travel through us and into all who follow. Whole communities unknowingly play out the violation and the damage for generations. Post-traumatic stress disorder is real. Sexual abuse is real. Domestic violence is real. Veteran suicide is real.

But with the power of creativity, awareness, compassion and attentive prevention we can "turn things around".

Ray Moult-Spiers' had a passion for big old classic cars.

The Consequence

It's all the souls who've gone before

The boom was lowered to the floor

The last one in the golden net

Is something he cannot forget

For all the souls who missed the boat

Are cast asunder just to float

Eternal seas which is his due.

But careful now you've hit a roo.

Raymond Moult-Spiers,
date unknown

APPENDIX

Evidenced Exhibitions 1945–94
Artist Raymond Moult-Spiers 1920–95

1945	Solo: Malaya, Thailand, Burma, Australia, 1941–45, Australian Red Cross Art Exhibition, Military Hospital, Sydney (23 paintings)
1946	Contemporary Art Society, Sydney
1950–55	City of Parramatta Art Prize Shows
1953	Solo: David Jones Walk Gallery, Sydney (52 paintings)
1954	An Exhibition of Art by Cumberland Painters, Baulkham Hills School of Arts, Sydney
1957	Two-person show with Ronald Hugh Kirk, Dominion Art Galleries, Sydney
1958	City of Parramatta Art Prize Show, George St, Parramatta
1959	City of Parramatta Art Prize Show, George St, Parramatta
1959	Five Young Contemporary Artists, Fairfield, Sydney
1959	Three-person show, Blood for Paint, roadside, Sydney
1960	City of Parramatta Art Prize Show, George St, Parramatta
1961	City of Parramatta Art Prize (winner)
1962	City of Parramatta Art Prize (winner, Contemporary Art)
1962	Australian Art Associates group exhibition, Civic Arcade, George St, Parramatta,
1964	Two-person show with Collinridge Rivett, Penthouse Gallery, Parramatta
1968	Historical Art Exhibition, Civic Centre, Fairfield, Sydney
1972	Solo, Penthouse Gallery, Murray Bros, Parramatta (38 paintings 16x21cm)
1988	Exhibition of 30 works at unknown venue, Sydney
1992	Studio Garrali, Cronulla (possibly represented Ray from 1965 to 1995)
1994	Mother Moon Father Sun, two-person show with Kimbo Webster, Dunwich Art Gallery and Museum, North Stradbroke Island, Brisbane

ABOUT THE AUTHOR

Julie Lenora Parsons is a professional arts practitioner and writer based in Fremantle. She is the author of *Rabbits and other Immigrants: the Alan Parsons story*, a compelling story of pioneering in the wheatbelt of Western Australia, that is now into a second edition. Julie illustrated this with colourful drawings and paintings supplemented with family photographs.

Julie was the lead author for *Dorothy Erickson AM, Metamorphosis, Mookaite and the Metropolis: the life and work of an artist jeweller* undertaken with Philippa O'Brien, Dr Kathryn Wells and Dr Erickson to be published by the Western Australian Museum in 2025. Julie contributed the biographical chapter "Following the Sun Compass".

Since 2013, Julie has written for arts media journal *Oz Arts*, with printed and online articles. The author's focus on art, history and performance led to a Masters in Creative Arts (2009), exploring the design history of the harlequin costume. Her strong explorative research skills were developed from a forty-year career as a practising artist working with complex public art proposals and theatrical production design commissions.

The author's broad range of works in the visual arts, as a painter, public artist, illustrator, and designer for performance appear in private and public art collections across Australia and internationally.

Julie wrote Raymond's story to heal intergenerational patterns of trauma, through the exploration and revelations of the enigmatic interconnectedness of bloodlines both spiritually and manifest.

ACKNOWLEDGEMENTS

I am grateful for the support of family and friends throughout the adventure and long process of painstakingly researching the authentic story of Raymond Moult-Spiers.

Full appreciation goes to blood-line family members, especially Anne Elliott, Gayle Woods, Leonard Brokensha, Rad Young, Eleanor Parsons, Jamey Claffey, and Penelope Moult-Spiers. Treasured friends who willingly gave their time and expertise were; Professor Anna Haebich AM, Peter Clarke, Indigo Eli, Kester Mackay, and Phil Woods.

With professional or researched contributions from Elizabeth Gondwe, Shirley Cowcher, Ambrose Reisch, and chief war diary transcriber Chris Elliott, who spent all summer transcribing Ray's words written in war-torn foolscap-sized books during World War Two. How Ray kept these hidden from the Japanese is a conundrum but how Chris transcribed them is another.

The initial structural edit was completed by Tricia Dearborn who set me up for a rewrite with the clarity of direction the book now has. The final manuscript was expertly edited by Kerry Davies whose attention to detail is awe-inspiring.

Special thank you to Dr. Dorothy Erickson AM.

REFERENCES & FURTHER READING

Resources here are categorised into subjects: art; Trove newspaper titles, art; Fairfield; horse trade; war; and various.

Art

Boericke, Art, and Shapiro, Barry, *Handmade Houses: A Guide to the Woodbutcher's Art*, Scrimshaw Press, San Francisco, CA, 1973.

Butler, Rex, and Donaldson, A.D.S., "Surrealism and Australia: Towards a World History of Surrealism", *Journal of Art Historiography*, no. 9, December 2013, https://arthistoriography.files.wordpress.com/2013/12/butler_donaldson.pdf (accessed 18 April 2019).

Catalano, Gary, *The Years of Hope: Australian Art and Criticism 1959–1968*, Oxford University Press, Melbourne, Vic., 1981.

Gleeson, James, "Exhibition with Talent", *The Sun* (Sydney), 15 July 1953, p. 25, https://trove.nla.gov.au/newspaper/article/230351839 (accessed 26 September 2019).

Hull, Herbert, "Prison Camp Artist", *Australia Magazine*, February 1953, pp. 32–33.

Mumford, Ron, *Echoes of War in Avoca: The Service and Sacrifice of a Small Rural Community in Two Wars,* District Historical Society, Avoca, NSW, 2011.

National Gallery of Australia, "Surreal Landscapes, Australian Surrealism: The Agapitos/Wilson Collection", *Art on View*, Autumn 2008, pp. 16–19, https://issuu.com/nationalgalleryofaustralia/docs/artonview_53 (accessed 15 February 2022).

Pascoe, Joe, "The Beautiful Wisdom of Art History", essay by Joe Pascoe", 1 March 2015, note to *Dada Lives*, exhibition curator Joe Pascoe, 3 March – 4 April 2015, http://insect.org.au/dada-lives (accessed 8 March.2022), https://static1.squarespace.com/static/520716b6e4b019bfc9d67d3f/t/54f7a68ce4b0ceb22a6fefda/1425516172425/Dada+lives%21+essay+FINAL3.pdf (accessed 10 April 2019).

Plate, Gina, "Life with the Lewers", Penrith Regional Gallery, *abridged from Michael Crayford, Australian Dictionary of Biography, Vol. 15, Melbourne University Press, 2000,* pp. 89–90, https://www.penrithregionalgallery.com.au/about-us/our-story/ (accessed 26 August 2020).

Reisch, Ambrose, "Hawkesbury River Artist 1988", https://ambrosereisch.com/ (accessed 7 and 26 August 2020); correspondence with Ambrose Reisch 8, 13 and 17 August 2020.

Stockburn, Emma, *The Art Union and History of the Arts in Parramatta*, Parramatta City Council, 2014, https://historyandheritage.cityofparramatta.nsw.gov.au/blog/2014/12/10/the-art-union-and-the-school-of-the-arts-in-parramatta (accessed 2 March 2022).

Trove Newspaper Titles, Art

"Sundry Shows: Artbursts", *The Bulletin*, vol. 74, no. 3832, 22 July 1953, https://nla.gov.au/nla.obj-526781244/view?sectionId=nla.obj-533327738&partId=nla.obj-526845262" \l "page/n18/mode/1up (accessed 15 February 2022).

"Sundry Shows: Artbursts, Two Contemporaries", *The Bulletin*, vol. 74, no. 3847, 4 November 1953, https://nla.gov.au/nla.obj-526823486/view?partId=nla.obj-526933598#page/n18/mode/1up (accessed 15 February 2022).

"Artist Raymond Moult Spiers", *The Sydney Morning Herald*, 16 July 1953, p. 6, https://trove.nla.gov.au/newspaper/article/18385270 (accessed 26 September 2019).

"Local Artist Exhibits", *The Biz* (Fairfield, NSW), 30 July 1953, p. 10. https://trove.nla.gov.au/newspaper/article/75602555 (accessed 28 March 2015).

"City Artist Executive of New Cultural Society", *The Cumberland Argus* (Parramatta, NSW), 9 May 1962, p. 4, https://trove.nla.gov.au/newspaper/article/131330970 (accessed 28 March 2015).

"Emotional Art in Exhibition", *The Daily Telegraph* (Sydney), 13 November 1946, p. 11, https://trove.nla.gov.au/newspaper/article/248362503 (accessed 25 September 2019).

"Executive Post for Horsley Park Artist", *The Biz* (Fairfield, NSW), 2 May 1962, p. 2, https://trove.nla.gov.au/newspaper/article/189950143 (accessed 26 September 2019).

"Horsley Storekeeper Learnt Painting in Prison Camp", *The Biz* (Fairfield, NSW), 12 February 1953, p. 4, https://trove.nla.gov.au/newspaper/article/75600228 (accessed 28 March 2015).

"Just Mere Chatter: Nicest Story of the Week", *The Sydney Morning Herald*, 19 July 1953, p. 26, https://trove.nla.gov.au/newspaper/article/18519272 (accessed 28 March 2015).

"Local Art on Display", *The Broadcaster* (Fairfield, NSW), 31 August 1955, p. 2, https://trove.nla.gov.au/newspaper/article/144074812 (accessed 26 September 2019).

"Raymond Moult-Spiers", *The Sydney Morning Herald*, Wednesday 15 July 1953, p.2, https://nla.gov.au/nla.news-article18388206 (accessed 28 March 2015).

"War Artist", *The Daily Telegraph* (Sydney), 16 July 1953, p.17, https://trove.nla.gov.au/newspaper/article/248583764 (accessed 26 September 2019).

Fairfield

"History, Horsley Park, New South Wales", in George Vance, *Fairfield – A History of the District*, 2nd ed, Council of the City of Fairfield, NSW, 1991, http://ourladyofvictories.org.au/our-parish/history (accessed 20 March 2019).

McLeod, Shirley, transcript of an oral history interview with Helen Kerfoot, conducted by Shirley McLeod, 3 September 2003, Part 2, pp.10–11, Fairfield City Heritage Collection, https://heritagecollection.fairfieldcity.nsw.gov.au/nodes/view/733 (accessed 20 March 2019).

Arfanis, Peter, *The Rivoli: Parramatta's Bygone Entertainment Venue*, Parramatta Council, Parramatta Heritage Centre, 2014, https://historyandheritage.cityofparramatta.nsw.gov.au/blog/2014/01/16/the-rivoli-parramattas-bygone-entertainment-venue (accessed 9 May 2019).

Horse Trade

Burke, Mary, *"Tinkers": Synge and the Cultural History of the Irish Traveller*, Oxford University Press, Oxford and New York, 2010.

Butts, Edward, "North-West Mounted Police", *The Canadian Encyclopedia*, 7 February 2006, http://www.thecanadianencyclopedia.ca/en/article/north-west-mounted-police (accessed 27 January 2018).

Davis, Beverley, *Timeline of the Development of the Horse*, Sino-Platonic Papers, no. 177, August 2007, University of Pennsylvania, http://sinoplatonic.org/complete/spp177_horses.pdf (accessed 6 April 2019).

Derry, Margaret Elsinor, *Horses in Society: A Story of Animal Breeding and Marketing Culture, 1800–1920*, University of Toronto Press, Toronto, 2006.

Johnson, Ben, "The Great Horse Manure Crisis of 1894", *Historic UK* (n.d.), https://www.historic-uk.com/HistoryUK/HistoryofBritain/Great-Horse-Manure-Crisis-of-1894/ (accessed 28 October 2019).

Kelly, W., and Kelly, N., *The Horses of the Royal Canadian Mounted Police: A Pictorial History*, D. W. Friesen and Sons Ltd, Doubleday, Canada, 1984.

Moore-Colyer, R. J., "Aspects of the Trade in British Pedigree Draught Horses with the United States and Canada, c. 1850–1920", *The Agricultural History Review*, vol. 48, no. 1, 2000, pp. 42–59, http://www.bahs.org.uk/AGHR/ARTICLES/48n1a3.pdf (accessed 6 April 2019).

Murphy, John L, review of "'Tinkers': Synge and the Cultural History of the Irish Traveller", *Electronic Journal of the Spanish Association for Irish Studies*. https://www.estudiosirlandeses.org/reviews/tinkers-synge-and-the-cultural-history-of-the-irish-traveller-2010 (accessed 3 March 2019).

North West Mounted Police Commemorative Association, "1891–1900: The Northern Frontier", https://www.nwmpca.ca/history-of-nwmp/1891-1900, (accessed 7 April 2019).

North West Mounted Police Commemorative Association, "The Horses Weren't All Black", http://www.nwmpca.ca/history-of-nwmp/the-horses-werent-all-black

War

Australian War Memorial, "Changi", https://www.awm.gov.au/articles/encyclopedia/pow/changi (accessed 12 November 2019).

Australian War Memorial, "2/19th Battalion", https://web.archive.org/web/20131219014048/http://www.awm.gov.au/units/unit_11270.asp (accessed 28 December 2019).

Bingham, Geoffrey C., "The Cat and the Clown", in *Laughing Gunner and Selected War Stories*, Troubadour Press Inc., Australia, 1992.

Bingham, Geoffrey C., *Love Is the Spur*, Eyrie Books, North Parramatta, NSW, 2004.

Brune, Peter, *Descent into Hell: The Fall of Singapore – Pudu and Changi – the Thai–Burma Railway*, Allen & Unwin, Sydney, NSW, 2014.

Burma Thailand Railway Memorial Association, "Hellfire Pass Memorial Project", 2019, http://www.btrma.org.au/?s=Hellfire+pass+memorial+project (accessed 19 November 2019).

Cooper, Carol, "The Story of Changi", COFEPOW (n.d.), https://www.cofepow.org.uk/armed-forces-stories-list/the-story-of-changi (accessed 28 December 2019).

Department of Veterans Affairs (DVA), "Burma–Thailand Railway and Hellfire Pass 1942 to 1943", DVA Anzac Portal, https://anzacportal.dva.gov.au/wars-and-missions/burma-thailand-railway-and-hellfire-pass-1942-1943 (accessed 3 March 2019).

Dunlop, E. E., *The War Diaries of Weary Dunlop: Java and The Burma–Thailand Railway 1942–1945*, Penguin Books, Australia, 1990.

Featherstone, Don, *Singapore 1942 End of Empire*, an Electric Pictures Production 2013, viewed 2015.

Flanagan, Richard, *The Narrow Road to the Deep North*, Vintage, Australia, 2013.

Forces War Records, "Prisoners of War of the Japanese 1939–1945" (n.d.), https://www.forces-war-records.co.uk/prisoners-of-war-of-the-japanese-1939-1945 (accessed 28 December 2019).

Hearder, Rosalind, "Memory, Methodology, and Myth: Some of the Challenges of Writing Australian Prisoner of War History", *Australian War Memorial*, www.awm.gov.au/articles/journal/j40/hearder (accessed 18 April 2019).

Hill, Anthony, *The Story of Billy Young: A Teenager in Changi, Sandakan and Outram Road*, Penguin, Melbourne, Vic, 2012.

Manning, Benjamin, *Embedded Behind Barbed Wire: Culture and the Economies of POW Camps* PhD thesis, University of New South Wales, 2011, http://unsworks.unsw.edu.au/fapi/datastream/unsworks:9876/SOURCE02?view=true (accessed 12 November 2019).

Moult-Spiers, Raymond, *Moult-Spiers' War Diaries and Other Writings* (unpublished).

Muir, Kristy, *The Hidden Cost of War: The Psychological Effect of the Second World War and Indonesian Confrontation on Australian Veterans and Their Families,* PhD thesis, University of Wollongong, 2003, https://ro.uow.edu.au/theses/863/ (accessed 8 October 2019).

Mumford, Ron, *Echoes of War in Avoca: The Service and Sacrifice of a Small Rural Community in Two Wars*. District Historical Society, Avoca, NSW, 2011.

Prisoner of War Memorial, "Raymond Moult-Spiers", http://www.powmemorialballarat.com.au/world-war-2-m-o.php (accessed 15 September 2022).

Unofficial History of the Australian and New Zealand Armed Services, "Changi Prison: Was It a 'Hell Hole'?" (n.d.), http://www.diggerhistory.info/pages-battles/ww2/changi/0-changi-cat-index.htm (accessed 16 November 2019).

Wahlert, Glenn Wayne, "Provost: Friend or Foe? The Development of an Australian Provost Service 1914–1945", Master's thesis, University of New South Wales, 1996. http://unsworks.unsw.edu.au/fapi/datastream/unsworks:52822/SOURCE01?view=true (accessed 8 May 2021).

Various

"Artificial Flower History", *How Products Are Made*, vol. 5 (n.d.), http://www.madehow.com/Volume-5/Artificial-Flower.html (accessed 27 January 2018).

Aviation Safety Network, "Aviation Safety Report", 3 February 1997, https://aviation-safety.net/wikibase/48753 (accessed 27 May 2021).

Coldrey, Barry, "Good British Stock: Child and Youth Migration to Australia", *National Archives of Australia*, Research Guide, 1999, http://guides.naa.gov.au/good-british-stock/chapter3/index.aspx (accessed 7 April 2019).

Parliament of Australia, "Chapter 2, Child Migration to Australia During the 20th Century", 2002, https://www.aph.gov.au/parliamentary_business/committees/senate/community_affairs/completed_inquiries/1999-02/child_migrat/report/c02 (accessed 28 February 2022).

Pickett, Charles, "Fields of Memories: The Scheyville Training Farm 1911–1964", Powerhouse Museum for NSW Migration Heritage Centre, 2006, https://www.migrationheritage.nsw.gov.au/exhibitions/fieldsofmemories/trainingfarm.html (accessed 17 May 2019).

www.ingramcontent.com/pod-product-compliance
Lightning Source LLC
Chambersburg PA
CBHW061147070526
44584CB00034B/4450